# Excel
## Get the Results You

# Year 9
# NAPLAN*-style
# Numeracy Tests

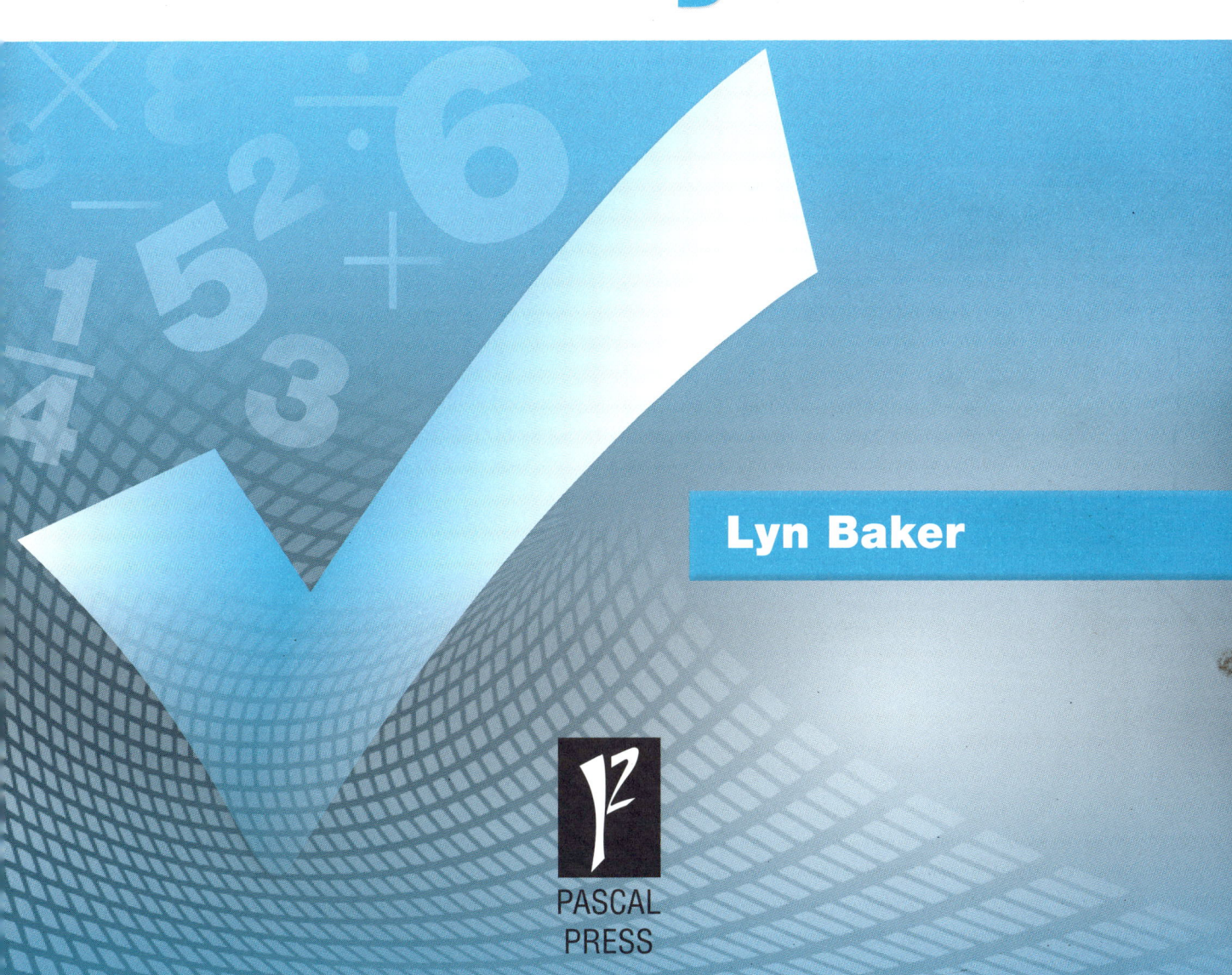

**Lyn Baker**

PASCAL PRESS

* This is not an officially endorsed publication of the NAPLAN program and is produced by Pascal Press independently of Australian governments.

© 2010 Lyn Baker and Pascal Press
Reprinted 2011
**New NAPLAN Test question formats added 2012**
Reprinted 2014

ISBN 978 1 74125 362 7

Pascal Press Pty Ltd
PO Box 250
Glebe NSW 2037
(02) 9557 4844
www.pascalpress.com.au

Publisher: Vivienne Joannou
Project editor: Mark Dixon
Edited by Rosemary Peers
Answers checked by Peter Little
Cover, page design and typesetting by DiZign Pty Ltd
Printed by Green Giant Press

**Reproduction and communication for educational purposes**
The Australian *Copyright Act 1968* (the Act) allows a maximum of one chapter or 10% of this book, whichever is the greater, to be copied by any educational institution for its educational purposes provided that the educational institution (or the body that administers it) has given a remuneration notice to Copyright Agency Limited (CAL) under the Act.

For details of the CAL licence for educational institutions contact:

Copyright Agency Limited
Level 15, 233 Castlereagh Street
Sydney NSW 2000
Telephone: (02) 9394 7600
Facsimile: (02) 9394 7601
Email: enquiry@copyright.com.au

**Reproduction and communication for other purposes**
Except as permitted under the Act (for example, any fair dealing for the purposes of study, research, criticism or review) no part of this book may be reproduced, stored in a retrieval system, or transmitted in any form or by any means without prior written permission. All inquiries should be made to the publisher at the address above.

While care has been taken in the preparation of this study guide, students should check with their teachers about the exact requirements or content of the tests for which they are sitting.

NAPLAN is a trademark of Australian Curriculum, Assessment and Reporting Authority (ACARA).

**Notice of liability**
The information contained in this book is distributed without warranty. While precautions have been taken in the preparation of this material, neither the authors nor Pascal Press shall have any liability to any person or entity with respect to any liability, loss or damage caused or alleged to be caused directly or indirectly by the instructions and content contained in the book.

All efforts have been made to gain permission for the copyright material reproduced in this book. In the event of any oversight, the publisher welcomes any information that will enable rectification of any reference or credit in subsequent editions.

# Contents

Introduction ..................................................... 2
The Strengths and Weaknesses Chart ......... 3

## Mini Tests

### Basic level questions

**Mini Test 1:** Basic Numbers  Non-calculator .................... 4
**Mini Test 2:** Basic Algebra  Non-calculator .................... 5
**Mini Test 3:** Basic Space  Non-calculator ...................... 6
**Mini Test 4:** Basic Numbers  Calculator Allowed ............... 7
**Mini Test 5:** Basic Measurement  Calculator Allowed .......... 8
**Mini Test 6:** Basic Chance and Data
  Calculator Allowed ............................................. 9
**Mini Test 7:** Mixed Questions  Non-calculator ................ 10
**Mini Test 8:** Mixed Questions  Calculator Allowed ........... 11

### Intermediate level questions

**Mini Test 9:** Numbers  Non-calculator ......................... 12
**Mini Test 10:** Algebra  Non-calculator ........................ 13
**Mini Test 11:** Plane Figures and Solids
  Non-calculator ................................................ 14
**Mini Test 12:** Measurement and Data
  Non-calculator ................................................ 15
**Mini Test 13:** Number Operations and Ratios
  Calculator Allowed ........................................... 16
**Mini Test 14:** Fractions, Decimals and
  Percentages  Calculator Allowed ............................. 17
**Mini Test 15:** Angles  Calculator Allowed .................... 18
**Mini Test 16:** Rates and Measurements
  Calculator Allowed ........................................... 19
**Mini Test 17:** Perimeter, Area and Volume
  Calculator Allowed ........................................... 20
**Mini Test 18:** Chance and Data  Calculator Allowed ......... 21

**Mini Test 19:** Mixed Questions  Non-calculator ............... 22
**Mini Test 20:** Mixed Questions  Calculator Allowed .......... 23

### Advanced level questions

**Mini Test 21:** Number  Non-calculator ......................... 24
**Mini Test 22:** Algebra  Non-calculator ........................ 25
**Mini Test 23:** Space, Measurement and Data
  Non-calculator ................................................ 26
**Mini Test 24:** Number  Calculator Allowed .................... 27
**Mini Test 25:** Algebra—Patterns, Expressions
  and Number Plane  Calculator Allowed ..................... 28
**Mini Test 26:** Algebra—Substitution and
  Equations  Calculator Allowed .............................. 29
**Mini Test 27:** Angles  Calculator Allowed .................... 30
**Mini Test 28:** Measurement  Calculator Allowed .............. 31
**Mini Test 29:** Plane Figures and Solids
  Calculator Allowed ........................................... 32
**Mini Test 30:** Chance and Data  Calculator Allowed ......... 33
**Mini Test 31:** Mixed Questions  Non-calculator ............... 34
**Mini Test 32:** Mixed Questions  Calculator Allowed .......... 35

## Sample Tests

Sample Test 1  Non-calculator ............................. 36
Sample Test 1  Calculator Allowed ....................... 44
Sample Test 2  Non-calculator ............................. 52
Sample Test 2  Calculator Allowed ....................... 60
Sample Test 3  Non-calculator ............................. 68
Sample Test 3  Calculator Allowed ....................... 76

## Answers

Mini Tests ................................................... 84
Sample Tests ............................................... 138

# INTRODUCTION

## THE YEAR 9 NAPLAN NUMERACY TESTS

### About the tests
- The Year 9 NAPLAN Numeracy Tests are divided into the Non-calculator and the Calculator Allowed tests—in which there are around 30 questions each.
- The students have 40 minutes to complete each test.
- The majority of the questions are multiple choice with the remaining questions being short answer.

### About the report
- When your child completes the NAPLAN Tests you, your child's teacher and the school each receive a comprehensive report. This report displays your child's results for the Numeracy Tests (as well as the Literacy Tests) on a graph in the form of levels; these are called achievement bands.
- In Year 9 there are six levels (achievement bands). They are Bands 5–10, with Band 5 being the lowest achievement band and Band 10 being the highest. Band 6 represents the national minimum standard for this year level.
- Your child's performance in the NAPLAN Numeracy Tests will be assessed and put into a level (band).

## ABOUT THIS BOOK

### The Mini Numeracy Tests
- In the first part of this book you will find 32 Non-calculator and Calculator Allowed tests. They are divided into three levels of difficulty:
  - Basic level
  - Intermediate level
  - Advanced level.
- Within each level, the key topics are covered, each with a full page of exercises for your child to practise.
- You will be able to see what level your child is at by finding the point where he or she starts having consistent difficulty with questions. For example, if your child answers most questions correctly up to the Intermediate level and then gets most questions wrong from then onwards, it is likely your child's ability is at an Intermediate level.
- You will be able to see your child's strengths and weaknesses in different topics by completing the Strengths and Weaknesses Chart (see page 3).
- You will also be able to give your child intensive practice in short tests which have time limits based on the actual Numeracy Test times.
- There are quick answers for every question so you can easily mark your child's work. Worked solutions are also included in case you need to show your child how to do a question.

### The Sample Numeracy Tests
- In the second part of this book we provide you with three Sample Tests, each with a Non-calculator and Calculator Allowed section.
- Your child will be able to practise doing the longer sample tests.
- With the answers and worked solutions, there is also a list of the different levels of difficulty for each question to help you identify which are the easier and harder questions in the tests.

### Tips for the tests
Students should make sure that they:
- read the questions carefully, again and again if necessary, and underline any important points
- take time to think and don't rush the questions
- are logical and work step by step though each problem
- take care with the multiple-choice questions as the common wrong answers will also be there
- remember with some multiple-choice questions it will be necessary to consider all the options
- make sure that the answers to short-answer questions make sense; for example, an item bought during a sale must cost less than it did originally
- know how to use their calculators for Calculator Allowed tests and take care to enter the correct information in the correct order
- check that they have answered every question.

# THE STRENGTHS AND WEAKNESSES CHART

- As your child completes each test, mark it using the answer section at the back and then fill in this chart to record his or her progress.
- You will be able to see at a glance your child's strengths and weaknesses in different topics and different strands of Numeracy.
- If you find your child needs more practice on specific topics, use the checklist of *Excel* books on the back cover to find the book to help you.

| Type of test | Level | Mini test | Topic | Mark |
|---|---|---|---|---|
| Non-calculator | Basic | 1 | Basic Numbers | /24 |
| Non-calculator | Basic | 2 | Basic Algebra | /20 |
| Non-calculator | Basic | 3 | Basic Space | /16 |
| Calculator Allowed | Basic | 4 | Basic Numbers | /22 |
| Calculator Allowed | Basic | 5 | Basic Measurement | /16 |
| Calculator Allowed | Basic | 6 | Basic Chance and Data | /12 |
| Non-calculator | Basic | 7 | Mixed Questions | /16 |
| Calculator Allowed | Basic | 8 | Mixed Questions | /16 |
| Non-calculator | Intermediate | 9 | Numbers | /20 |
| Non-calculator | Intermediate | 10 | Algebra | /16 |
| Non-calculator | Intermediate | 11 | Plane Figures and Solids | /12 |
| Non-calculator | Intermediate | 12 | Measurement and Data | /15 |
| Calculator Allowed | Intermediate | 13 | Number Operations and Ratios | /20 |
| Calculator Allowed | Intermediate | 14 | Fractions, Decimals and Percentages | /16 |
| Calculator Allowed | Intermediate | 15 | Angles | /16 |
| Calculator Allowed | Intermediate | 16 | Rates and Measurements | /16 |
| Calculator Allowed | Intermediate | 17 | Perimeter, Area and Volume | /16 |
| Calculator Allowed | Intermediate | 18 | Chance and Data | /16 |
| Non-calculator | Intermediate | 19 | Mixed Questions | /16 |
| Calculator Allowed | Intermediate | 20 | Mixed Questions | /16 |
| Non-calculator | Advanced | 21 | Number | /18 |
| Non-calculator | Advanced | 22 | Algebra | /18 |
| Non-calculator | Advanced | 23 | Space, Measurement and Data | /12 |
| Calculator Allowed | Advanced | 24 | Number | /18 |
| Calculator Allowed | Advanced | 25 | Algebra—Patterns, Expressions and Number Plane | /16 |
| Calculator Allowed | Advanced | 26 | Algebra—Substitution and Equations | /18 |
| Calculator Allowed | Advanced | 27 | Angles | /16 |
| Calculator Allowed | Advanced | 28 | Measurement | /15 |
| Calculator Allowed | Advanced | 29 | Plane Figures and Solids | /12 |
| Calculator Allowed | Advanced | 30 | Chance and Data | /12 |
| Non-calculator | Advanced | 31 | Mixed Questions | /16 |
| Calculator Allowed | Advanced | 32 | Mixed Questions | /16 |

## NON-CALCULATOR — Basic level questions
## Mini Test 1: Basic Numbers
**20 min**

1. Which of these has the same value as $18 \times 37 - 26 \times 18$?
   A $18 \times 11$  B $19 \times 8$
   C $37 \times 8$  D $26 \times 19$

2. A positive number was multiplied by itself and then 8 was subtracted. The answer was 17. What was the number? **5**

3. 25% of Rochelle's income is spent on rent. If Rochelle earns $1280 per week, how much is her weekly rent? **$320**

4. Which is the best estimate for $87 + 43 \times 28 - 19$?
   A $80 + 40 \times 20 - 10$
   B $90 + 50 \times 20 - 20$
   C $80 + 50 \times 30 - 20$
   D $90 + 40 \times 30 - 20$

5. The arrow points to a position on the number line.
   
   What number is at this position?
   A −1  B −2  C −3  D −5

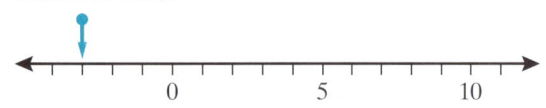

6. Which is **not** equal to 20?
   A $2 + 3 \times 6$  B $4 + 6 \times 2$
   C $2 \times 5 \times 2$  D $14 - 3 + 9$

7. The area of a farm is 56 823 km². What is this area to the nearest thousand square kilometres? **57 000** km²

8. In a group of 150 students, 20% are in Year 9. How many of the students are in Year 9?
   A 30  B 45  C 50  D 75

9. Xanthe bought 6 kg of grapes. The grapes were selling for $2.49 per kilogram. Which is closest to the amount Xanthe paid?
   A $12  B $15  C $18  D $20

10. $36 \div 12 = 12 \div$ ▢
    What is ▢?

11. Which is another way of writing $3^4$?
    A $3 \times 4$  B $3 \times 3 \times 3 \times 3$
    C $4 \times 4 \times 4$  D $3 \times 4 \times 3 \times 4$

12. What is 15% of 180? **27**

13. Henry bought 3 pens for $1.65. What was the average price per pen? $ **55c**

14. Paris divided 234 by a number and got 2.34 as her answer. What number did Paris divide by? **100**

15. $\frac{3}{4}$ of a number is 24. What is the number? **32**

16. $632 \times 35 = 22\,120$
    What is $6.32 \times 3.5$?
    A 0.2212  B 2.212  C 22.12  D 221.2

17. The ratio of wet days to sunny days on a holiday was 3:2. There were 12 wet days. How many sunny days were there?
    A 6  B 8  C 9  D 18

18. Tia has 300 shares in a business. This is 20% of the total number of shares. How many shares are there? **1500**

19. Which is the largest?
    A 0.2006  B 0.108  C 0.039  D 0.27

20. What number is halfway between 0.2 and 0.7? **0.45**

21. $\frac{7}{10} + \frac{13}{100} = ?$
    A 0.83  B 0.2  C 0.02  D 0.713

22. $\frac{1}{6}$ of the people at a lecture are children. If there are 60 children at the lecture, how many adults are there? **300**

23. $12 + 1.2 + 0.12 = ?$
    A 12.14  B 12.44  C 13.14  D 13.32

24. $\sqrt{70}$ is between
    A 5 and 6  B 6 and 7
    C 7 and 8  D 8 and 9

Answers and explanations on pages 84–85

# NON-CALCULATOR — Basic level questions
## Mini Test 2: Basic Algebra
**20 MIN**

**1** If $k = 5$, what is the value of $3k$?
A 8    **B 15**    C 35    D 125

**2** What is the next number in this pattern?
1, 3, 7, 15, 31, **63**

**3** The table shows the values of □ and ○, which are related by a rule.

| □ | 1 | 3 | 5 | 7 | 9 | 11 |
|---|---|---|---|---|---|----|
| ○ | 3 | 7 | 11 | **15** | 19 | 23 |

What is ○ when □ = 7?
A 13    B 14    **C 15**    D 17

**4** If $p = 3$ and $q = 4$, what is the value of $pq$?
A 7    **B 12**    C 16    D 34

**5** A rule for a pattern is: 'double the previous number and add 3'. The first number in the pattern is 1. What is the fourth number? **2a**

**6** What is the next number in this pattern?
2, 2.6, 3.2, 3.8, 4.4, **5**

**7** Pins are used to make this pattern of octagons.

The rule is 'number of pins = 6 × number of octagons + 2'. How many pins are needed if the pattern has 12 octagons? **96**

**8** A rule for $y$ in terms of $x$ is $y = 4x + 3$. What is the value of $y$ when $x = 2$?
**A 11**    B 9    C 45    D 18

**9** Which point does **not** lie in the shaded region?
A (3, 3)
B (1, 4)
C (5, 2)
**D (4, 1)**

**10** Which is equivalent to $3t + 2t + 4t$?
**A $9t$**    B $24t$    C $9t^3$    D $24t^3$

**11** Charlie wrote down the first three numbers in a pattern: 4.3, 3.6, 2.9
What is the rule to find the next number in this pattern?
**A decrease by 0.7**    B increase by 0.7
C decrease by 0.9    D increase by 0.9

**12** ⊗ = 3 and △ = 4
3⊗ + ◇ = △ + △    ◇ = ?
A 2    B 3    C 4    **D 5**

**13** Claire wrote down the first five numbers in a pattern: 3, 6, 9, 12, 15
Which is **not** a number in this pattern?
A 36    B 45    **C 67**    D 99

**14** Which rule connects $x$ and $y$?

| x | 1 | 2 | 3 | 4 | 5 |
|---|---|---|---|---|---|
| y | 3 | 7 | 11 | 15 | 19 |

A $y = x + 2$    B $y = 3 \times x$
**C $y = 4 \times x - 1$**    D $y = 2 \times x + 1$

**15** Kevin wrote down the first five numbers in a pattern: 2, 7, 12, 17, 22    5×21−3
What is the 21st number in this pattern?
A 97    **B 102**    C 107    D 112

**16** If $a = 6$ and $b = 5$, what is the value of $ab - b$? 30−5=
A 1    B 6    C 21    **D 25**

**17** Kylie has written down the first five numbers in a pattern: 2, 5, 8, 11, 14
What is the tenth number in this pattern? **29**

**18** $2x + 1 = 25$
What is the value of $x$?
A 16    B 15    **C 12**    D 4

**19** Sam wrote out a pattern using symbols:
♦♥♣♠♦♥♣♠♦♥♣♠♦♥♣♠…
What is the 50th symbol in the pattern?
A ♦    **B ♥**    C ♣    D ♠

**20** Joan is making a pattern with matches.

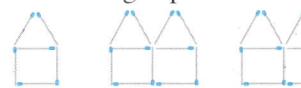

First shape    Second shape    Third shape

How many matches will be needed for the fifth shape? **26**

# NON-CALCULATOR — Basic level questions
## Mini Test 3: Basic Space

**1** This object is made from 12 cubes. What is the view from the top? 
A  B  C  **D** ✓

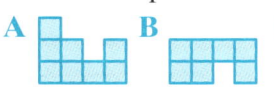

**2** Which is a reflex angle?
A  **B** ✓  C  D

**3** Sandra is standing at the lookout facing Heron Island.
In what direction is she facing? 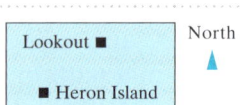
A north-west  B north-east
**C** ✓ south-west  D south-east

**4** Which is **not** the net of a cube?
A  B  **C** ✓  D

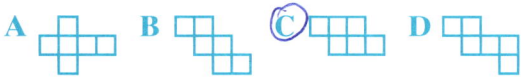

**5** A regular octagon is cut into three pieces as shown in the diagram. The top piece is what shape?
A rectangle  B parallelogram 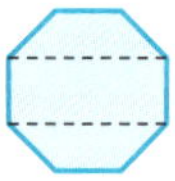
C rhombus  **D** ✓ trapezium

**6** Which triangle is isosceles? = two equal sides
A  B  C  **D** ✓

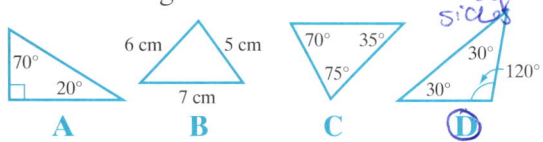

**7** Wayne had two identical objects, each made from three cubes. How many of the following can be formed by joining Wayne's two objects? 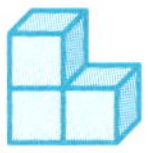 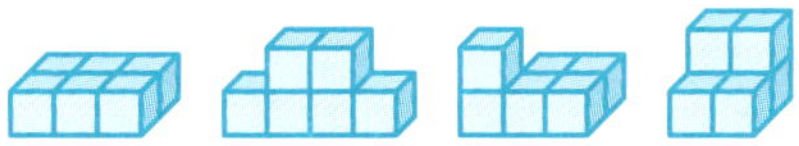
A 4  **B** ✓ 3 only  C 2 only  D 1 only

**8** Which dotted line is a line of symmetry?
A  **B** ✓  C  D

**9** The diagram shows the top view of a solid. What is the solid?
A square prism  **B** ✓ square pyramid 
C triangular prism  D triangular pyramid

**10** What is the value of $x$ in this diagram?
(40°, $x°$, 30°)
A 70  **B** ✓ 110  C 140  D 150

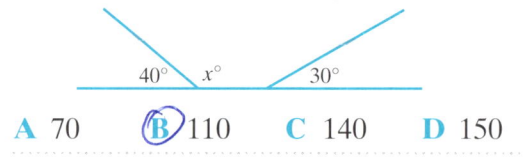

**11** This arrow → is turned through 270° in a clockwise direction. How does it look now?
**A** ✓ ↑  B ↓  C ←  D →

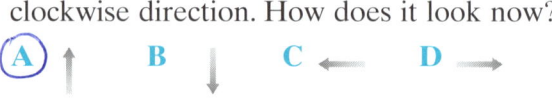

**12** Zara writes her initial on a card. She flips the card over its left side so that the initial cannot be seen. She then flips the card over the top edge so the initial can be seen again. How does it look now?
**A** ✓ Z  B Ƨ  C И  D N 

**13** Edward was travelling north-west in Station Street. He turned left into Ocean Drive at the roundabout and then took the first street on the right. Into which street did Edward turn?
**A** ✓ John Street
B Beach Street
C Hill Street
D King Street

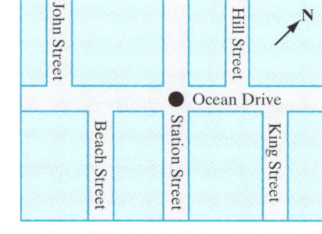

**14** A rectangular prism has
**A** ✓ 6 faces and 8 edges.
B 6 edges and 8 vertices.
C 8 vertices and 12 edges.
D 6 vertices and 12 edges.

**15** Which transformation could move P to P¹?
A translation  **B** ✓ rotation
C reflection in a horizontal line
D reflection in a vertical line

**16** An angle of 190° is what type of angle?
A right  B reflex  C acute  **D** ✓ obtuse

**CALCULATOR ALLOWED** — **Basic level questions** — 20 MIN

## Mini Test 4: Basic Numbers

**1** Jenna bought a dozen oranges for $10.20. What was the average price per orange? $ ☐

**2** What fraction of 36 is 24?
A $\frac{2}{3}$   B $\frac{3}{2}$   C $\frac{3}{4}$   D $\frac{4}{3}$

**3** $\sqrt{36 + 64} = ?$
A 10   B 12   C 13   D 14

**4** 15% of all students in Year 11 at River High School have a driving licence. If there are 120 students in Year 11, how many have a driving licence?
A 60   B 18   C 8   D 6

**5** Jye bought 4 hamburgers and 3 drinks for $14.50. The hamburgers cost $2.50 each. How much was each drink? $ ☐

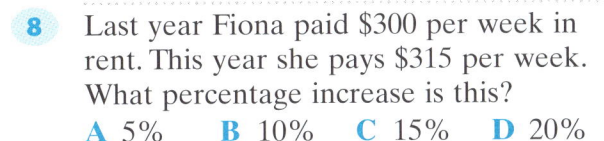

**6** Nathan divided 2686 by a number and the answer was 34. By what number did Nathan divide? ☐

**7** Which of these is between $15^2$ and $16^2$?
A 150   B 200   C 250   D 300

**8** Last year Fiona paid $300 per week in rent. This year she pays $315 per week. What percentage increase is this?
A 5%   B 10%   C 15%   D 20%

**9** A box holds 70 photos. 28 of the photos are black and white. What fraction of the photos is black and white?
A $\frac{2}{5}$   B $\frac{3}{5}$   C $\frac{5}{2}$   D $\frac{5}{3}$

**10** Jeremy had a box of 24 chocolates. He ate 25% of the chocolates. How many were left? ☐

**11** The ratio of the length to the width of a rectangle is 4:3. The rectangle is 84 cm long. How wide is the rectangle?
A 36 cm   B 48 cm   C 56 cm   D 63 cm

**12** What is the value of $\frac{63.2 + 16.8}{4 - 1.5}$?
A 65.9   B 18.5   C 69.92   D 32

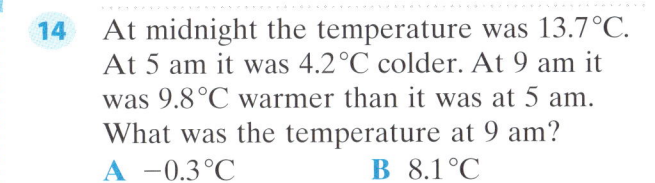

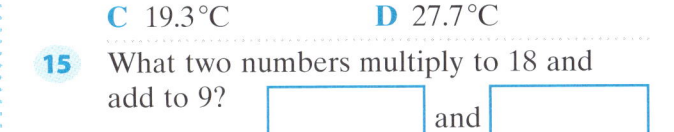

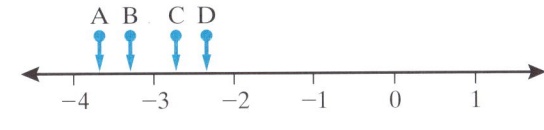

**13** The cost of 8 tickets is $108.00. What would 3 of the same tickets cost? $ ☐

**14** At midnight the temperature was 13.7°C. At 5 am it was 4.2°C colder. At 9 am it was 9.8°C warmer than it was at 5 am. What was the temperature at 9 am?
A −0.3°C   B 8.1°C   C 19.3°C   D 27.7°C

**15** What two numbers multiply to 18 and add to 9? ☐ and ☐

**16** Which arrow shows the position of $-3\frac{1}{3}$ on the number line?

A A   B B   C C   D D

**17** $36 \times \square = 27$
What is the value of ☐?
A $\frac{2}{3}$   B $\frac{3}{4}$   C $\frac{3}{2}$   D $\frac{4}{3}$

**18** There were 20 balloons left in the packet. The other 5 had been inflated. What percentage of the balloons had been inflated?
A 5%   B 10%   C 20%   D 25%

**19** Leanne's weekly bus ticket costs $15.50. A daily return ticket costs $3.75. If Leanne catches the bus on 5 days one week, how much does she save by buying a weekly ticket? $ ☐

**20** Suzi's shop took $2375 on Monday. This was a reduction of $685 on her takings for Saturday. What were her takings on Saturday? $ ☐

**21** Jimmy paid $500 off his credit card bill. This was 20% of the bill. How much was Jimmy's credit card bill?
A $100   B $250   C $1000   D $2500

**22** The population of Red Island was given as 8 million to the nearest million. Which could be the population of Red Island?
A 8 512 782   B 7 216 928   C 7 658 107   D 7 040 315

Answers and explanations on pages 88–89

**CALCULATOR ALLOWED** — **Basic level questions**

## Mini Test 5: Basic Measurement

**15 MIN**

**1** Ben travels 300 km in 4 hours. What is his average speed in kilometres per hour?
A 60   B 75   C 90   D 120

**2** Two places are 8.6 cm apart on a map. On the map 1 cm represents 15 km. What is the actual distance between the two places?
A 57 km   B 64 km   C 174 km   D 129 km

**3** Which jug contains the most juice? 
A   B   C   D

**4** The train arrived at the station at 2:38 pm and left at 3:11 pm. How many minutes was the train at the station?
A 27   B 33   C 49   D 51

**5** Which rectangle has the largest area?
A 19 m × 8 m
B 16 m × 9 m
C 13 m × 13 m
D 35 m × 4 m

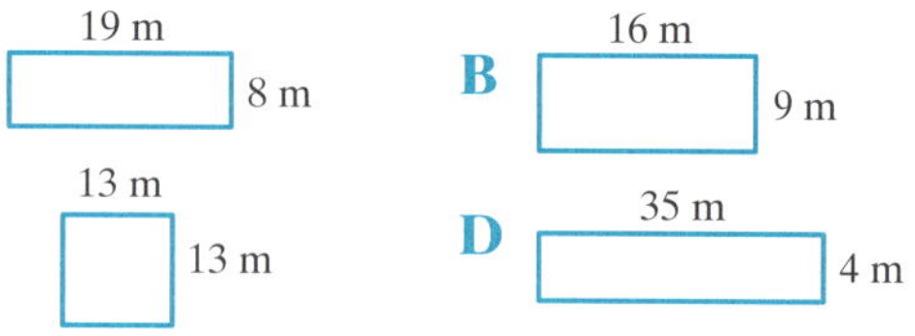

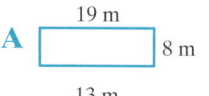

**6** 1 kilometre and 50 metres is the same as
A 1.05 km   B 1.5 km
C 1.005 km   D 100050 m

**7** This balance shows that 3 drums and 2 boxes balance 3 boxes and 1 drum. 
How many drums would balance 4 boxes?
A 2   B 4   C 6   D 8

**8** A car uses petrol at the rate of 8 litres for every 100 km travelled. How far will the car travel on a full tank of 60 litres? ☐ km

**9** Rosemary sees this sign as she drives along the highway to Red Hill. Rosemary knows that Red Hill is between Acacia and Sunshine and is 87 km from Sunshine.

| | km |
|---|---|
| Acacia | 187 |
| Sunshine | 453 |

What is the distance from Acacia to Red Hill? ☐ km

**10** Which calculation will give the area of the shaded triangle (in square units)?

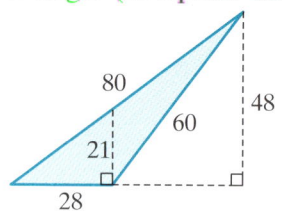

A $\frac{1}{2} \times 28 \times 48$   B $\frac{1}{2} \times 28 \times 60$
C $\frac{1}{2} \times 28 \times 80$   D $\frac{1}{2} \times 28 \times 21$

**11** What is the perimeter of this shape? 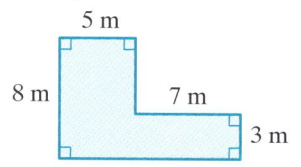
A 23 m   B 35 m   C 40 m   D 46 m

**12** What is the length of the nail in millimetres? 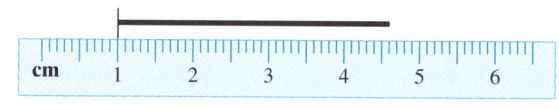
A 34   B 36   C 44   D 46

**13** A square has perimeter 64 m. What is the length of each side? ☐ m

**14** Anna rode 5 km in 20 minutes. What was her average speed in kilometres per hour?
A 4   B 10   C 15   D 25

**15** What is the time $3\frac{3}{4}$ hours after 10:20 am?
A 2:05 pm   B 2:35 pm
C 1:05 pm   D 1:35 pm

**16** The perimeter of this rectangle is 26 m.

What is the length of the rectangle? ☐ m

8    Answers and explanations on pages 89–90

**CALCULATOR ALLOWED** — **Basic level questions**

## Mini Test 6: Basic Chance and Data

**15 min**

**1** A die is tossed once. What is the chance that 5 is shown on the uppermost face?
A $\frac{1}{2}$    B $\frac{1}{4}$    C $\frac{1}{5}$    D $\frac{1}{6}$

**2** Dianne recorded the number of minutes it took to drive home from work each afternoon last week.
What was the average time?

| Day | Time (minutes) |
|---|---|
| Monday | 25 |
| Tuesday | 35 |
| Wednesday | 45 |
| Thursday | 40 |
| Friday | 55 |

☐ min

**3** Jon checked 60 players in his club to see if they had paid their fees. Some of the results are shown in the table.

|  | Paid | Unpaid |
|---|---|---|
| Seniors | 8 |  |
| Juniors | 22 | 13 |

How many seniors had unpaid fees? ☐

**4** The graph shows the number of computers in all the houses in a street.

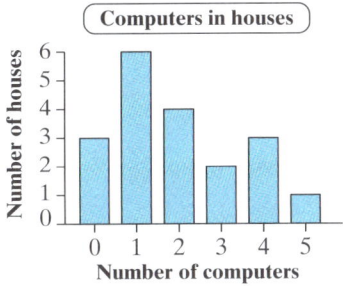

How many computers were there, altogether, in the street? ☐

**5** A jar holds 5 red, 6 yellow, 4 green and 3 black jelly beans. Without looking, Amy takes a jelly bean from the jar. What is the chance that it is yellow?
A $\frac{1}{3}$    B $\frac{1}{4}$    C $\frac{1}{5}$    D $\frac{1}{6}$

**6** After 6 games, Shaun's average (mean) number of points scored per game was 3.5. How many points had Shaun scored altogether? ☐

**7** The graph shows the age and price of four cars for sale at Jim's Autos. Which statement is correct? 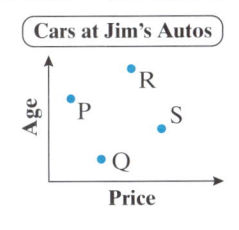
A Car Q is younger and cheaper than car P.
B Car R is younger and cheaper than car S.
C Car P is younger and cheaper than car R.
D Car S is younger and cheaper than car Q.

**8** The number of customers at a store in an hour (over 5-minute intervals) was recorded.
0, 1, 2, 2, 4, 5, 7, 7, 7, 8, 8, 9
What was the median?
A 5    B 6    C 7    D 9

**9** This dot plot was drawn to illustrate some scores. What is the mode? 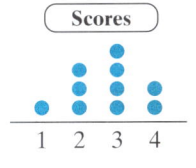
A 4    B 3
C 2    D 1

**10** In which bucket is the chance of choosing a white ball one in four?
A    B    C    D

**11** The ages of ten students at a surf school are 16, 17, 17, 19, 20, 23, 28, 31, 35 and 41. Their ages, and that of an 11th person, were then placed in a stem-and-leaf plot.

Ages of surf students
```
1 | 6 7 7 9
2 | 0 3 7 8
3 | 1 5
4 | 1
```
Key: 4 | 1 = Age of 41

How old was that 11th person? ☐

**12** There are 30 apples in a box. 18 are red and the rest are green. Brad takes an apple from the box without looking. What is the chance that the apple is green?
A $\frac{2}{5}$    B $\frac{1}{3}$    C $\frac{3}{5}$    D $\frac{1}{12}$

Answers and explanations on pages 91–92

# NON-CALCULATOR — Basic level questions
## Mini Test 7: Mixed Questions

**1** What number comes next in this pattern?

1007, 1005, 1003, 1001, ☐

**2** $12 \times 8 = 6 \times \square$
What is the missing number?

**3** Which does **not** have the same value as $4 \times 7$?
- **A** $3 \times 9 + 1$
- **B** $5 \times 5 + 3$
- **C** $10 \times 3 - 2$
- **D** $2 \times 12 + 5$

**4** This map shows the position of some objects in a garden. What is both south of the shed and east of the statue?
- **A** Bench
- **B** Bridge
- **C** Gazebo
- **D** Pond

**5** Sid travelled 350 km in 5 hours. What was his average speed in kilometres per hour?
- **A** 75  **B** 70  **C** 65  **D** 60

**6** Which shows a reflex angle?

**7** Which time is the same as that shown on this clock? `15:30`
- **A** 3:30 pm
- **B** 5:30 pm
- **C** 7:30 pm
- **D** 5:30 am

**8** 25% of tickets to a concert have not been sold. If there are 500 tickets altogether, how many have been sold?

**9** The areas of three of these rectangles are the same. Which rectangle has an area different to the other three?
- **A** 9 m × 4 m
- **B** 6 m × 6 m
- **C** 12 m × 3 m
- **D** 8 m × 5 m

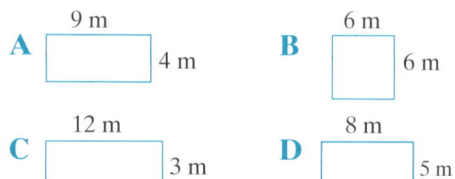

**10** $87 \times 42 = 3654$
What is $8.7 \times 0.42$?
- **A** 0.3654  **B** 3.654  **C** 36.54  **D** 365.4

**11** Adele is making a pattern with matches.

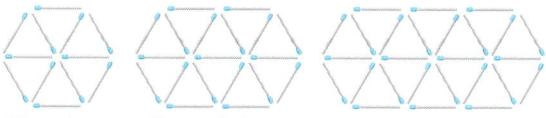

First shape   Second shape   Third shape

How many matches will she need for the next (fourth) shape?

**12** Which spinner has a one in four chance of landing on 2?

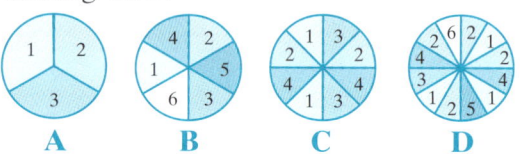

A   B   C   D

**13** This object is made from ten cubes. What is the view from the right side?

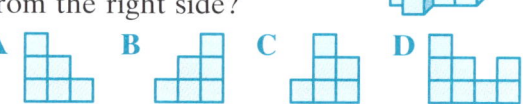

A   B   C   D

**14** Which is closest in value to $\sqrt{500}$?
- **A** 15  **B** 22  **C** 35  **D** 70

**15** The amounts raised for a charity by four friends are shown in the table.

| Name | Amount |
| --- | --- |
| Adam | $350 |
| Brian | $250 |
| Sarah | $400 |
| Louise | $300 |

What was the average (mean) amount raised? $ ☐

**16** This pictograph shows the number of bags of fruit sold by a farmer from her roadside stall one week.

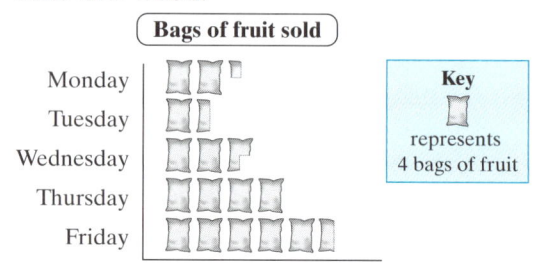

Bags of fruit sold

Monday
Tuesday
Wednesday
Thursday
Friday

Key: represents 4 bags of fruit

On what day were 10 more bags sold than on Tuesday?
- **A** Monday
- **B** Wednesday
- **C** Thursday
- **D** Friday

**CALCULATOR ALLOWED** — **Basic level questions** — 15 MIN

# Mini Test 8: Mixed Questions

**1** The map shows the location of four towns. What direction is Saxon from Portland?

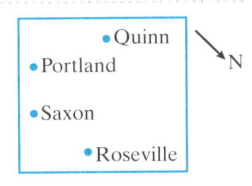

(Map shows: Quinn, Portland, Saxon, Roseville; N arrow pointing north-east)

- A north-east
- B north-west
- C south
- D south-west

**2** Narelle arrived at work at 8:40 am and left at 2:15 pm. How long was Narelle at work?
- A 5 h 25 min
- B 5 h 35 min
- C 6 h 25 min
- D 6 h 35 min

**3** Ron bought a table during a sale where 20% was taken off the marked price of all goods. The marked price of the table was $1200. How much did Ron pay?  $ ☐

**4** If $t = 3$, what is the value of $4t$?
- A 7
- B 12
- C 34
- D 43

**5** A tin holds 9 black, 5 blue, 7 red and 19 white buttons. If a button is taken from the tin without looking, what is the probability that it is blue?
- A $\frac{1}{3}$
- B $\frac{1}{4}$
- C $\frac{1}{5}$
- D $\frac{1}{8}$

**6** Which arrow shows the position of $-1.4$ on the number line?

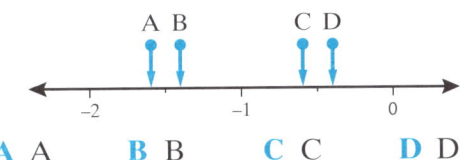

(Number line with arrows A, B near $-2$ to $-1$, and C, D near $-1$ to $0$)

- A A
- B B
- C C
- D D

**7** Two towns are 5.6 cm apart on a map. On the map, 1 cm represents 20 km. How far apart are the actual towns?
- A 28 km
- B 76 km
- C 112 km
- D 280 km

**8** Vera drew these three rectangles.

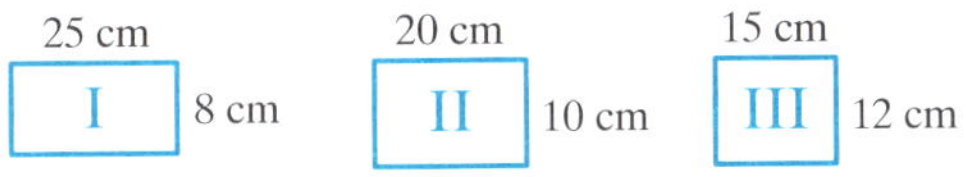

I: 25 cm × 8 cm   II: 20 cm × 10 cm   III: 15 cm × 12 cm

Which rectangles have the same area?
- A I and II only
- B I and III only
- C II and III only
- D I, II and III

**9** What is the average (mean) of 23, 25 and 48?  ☐

**10** Which is the net of this prism?

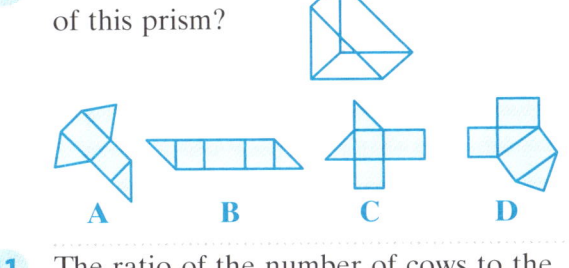

(Options A, B, C, D showing different nets)

**11** The ratio of the number of cows to the number of horses on a property is 5:2. There are 350 cows. How many horses are there?
- A 175
- B 100
- C 140
- D 150

**12** The table shows the area of each state to the nearest thousand square kilometres.

| State | Area (km²) |
|---|---|
| NSW | 802 000 |
| Vic | 228 000 |
| Qld | 1 727 000 |
| SA | 984 000 |
| WA | 2 526 000 |
| Tas | 68 000 |
| NT | 1 346 000 |
| ACT | 2 000 |

How much greater is the area of Western Australia than that of New South Wales and South Australia combined?  ☐ km²

**13** Margaret was using the rule 'double the previous number and add 1' to get the next number in a pattern. The first number was 3. What was the fifth number?  ☐

**14** A train travelled 275 km in $2\frac{1}{2}$ hours. What was its average speed?  ☐ km/h

**15** What is the perimeter of this shape?
- A 195 m
- B 200 m
- C 270 m
- D 285 m

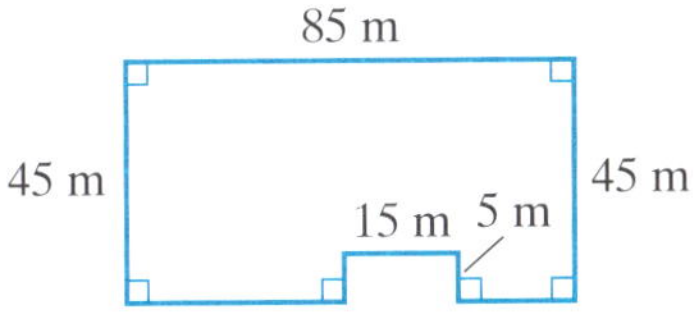

(Shape with sides 85 m, 45 m, 15 m, 5 m, 45 m)

**16** Which diagram shows the result when this shape is rotated through 90° in an anticlockwise direction?

(Options A, B, C, D showing triangles in different orientations)

**NON-CALCULATOR** | **Intermediate level questions**

## Mini Test 9: Numbers

25 MIN

**1** What is 4.2 ÷ 0.2?
  A 0.021   B 0.21   C 2.1   D 21

**2** $\frac{3}{4}$ of a number is 36.
What is $\frac{2}{3}$ of the number? ☐

**3** Tim's phone bill last month was $80. This month it is $100. What percentage increase is this?
  A 20%   B 25%   C 40%   D 80%

**4** What is $12 \div \frac{1}{2}$?
  A 6   B 8   C 20   D 24

**5** Which is equivalent to $\frac{5}{8}$?
  A $\frac{5+2}{8+2}$   B $\frac{5-2}{8-2}$   C $\frac{5 \times 2}{8 \times 2}$   D $\frac{5^2}{8^2}$

**6** Which number is the largest?
  A 0.3   B 0.05   C 0.006   D 0.123

**7** Which fraction is equal to $4\frac{2}{5}$?
  A $\frac{13}{5}$   B $\frac{22}{5}$   C $\frac{18}{5}$   D $\frac{30}{5}$

**8** Of the 80 children in Year 1 at a school, 50 are girls. What is the ratio of girls to boys?
  A 5 to 8   B 3 to 5   C 5 to 3   D 8 to 5

**9** The temperature at midnight was −3°C. It was 5°C colder at 6 am. At 9 am it was 7°C warmer than it was at 6 am. What was the temperature at 9 am?
  A −5°C   B 9°C   C 1°C   D −1°C

**10** On Tuesday, Sandi slashed 30% of a paddock. On Wednesday, she slashed 50% of the remainder of the paddock. Sandi finished slashing the paddock on Thursday. What percentage of the whole paddock did Sandi slash on Thursday? ☐%

**11** $\sqrt{300}$ is between
  A 11 and 14   B 14 and 17
  C 17 and 20   D 120 and 160

**12** A recipe for 1 dozen scones uses $\frac{3}{4}$ cup of water. How many cups of water would be needed to make 2 dozen scones?
  A $\frac{3}{4}$   B $1\frac{1}{4}$   C $1\frac{1}{2}$   D $1\frac{3}{4}$

**13** What is the value of $\frac{4+12}{2 \times 4}$?
  A 2   B 6   C 32   D 40

**14** Kieran bought 2 loaves of bread and a $3 bottle of juice for $11.00. What would 3 loaves of bread and 2 bottles of the juice cost?
  A $15   B $16   C $17   D $18

**15** What number is exactly halfway between 1.84 and 3.46? ☐

**16** $3 - 1\frac{1}{5} = ?$
  A $1\frac{1}{5}$   B $1\frac{4}{5}$   C $2\frac{1}{5}$   D $2\frac{4}{5}$

**17** $20 \times \square = 12$
What is the value of ☐?
  A $\frac{3}{5}$   B $\frac{5}{3}$   C $\frac{3}{4}$   D $\frac{4}{3}$

**18** $\frac{3}{5}$ of the jelly beans in a jar are red and $\frac{1}{4}$ are black. The rest are yellow. What fraction of the jelly beans is yellow?
  A $\frac{3}{20}$   B $\frac{5}{9}$   C $\frac{2}{3}$   D $\frac{1}{5}$

**19** A farm has cows, horses, pigs, goats and sheep. Jackson counted 50 animals. Some of the results are shown in the table.

| Animal | Cow | Horse | Pig | Goat | Sheep |
|---|---|---|---|---|---|
| Number | 16 | 13 |  | 7 | 6 |

What percentage were pigs? ☐%

**20** The ratio of men to women to children competing at a sports event is 5 to 3 to 4. There are 120 competitors. How many more men than women are competing?
  A 10   B 20   C 30   D 50

**NON-CALCULATOR** — **Intermediate level questions** — 20 MIN

# Mini Test 10: Algebra

**1** When $k = -5$, what is the value of $4k$?
  **A** $-9$  **B** $-1$  **C** $-20$  **D** $-45$

**2** Which is equivalent to $3x + 5 + 2x$?
  **A** $5x + 5$  **B** $10x$  **C** $5x^2 + 5$  **D** $10x^2$

**3** Matches are used to make this pattern of triangles.

  In this pattern the rule for the number of matches is
  **A** $2 \times$ number of triangles
  **B** $3 \times$ number of triangles
  **C** $2 \times$ number of triangles $+ 1$
  **D** $3 \times$ number of triangles $- 1$

**4** What is the number 2 less than $x$?
  **A** $-2x$  **B** $2 - x$  **C** $x - 2$  **D** $-2 - x$

**5** Jordan is making a pattern with matches.

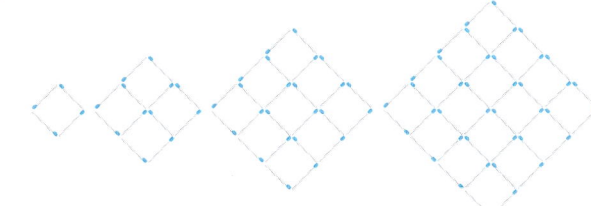

  First   Second   Third   Fourth

  How many matches will be needed for the fifth shape? ☐

**6** $y = 2x - 3$
  $y = x + 5$
  Which value of $x$ satisfies both these equations at the same time?
  **A** $x = -2$  **B** $x = 2$  **C** $x = 4$  **D** $x = 8$

**7** Which expression gives the area of this shape? 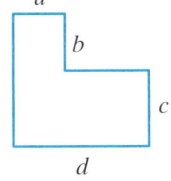
  **A** $(a \times b) + (c \times d)$
  **B** $(a \times c) + (b \times d)$
  **C** $(a \times d) + (b \times d)$
  **D** $(a \times d) + (b \times c)$

**8** Which value of $x$ does **not** satisfy the inequality $2x - 3 \leq 8$?
  **A** $x = -4$  **B** $x = 0$  **C** $x = 5\frac{1}{2}$  **D** $x = 7$

**9** What is the rule connecting $x$ and $y$?

  | $x$ | 1 | 2 | 3 | 4 | 5 |
  |---|---|---|---|---|---|
  | $y$ | 1 | 4 | 7 | 10 | 13 |

  **A** $y = x$  **B** $y = 2x - 1$
  **C** $y = 3x - 2$  **D** $y = 4x - 3$

**10** Adele wrote out the first five numbers in a pattern: 1, 4, 9, 16, 25
  What is the tenth number in this pattern? ☐

**11** A rule connecting $x$ and $y$ is $y = 4x - 7$.
  What is the value of $y$ when $x = 2\frac{1}{2}$?
  **A** $1\frac{1}{2}$  **B** $3$  **C** $4\frac{1}{2}$  **D** $7$

**12** Which expression is equivalent to $3(p + 5)$?
  **A** $p + 15$  **B** $3p + 15$
  **C** $3p + 5$  **D** $15p$

**13** Natasha is drawing a rectangle on a grid. She has marked three of the points.

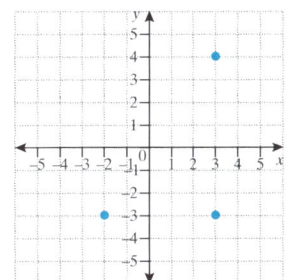

  Where will the fourth point go?
  **A** $(2, -4)$  **B** $(-2, 4)$  **C** $(4, -2)$  **D** $(-4, 2)$

**14** $3x - 7 = x + 3$
  What value of $x$ will satisfy this equation?
  **A** $x = 2$  **B** $x = 3$  **C** $x = 4$  **D** $x = 5$

**15** Which is equal to $m^2$?
  **A** $m + 2$  **B** $m \times 2$  **C** $m + m$  **D** $m \times m$

**16** Jamal is using matches to make a pattern of octagons.

  What is the rule for the number of matches when there are $n$ octagons?
  **A** $7n + 1$  **B** $7n - 1$  **C** $8n$  **D** $8n - 1$

Answers and explanations on pages 97–98

# NON-CALCULATOR — Intermediate level questions
## Mini Test 11: Plane Figures and Solids

**1** A cut is made in this cone as shown in the diagram. Which shows the shape of the cross-section made by the cut?

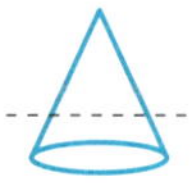

A  ⬭   B ◯   C △   D ⌒

**2** For which shape are the opposite sides **not always** equal?
A rectangle   B rhombus
C square   D trapezium

**3** The opposite faces of a standard die always add to 7. Which is **not** the net of a standard die?

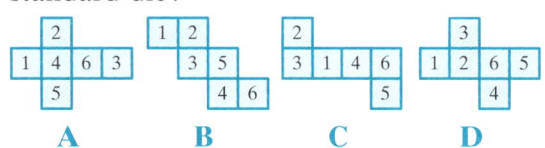

A   B   C   D

**4** What fraction of this rectangle is shaded? 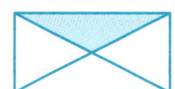
A less than $\frac{1}{4}$
B exactly $\frac{1}{4}$   C more than $\frac{1}{4}$
D there is not enough information

**5** For which object is the sum of the number of edges and number of vertices three times the number of faces?
A triangular prism
B triangular pyramid
C rectangular prism
D rectangular pyramid

**6** Which statement is **not** correct?
A The adjacent sides of a rhombus are always equal.
B The opposite sides of a parallelogram are always equal.
C The diagonals of a parallelogram are always equal.
D The diagonals of a square always meet at right angles.

**7** Consider this rectangular prism. Which edge is **not** perpendicular to AB? 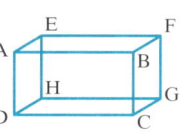
A AD   B AH
C BC   D BE

**8** Shelly made this solid object from 48 cubes. She painted the outside of her object green. Sally then broke her object apart again into the 48 individual cubes. How many of these cubes have exactly one green face? 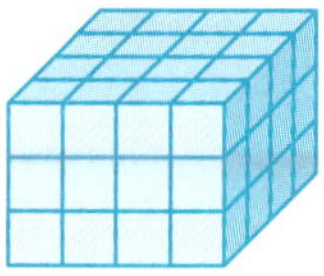
A 20   B 16   C 12   D 8

**9** An equilateral triangle is cut along one of its axes of symmetry. Which description applies to the two resulting triangles?
A acute-angled and isosceles
B obtuse-angled and isosceles
C right-angled and isosceles
D right-angled and scalene

**10** Mark made a 3D object from identical cubes. He then drew a front view and a side view.

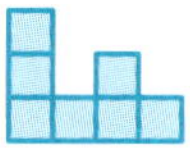

Front 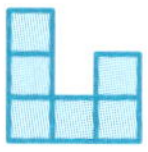   Side

Which **cannot** be a top view of Mark's object?

A   B   C   D

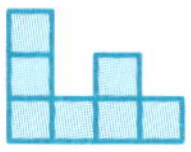

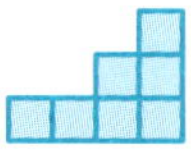

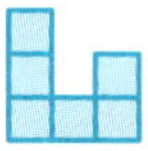

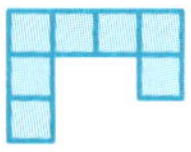

**11** Maria is paving a square area with triangular tiles.

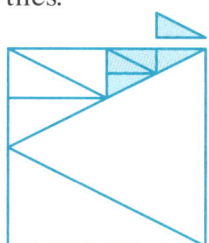

How many tiles will she need altogether?

**12** The six faces of a cube show six different symbols (a small dot, a large dot, a triangle, a square, a circle and a cross). Here are two different views of this cube:

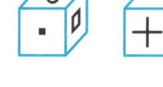

What symbol is on the face opposite the face showing the large dot?
A ◯   B □   C △   D +

**NON-CALCULATOR** — **Intermediate level questions**

# Mini Test 12: Measurement and Data

**20 MIN**

**1** The area of this rectangle is 85 cm². 

85 cm²   5 cm

What is the length of the rectangle? ☐ cm

**2** A bag holds 12 red, 15 blue, 9 yellow and 6 green marbles. Without looking, Cate takes a marble from the bag. What is the chance that the marble is green?
A $\frac{1}{4}$   B $\frac{1}{5}$   C $\frac{1}{6}$   D $\frac{1}{7}$

**3** Glenda counted the different types of vehicles that went past her house one hour and showed the results in a divided bar chart.

**Vehicles passing Glenda's house**

| Motorbikes | Cycles | Trucks | Cars |

If there were 18 motorbikes, how many trucks were there? ☐

**4** 1.2 kg and 1500 g is the same as
A 1.215 kg   B 1.35 kg
C 2.215 kg   D 2.7 kg

**5** Each week, Albert's class does a test marked out of 10. After seven tests Albert's mean (average) mark is 8. Albert scores 10 in his eighth test. Which is closest to his mean after eight tests?
A 8   B 8.3   C 8.8   D 9.4

**6** In $3\frac{1}{2}$ hours, Daphne drove 240 km. Her average speed for the first 2 hours was 70 kilometres per hour. How far did she travel in the last $1\frac{1}{2}$ hours? ☐ km

**7** Grant is building a fence. He has positioned the two end posts 100 metres apart and needs to place other posts at 5-metre intervals as shown in the diagram.

(not to scale)
100 m
5 m

How many other posts does Grant need?
A 19   B 20   C 21   D 25

**8** Here is a set of five scores: 4, 2, 6, 4, 4
Which is equal to 4?
A mode only
B mode and range only
C mode, mean and range only
D mode, mean, median and range

**9** A rectangle has a perimeter of 24 metres. The shorter sides are 5 metres long. How long are the longer sides? ☐ m

**10** In a straight line, the distance from Y to Z is three times the distance from X to Y. The distance from X to Z is 60 km.

60 km   (not to scale)
X   Y   Z

What is the distance from X to Y?
A 12 km   B 15 km   C 18 km   D 20 km

**11** Netta is weighing flour. She needs 1.5 kg. About how much more flour does she need?
A 250 g   B 400 g
C 600 g   D 900 g

**12** There are 40 pegs in a basket. 15 pegs are yellow and the rest are green. Without looking, Greg takes a peg from the basket. What is the probability that it is green?
A $\frac{3}{8}$   B $\frac{1}{2}$   C $\frac{5}{8}$   D $\frac{1}{15}$

**13** Consider these scores: 3, 5, 5, 8, 12
Which changes if the score of 8 is removed?
A mean   B median   C mode   D range

**14** A car uses fuel at the rate of 8 litres per 100 km travelled. How much fuel will it use to travel 625 km? ☐ litres

**15** A plane arrived in Hobart at 1:20 pm after a $3\frac{3}{4}$ hour flight from Brisbane. What time did it leave Brisbane?
A 9:35 am   B 9:45 am
C 10:15 am   D 10:35 am

15   Answers and explanations on pages 100–101

**CALCULATOR ALLOWED** — **Intermediate level questions** — 25 MIN

## Mini Test 13: Number Operations and Ratios

**1** A positive number was multiplied by itself. The answer was 8649. What was the number?

**2** Isabel was supposed to multiply a number by 17 and then subtract 25 but instead she multiplied by 25 and then subtracted 17. Her answer was 1008. What should it have been?

**3** The ratio of cars to trucks on a road was 7 to 2. If there were 126 cars, how many cars and trucks were there altogether?
A 144    B 154    C 162    D 441

**4** What two numbers multiply to 12 and add to 13? ☐ and ☐

**5** Which is equal to $12^2 + 16^2$?
A $20^2$    B $24^2$    C $28^2$    D $32^2$

**6** Of the 30 medals won by a country in the Olympic games, 9 were gold and 6 were silver. What was the ratio of gold to silver to bronze medals?
A 5:3:2    B 5:2:3    C 2:3:5    D 3:2:5

**7** Which is a factor of both 87 and 111?
A 3    B 7    C 11    D 37

**8** A packet of two hinges costs $11.90 and a packet of five of those hinges costs $27.50. Pia wants to buy 12 hinges. What is the least amount that she can pay? $

**9** Which is equivalent to $4^3$?
A $2 \times 2 \times 2$
B $2 \times 2 \times 2 \times 2$
C $2 \times 2 \times 2 \times 2 \times 2$
D $2 \times 2 \times 2 \times 2 \times 2 \times 2$

**10** Which is **not** equal to 20?
A $40 \div 8 \times 4$    B $3 \times 8 - 2 \times 2$
C $3 + 7 \times 2$    D $32 - 3 \times 4$

**11** Callum's fortnightly train ticket costs $21.20. A daily return ticket costs $2.60. How much does Callum save each day by buying a fortnightly ticket instead of ten daily return tickets? $

**12** The table shows the maximum and minimum temperatures for four towns, one day last winter.

| Town | Sullivan | Lotus | Paxton | Kenton |
|---|---|---|---|---|
| Maximum (°C) | 15 | 12 | 7 | −1 |
| Minimum (°C) | −1 | −5 | −8 | −12 |

Which town had the biggest difference between its maximum and minimum temperature?
A Sullivan    B Lotus
C Paxton    D Kenton

**13** There were 120 adults at a meeting. The ratio of men to women at the meeting was 7 to 5. How many more men than women were at the meeting?
A 2    B 10    C 12    D 20

**14** Together a loaf of bread and a packet of biscuits cost $5.50. The bread cost 50 cents more than the biscuits. How much was the bread? $

**15** Neil paid $8.60 when he bought 2.5 kg of carrots. Which calculation would give the cost of 7 kg of the carrots?
A $2.5 \div \$8.60 \times 7$    B $7 \div \$8.60 \times 2.5$
C $\$8.60 \div 2.5 \times 7$    D $\$8.60 \div 7 \times 2.5$

**16** Nelly put 3 sweets in each of nine bags and had 5 sweets left over. If she wanted to put 4 sweets in each of 12 bags, how many more sweets would she need?

**17** Which is **not** correct?
A $4 \leq 7$    B $-5 < -8$
C $-2 > -3$    D $6 \geq -1$

**18** Jess and Jo share $3600 in the ratio 5 to 4. What is Jo's share?
A $1600    B $1700    C $1800    D $2000

**19** $\sqrt{1600 + 81} =$
A 41    B 49    C 121    D 129

**20** Brandon paid $2000 deposit and monthly payments of $360 for 2 years when he bought a car. How much extra did he pay than the cash price of $8000? $

16    Answers and explanations on pages 101–103

**CALCULATOR ALLOWED** — **Intermediate level questions** — 20 MIN

## Mini Test 14: Fractions, Decimals and Percentages

**1** What number is exactly halfway between $2\frac{3}{4}$ and $4\frac{1}{4}$?
 A 3  B $3\frac{1}{4}$  C $3\frac{1}{2}$  D $3\frac{3}{4}$

**2** Caleb bought a pair of boots which were on sale at 40% off the marked price. The marked price of the boots was $120. How much did Caleb pay?
 A $48  B $64  C $72  D $80

**3** What is the value of $\frac{18.4 - 6.8}{4 \div 0.2}$?
 A 0.58  B 9.9  C 14.5  D 18.06

**4** Jorja ate 40% of a pie on Saturday and ate 40% of the remaining pie on Sunday. How much of the pie remained on Monday?
 A 40%  B 36%  C 16%  D 0

**5** Liam spends $\frac{2}{5}$ of his weekly income on rent and $\frac{1}{4}$ on food. If the amount he spends on food is $225, how much is his weekly rent? $ ____

**6** Alexander scored these marks in his exams.

| Subject | Mark |
|---|---|
| English | 37 out of 50 |
| Maths | 51 out of 60 |
| Science | 56 out of 70 |
| History | 19 out of 25 |

In which subject did Alexander achieve his best result?
 A English  B Maths
 C Science  D History

**7** Yesterday, Alison completed 25 laps of the pool. Today she completed 30 laps. What percentage increase is this?
 A 20%  B 25%  C 30%  D 55%

**8** Which set of decimals is in order from lowest to highest?
 A 0.3, 0.05, 0.048, 0.107
 B 0.05, 0.048, 0.3, 0.107
 C 0.05, 0.3, 0.048, 0.107
 D 0.048, 0.05, 0.107, 0.3

**9** Some friends shared the cost of starting a business. Sally paid $3000. This was 12% of the total cost. Jim paid 15% of the cost. How much did Jim pay? $ ____

**10** Which is the largest?
 A 0.56  B $\frac{5}{6}$  C 65%  D $\frac{4}{5}$

**11** When rounded off to one decimal place 3.2185 and 7.462 become
 A 3.2 and 7.4  B 3.3 and 7.4
 C 3.2 and 7.5  D 3.3 and 7.5

**12** There are 200 animals on a farm. One-fifth of the animals are sheep and the rest are cattle. 40% of the cattle are calves. How many calves are on the farm?
 A 16  B 24  C 40  D 64

**13** What number is exactly halfway between 0.35 and 0.63? ____

**14** A recipe to make 16 biscuits uses $\frac{3}{4}$ cup of honey. Jamie wants to make 4 dozen of the biscuits. How many cups of honey should she use?
 A $1\frac{1}{3}$  B $2\frac{1}{4}$  C 3  D $3\frac{1}{2}$

**15** 200 spectators were asked which field event they preferred at an athletics meet. Some of the results are shown in the table.

| Event | Number |
|---|---|
| Discus | 37 |
| Javelin | 29 |
| Shot-put | 36 |
| High jump |  |
| Long jump | 48 |

What percentage preferred the high jump?
 A 25%  B 35%  C 40%  D 50%

**16** What is the value of $\frac{\frac{3}{4} - \frac{1}{2}}{8}$?
 A 32  B 2  C $\frac{11}{16}$  D $\frac{1}{32}$

**CALCULATOR ALLOWED** — Intermediate level questions

# Mini Test 15: Angles

**20 min**

**1** What is the size of ∠PQR? ▢°

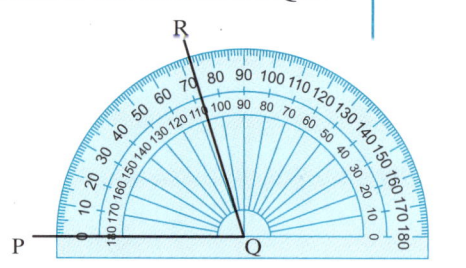

**2** What is the value of y? ▢

**3** Which is the best estimate for the size of this angle?
A 70°   B 110°   C 140°   D 170° 

**4** Which of these (when drawn accurately) is an isosceles triangle?
A (50°, 60°)   B (40°, 70°)   C (30°, 65°, 20°)   D (75°)

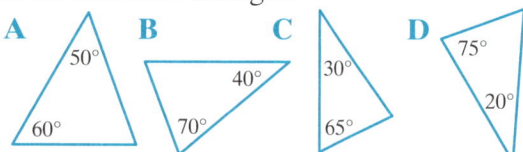

**5** A regular hexagon is divided into two trapeziums. 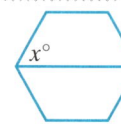 What is the value of x? ▢

**6** What is the value of a? (120°, 110°, 80°, a°) ▢

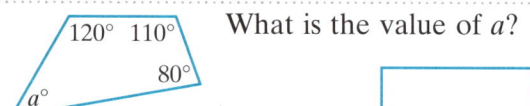

**7** What is the value of x? (130°, x°) ▢

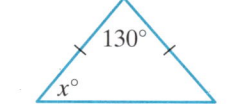

**8** What is the value of m? (m°, m°) ▢

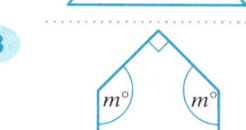

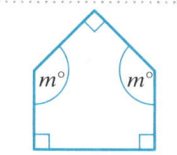

**9** What is the value of z? (40°, 120°, z°) ▢

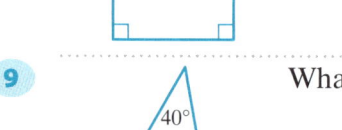

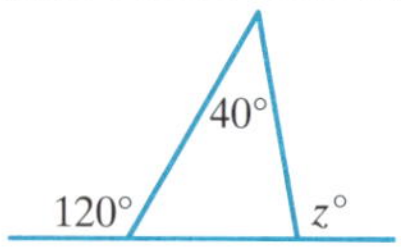

**10** This diagram is made up of a rectangle and an equilateral triangle. x = ▢

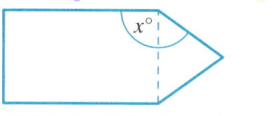

**11** A trapezium has two angles of 110° and its other angles are equal to each other. What size is each of those remaining angles? ▢°

**12** Which description applies to triangle CBD? 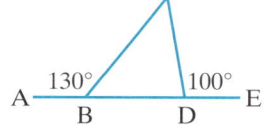
A acute-angled, isosceles
B acute-angled, scalene
C obtuse-angled, isosceles
D obtuse-angled, scalene
(A — 130° — B — D — 100° — E, C above)

**13** Which of these (when drawn accurately) is a right-angled triangle?
A (47°, 53°)   B (39°, 71°)   C (36°, 64°)   D (58°, 32°)

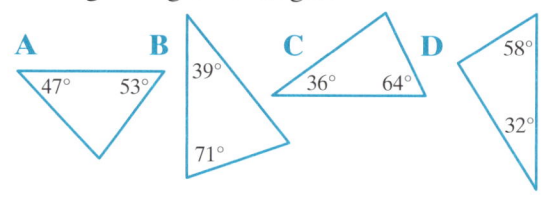

**14** What is the value of a? (100°, 40°, 30°, a°) ▢

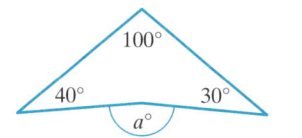

**15** In this diagram, AE is a straight line. (70°, 30°, 60° at G and F)
What is the size of ∠BGC?
A 30°   B 40°   C 80°   D 100°

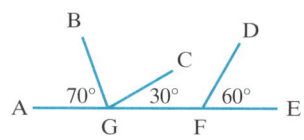

**16** What is the value of x? ▢

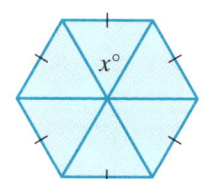

Answers and explanations on pages 104–106

**CALCULATOR ALLOWED** — **Intermediate level questions** — **20 MIN**

## Mini Test 16: Rates and Measurements

**1** A milk vat has a capacity of 9.75 kL. How many litres of milk does the vat hold when full?
A 9075  B 9750  C 97 500  D 975 000

**2** The diagram shows the course of a 21 km half-marathon, which starts and finishes at the same point.

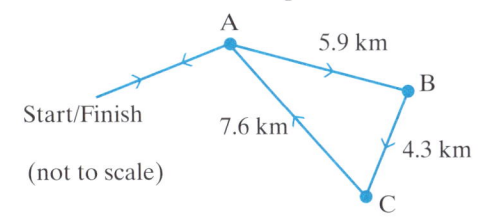

How long is it from the start to A? ☐ km

**3** Steven ran a 21 km half-marathon. His average speed was 9 kilometres per hour. How long did he take to complete the race?
A 2 h 3 min     B 2 h 20 min
C 2 h 33 min    D 2 h 40 min

**4** 1 kilogram and 75 grams is the same as
A 1.0075 kg    B 1.00075 kg
C 1.75 kg      D 1.075 kg

**5** A car uses petrol at the rate of 7.5 litres per 100 km travelled. Approximately how much petrol will it use to travel 750 km?
A 10 L  B 60 L  C 75 L  D 100 L

**6** A tap is dripping and fills a 7.2 litre bucket in one hour. At which rate is the water flowing?
A 2 millilitres per second
B 4 millilitres per second
C 6 millilitres per second
D 8 millilitres per second

**7** When it is 7:30 am in London, it is 3:30 pm in Perth on the same day. When it is 7:30 am Monday in Perth, what time is it in London?
A 3:30 pm Monday  B 11:30 pm Monday
C 3:30 pm Sunday  D 11:30 pm Sunday

**8** 3 hours and 15 minutes is the same as
A 315 min   B 325 min
C 3.15 h    D 3.25 h

**9** The diameter of a 20-cent piece is about 28 mm. Kemal has a line of 20-cent pieces stretching 5.6 metres.

5.6 m (not to scale)

What is the total value of Kemal's line?
A $4  B $10  C $40  D $100

**10** This bottle has some juice in it. If Jan fills three glasses, each holding 250 mL, from the bottle, how much juice (in millilitres) will remain in the bottle? ☐ mL

**11** Candy left home at 9:30 am and arrived at her friend's house at 11:00 am. If the distance Candy travelled was 108 km, what was her average speed?
A 54 km/h     B 72 km/h
C 83 km/h     D 108 km/h

**12** A bus travelled 330 km at an average speed of 60 kilometres per hour. The bus trip began at 10:30 am. When did it finish?
A 3:00 pm   B 3:20 pm
C 4:00 pm   D 4:20 pm

**13** 4 kilometres and 80 metres is the same as
A 4.08 km   B 4.8 km
C 480 m     D 400 080 m

**14** Eden is laying paving tiles to make a path as shown in the diagram.

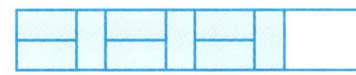

The path is to be 6 metres long and each tile is 40 cm long and 20 cm wide. How many tiles will she need? ☐

**15** On a trip of 625 km, a car used 50 litres of petrol. What is the rate of fuel consumption in litres per 100 km? ☐ L/100 km

**16** 9 cm and 15 mm is the same as
A 9.15 cm   B 915 mm
C 10.5 cm   D 1015 mm

**CALCULATOR ALLOWED** — **Intermediate level questions** — **20 MIN**

## Mini Test 17: Perimeter, Area and Volume

**1** The perimeter of a square is 4 metres. What is the area of the square?
   **A** 1 m²    **B** 2 m²    **C** 4 m²    **D** 16 m²

**2** The dimensions of a rectangular prism are double those of a smaller rectangular prism. How many times larger is the volume of the first prism than that of the smaller prism?
   **A** 2    **B** 4    **C** 6    **D** 8

**3** The area of a rectangle is 84 cm². The width of the rectangle is 6 cm. What is the length of the rectangle? ☐ cm

**4** All six faces of this cube are to be painted. What is the total area of all the faces, in square centimetres? (7 cm)
   **A** 196    **B** 252    **C** 294    **D** 343

**5** The area of a square is 36 cm². What is the perimeter of the square? ☐ cm

**6** The diagram shows the plan of a backyard. What is the area of the yard in square metres? (15 m, 28 m, 11 m, 9 m)
   **A** 417    **B** 519    **C** 537    **D** 1580

**7** The diameter of a circle is 48 cm. Which is the best approximation for the circumference?
   **A** 150 cm    **B** 180 cm
   **C** 300 cm    **D** 580 cm

**8** What is the area of this triangle in square metres? (5 m, 12 m, 13 m)
   **A** 30    **B** 32.5    **C** 65    **D** 78

**9** A piece of wire is bent to form a regular hexagon, each side of which is 3 cm long. The wire is straightened and then bent again to form a square. What is the length of each side of the square? ☐ cm

**10** Which rectangular prism has the greatest volume?
   **A** 7 m, 4 m, 3 m
   **B** 3 m, 9 m, 3 m
   **C** 8 m, 5 m, 2 m
   **D** 11 m, 4 m, 2 m

**11** A fish tank has a rectangular base that is 50 cm long and 30 cm wide. The tank holds water to a depth of 20 cm. Given that 1 m³ = 1000 L, how many litres will the fish tank hold?
   **A** 3000    **B** 300    **C** 30    **D** 3

**12** What is the area of this rectangle? (2 m, 90 cm)
   **A** 180 cm²    **B** 1.8 m²
   **C** 18 m²    **D** 180 m²

**13** The volume of this rectangular prism is 480 cubic metres. What is the height of the prism? (12 m, 8 m) ☐ m

**14** The cross-section of this prism is a regular hexagon of side length 10 cm. The height of the prism is 9 cm and each hexagonal face has an area of 260 cm². What is the total area of all the faces? (260 cm², 9 cm, 10 cm) ☐ cm²

**15** The diagram shows the end wall of a shed that needs to be painted. What is the area of the wall? (3 m, 5 m, 14 m) ☐ m²

**16** A rectangular swimming pool 18 metres long and 15 metres wide is to have a 1-metre wide path on all four sides. The path is to be paved. What is the area that needs to be paved?
   **A** 34 m²    **B** 48 m²    **C** 52 m²    **D** 70 m²

# Mini Test 18: Chance and Data

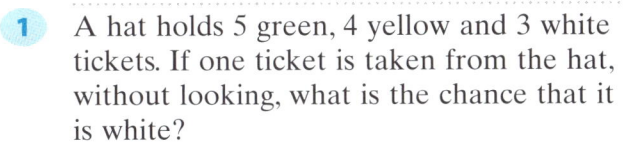

**CALCULATOR ALLOWED** — Intermediate level questions — 20 MIN

**1** A hat holds 5 green, 4 yellow and 3 white tickets. If one ticket is taken from the hat, without looking, what is the chance that it is white?
A $\frac{1}{6}$  B $\frac{1}{5}$  C $\frac{1}{4}$  D $\frac{1}{3}$

**2** When two dice are tossed, in how many ways can you get a total of 6?
A 3  B 4  C 5  D 6

**3** This spinner is to be spun 30 times. Which number would you expect to get 6 times? 
A 4  B 3
C 2  D 1

**4** A table was drawn up to show whether boys and girls attending a camp lived in the city or country. Some of the entries in the table are missing.

|  | City | Country | Total |
|---|---|---|---|
| Boys | 85 |  | 123 |
| Girls |  |  |  |
| Total | 168 |  | 250 |

How many girls were from the country?

**5** The sector graph shows the make-up of 300 people on a cruise. 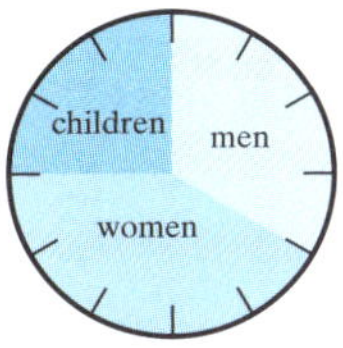
Which is the best estimate for the number of women on the cruise?
A 70  B 90  C 110  D 130

This stem-and-leaf plot is used for questions 6, 7 and 8. It shows the marks received by members of a class in an exam.

**Marks for Class 9P**
```
5 | 7 9
6 | 0 2 4 5 8 9 9 9
7 | 1 3 4 6 6 7 8
8 | 0 2 5 5 7 9
9 | 3 8
```
Key: 9 | 3 is a score of 93

**6** What is the range?

**7** What is the mode?

**8** What is the median?

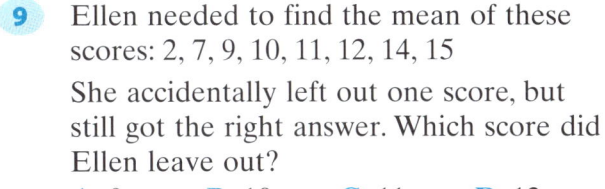

**9** Ellen needed to find the mean of these scores: 2, 7, 9, 10, 11, 12, 14, 15
She accidentally left out one score, but still got the right answer. Which score did Ellen leave out?
A 9  B 10  C 11  D 12

**10** Max recorded the colour of the bicycles at his school.

| Colour | Red | Black | Blue | Green | Pink |
|---|---|---|---|---|---|
| Number | 23 | 8 | 16 | 6 | 11 |

Based on these results, what is the probability that a bicycle is blue?
A $\frac{1}{3}$  B $\frac{1}{4}$  C $\frac{1}{5}$  D $\frac{1}{6}$

This graph is used for questions 11, 12, 13. It is used to convert amounts in other currencies to amounts in Australian dollars.

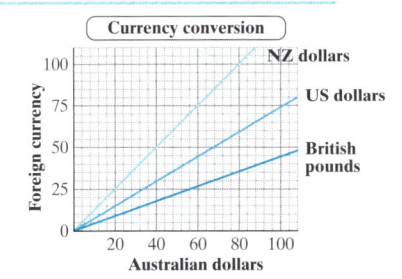

**11** How many British pounds will you get for $80 Australian? ⬚ British pounds

**12** How many Australian dollars will you get for 60 New Zealand dollars? $ ⬚

**13** How many New Zealand dollars will you get for 30 US dollars? ⬚ NZ dollars

**14** The 40 participants in a fun run raised an average of $20 per person for charity. How much was raised altogether? $ ⬚

**15** Of the 200 students in Year 9, 120 came to school by bus. If a student is chosen at random from Year 9, what is the probability that he or she did **not** come by bus?
A $\frac{2}{5}$  B $\frac{3}{5}$  C $\frac{1}{3}$  D $\frac{2}{3}$

**16** Consider these scores: 5, 8, 8, 11, 13
Which is **not** equal to 8?
A mean  B mode  C median  D range

Answers and explanations on pages 109–110

# NON-CALCULATOR — Intermediate level questions
## Mini Test 19: Mixed Questions
**20 MIN**

1. Which fraction is equal to $3\frac{2}{5}$?
   A $\frac{11}{5}$   B $\frac{14}{5}$   C $\frac{16}{5}$   D $\frac{17}{5}$

2. What type of angle is ∠AOB?

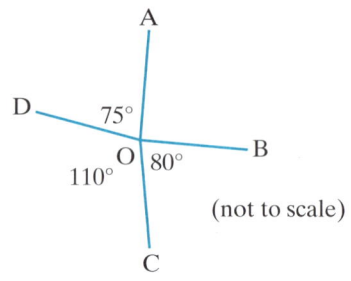

   (angles at O: 75°, 80°, 110°) (not to scale)

   A obtuse   B acute   C reflex   D right

3. A photo was 10 cm long and 8 cm wide. It was enlarged so that it is now 40 cm wide. How long is the enlarged photo? ☐ cm

4. What is the value of $3xy$ when $x = -2$ and $y = 4$?
   A −24   B −5   C 4   D 10

5. The average (mean) of five scores is 7. When an extra score is included, the new average is 8. What was the extra score?
   A 1   B 8   C 11   D 13

6. Which expression is equal to $56 \times 17 - 12 \times 56$?
   A $56 \times 5$    B $17 \times 12$
   C $39 \times 44$   D $29 \times 56$

7. What is $0.2 \div 0.04$?
   A 0.005   B 0.05   C 0.5   D 5

8. A bucket holds 8 blue, 12 red and 4 white balls. Without looking, Toby takes a ball from the bucket. What is the probability that it is white?
   A $\frac{1}{3}$   B $\frac{1}{4}$   C $\frac{1}{5}$   D $\frac{1}{6}$

9. $2h + 7 = 23$
   What is the value of $h$ in this equation?   $h = $ ☐

10. The ratio of boys to girls in a class is 5 to 4. There are 27 students in the class. How many more boys than girls are in the class?
    A 1   B 2   C 3   D 4

11. Which statement about a rhombus is **not always** correct?
    A The opposite sides are equal.
    B The diagonals are equal.
    C The opposite sides are parallel.
    D The adjacent sides are equal.

12. Liz needs to plot the points (2, −3), (3, −2), (−2, 3) and (−3, 2) on a grid. She has plotted three of the points. 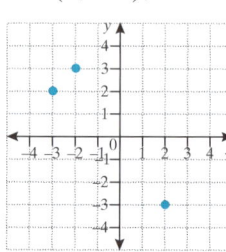
    Which point does Liz still need to plot?
    A (2, −3)   B (3, −2)
    C (−2, 3)   D (−3, 2)

13. There were 12 000 entrants in a dance competition. 30% of the entrants were called to the first audition. Of those, $\frac{1}{4}$ were asked to a second audition. 20% of those at the second audition were interviewed and $\frac{1}{3}$ of those interviewed were chosen. How many dancers were chosen? ☐

14. $m + n = 4$
    $m - n = -6$
    Which values of $m$ and $n$ satisfy both these equations?
    A $m = 1$ and $n = 3$
    B $m = 2$ and $n = 2$
    C $m = -1$ and $n = 5$
    D $m = -2$ and $n = 4$

15. The area of a rectangle is 20 m². The width of the rectangle is 4 m. What is the perimeter of the rectangle?
    A 9 m   B 10 m   C 18 m   D 20 m

16. Bill made this solid object using 30 identical cubes. He painted it green before pulling it apart. 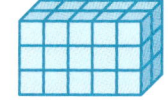
    Which statement is **not** correct?
    A No cubes have no painted faces.
    B 8 cubes have exactly one painted face.
    C 16 cubes have exactly two painted faces.
    D 8 cubes have three painted faces.

Answers and explanations on pages 110–112

**CALCULATOR ALLOWED** — **Intermediate level questions** — **20 MIN**

# Mini Test 20: Mixed Questions

**1** What is the total area of all the faces of this rectangular prism? (3 m, 6 m, 4 m)
A 54 m²    B 61 m²    C 72 m²    D 108 m²

**2** What is the size of ∠XYZ?

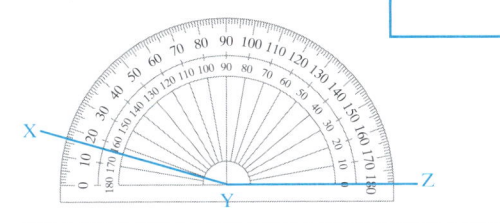

**3** Lisa has a total of 96 books. She has three times as many paperbacks as hardcover books. How many paperback books does Lisa have?

**4** How many hours and minutes are between 6:42 am and 3:24 pm on the same day?
A 8 h 42 min    B 9 h 18 min
C 9 h 22 min    D 9 h 42 min

**5** The arrow points to a position on the number line. What number is at the position indicated by the arrow?

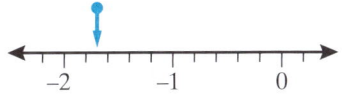

**6** Harry had a cube and a pyramid. The square base of the pyramid was the same size as each face of the cube. Harry stuck the base of the pyramid to one face of the cube. How many more edges than faces does the resulting solid have?
A 6    B 7    C 8    D 9

**7** PQRS is a rectangle. What is the value of x?   PQ = (2x − 5) cm, SR = (x + 4) cm
A 3    B 4
C 9    D 13

**8** The number of pets owned by nine friends is shown in the list.

| Number of pets | 0, 0, 1, 1, 1, 2, 2, 3, 5 |

Which is the largest?
A mean    B mode
C median    D range

**9** In class 9K there are 28 students and the ratio of boys to girls is 2 to 5. In class 9Y there are 21 boys. The ratio of boys to girls in 9Y is 7 to 3. How many more girls than boys are in the two classes?
A 0    B 1    C 7    D 17

**10** The diagram shows a rectangle and two equilateral triangles. What is the value of $x$?

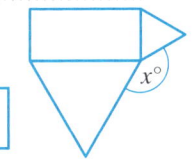

**11** $\frac{2}{5}$ of the pens in a box are blue and $\frac{1}{3}$ are black. The remaining 12 pens are red. How many pens are in the box?

**12** This table of values has been drawn up for values of $x$ and $y$ obeying a rule.

| x | 1 | 3 | 5 | 7 | 9 |
|---|---|---|---|---|---|
| y | 1 | 2 | 3 | 4 | 5 |

What is the rule?
A $y = \frac{1}{2}x + 1$    B $y = \frac{1}{2}(x + 1)$
C $y = 2(x + 1)$    D $y = 2x - 1$

**13** Over the last six years the value of a house has increased by 60%. The house is now valued at $320 000. What was its value six years ago? $

**14** Four children compared their ages. The diagram shows the result. Who is the oldest?

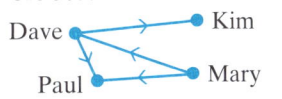

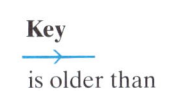

Key: → is older than

A Dave    B Mary    C Paul    D Kim

**15** The map, drawn to scale, shows the route of a walk of length 1.5 km. What scale is used on the map?
A 1 unit = 25 m
B 1 unit = 30 m
C 1 unit = 50 m
D 1 unit = 60 m

**16** What number is 3 less than 5 times $n$?
A $2n$    B $3 - 5n$
C $3 + 5n$    D $5n - 3$

Answers and explanations on pages 112–114

# NON-CALCULATOR — Advanced level questions
## Mini Test 21: Number

**25 MIN**

**1.** Which set of fractions is arranged from lowest to highest?
A $\frac{3}{5}, \frac{5}{8}, \frac{7}{10}, \frac{13}{20}$
B $\frac{3}{5}, \frac{5}{8}, \frac{13}{20}, \frac{7}{10}$
C $\frac{13}{20}, \frac{7}{10}, \frac{5}{8}, \frac{3}{5}$
D $\frac{5}{8}, \frac{13}{20}, \frac{3}{5}, \frac{7}{10}$

**2.** Which has the same value as $9^4$?
A $4^9$  B $6^3$  C $3^6$  D $3^8$

**3.** 30% of the competitors representing a club received a medal. Of these, 20% received a gold medal. What percentage of the club's competitors received a gold medal? ☐ %

**4.** Which is **not** equal to 0.32?
A $0.4 \times 0.8$  B $0.12 + 0.2$
C $6.4 \div 0.2$  D $1 - 0.68$

**5.** Which has the largest value?
A $\frac{1}{8}$  B $0.16$  C $8\%$  D $\frac{1}{9}$

**6.** What is the value of $(0.3)^2$?
A $0.09$  B $0.9$  C $0.6$  D $0.33$

**7.** There were 28 students in a class. The ratio of boys to girls was 5 to 2. Two more girls joined the class. What is the new ratio of boys to girls?
A 5:2  B 5:4  C 3:2  D 2:1

**8.** The price of a television was $600. During a sale this price was reduced by 10%. Which calculation gives the sale price?
A $600 - 10$  B $600 - 0.1$
C $600 \times 0.1$  D $600 \times 0.9$

**9.** Which two numbers multiply to $-18$ and add to $-7$? ☐ and ☐

**10.** What is $\sqrt{0.01}$?
A $0.1$  B $0.01$  C $0.001$  D $0.0001$

**11.** Which shows 60 written as a product of its prime factors?
A $3 \times 4 \times 5$  B $2 \times 3 \times 5$
C $2 \times 2 \times 3 \times 5$  D $2 \times 3 \times 3 \times 5$

**12.** Which has the largest value?
A $\frac{1}{3}$  B $\frac{2}{5}$  C $\frac{3}{10}$  D $\frac{11}{30}$

**13.** What number is halfway between $\frac{1}{3}$ and $\frac{1}{5}$?
A $\frac{1}{4}$  B $\frac{4}{15}$  C $\frac{1}{2}$  D $\frac{3}{8}$

**14.** $\frac{3}{4}$ of an amount is $180. What is $\frac{2}{3}$ of the amount? $ ☐

**15.** Which statement is correct?
A $0.3 < 0.08$  B $-0.7 > -0.6$
C $0.123 > 0.4$  D $-0.9 < -0.75$

**16.** In 1991, Cathy turned 16. At her birthday party she met Jade, who was also celebrating her birthday. Jade was $\frac{1}{4}$ of Cathy's age. On their birthday in 2011, what fraction of Cathy's age will Jade then be?
A $\frac{1}{4}$  B $\frac{4}{7}$  C $\frac{2}{3}$  D $\frac{3}{4}$

**17.** There were 60 people at a party. The ratio of adults to children was 7 to 5. Later, 20 people left the party. The new ratio of adults to children was 5 to 3. How many adults and children left the party?
A 10 adults and 10 children
B 12 adults and 8 children
C 8 adults and 12 children
D 15 adults and 5 children

**18.** A packet has balloons in colours of red, white and blue. $\frac{5}{12}$ of the balloons are red and $\frac{1}{3}$ are blue. What fraction of the balloons is white?
A $\frac{1}{15}$  B $\frac{1}{12}$  C $\frac{1}{4}$  D $\frac{1}{3}$

Answers and explanations on pages 114–116

# NON-CALCULATOR — Advanced level questions
## Mini Test 22: Algebra

**1** Which expression is equivalent to $-5x + 3$?
  A $-2x$  B $-3 + 5x$
  C $5x - 3$  D $3 - 5x$

**2** When $t = -2$, what is the value of $3t^2$?
  A 12  B $-12$  C 36  D $-36$

**3** The smallest number in a set of three consecutive whole numbers is given the value $x$. What is the value of the largest number in the set?
  A $z$  B $x + 2$  C $x + 3$  D $x + 4$

**4** $7p - 2 = 3p + 6$
  What value of $p$ will satisfy this equation?  $p = \boxed{\phantom{000}}$

**5** $3(2a - 2) + 5a + 4 =$
  A $10a + 2$  B $10a + 10$
  C $11a - 2$  D $11a + 2$

**6** A rule for $y$ in terms of $x$ is $y = 3x + 5$. If $y = 38$, what is the value of $x$?  $x = \boxed{\phantom{000}}$

**7** In a certain situation, the inequality $y > 3x - 7$ is true for all values of $x$ between 1 and 12. Which pair of values **does not** satisfy the inequality?
  A $x = 10$ and $y = 24$  B $x = 5$ and $y = 10$
  C $x = 2$ and $y = 0$  D $x = 7$ and $y = 12$

**8** Which expression is **not** equivalent to $3x^2 + 7x - 4$?
  A $7x - 4 + 3x^2$  B $-4 + 7x + 3x^2$
  C $4 - 7x - 3x^2$  D $3x^2 - 4 + 7x$

**9** $5m + 4 = 3m - 8$
  What is the value of $m$?
  A $-6$  B $-2$  C $-1\frac{1}{2}$  D $2$

**10** Which of these points lies on the straight line joining $(3, 4)$ and $(14, 15)$?
  A $(6, 5)$  B $(10, 11)$  C $(9, 12)$  D $(8, 8)$

**11** $x + y = 7$
  $x - y = 3$
  Which values of $x$ and $y$ satisfy both these equations?
  $x = \boxed{\phantom{000}}$ and $y = \boxed{\phantom{000}}$

**12** It is known that, for all values of $x$,
  $4(5x - 1) + 3 + \boxed{?} = 15x - 1$
  What is the missing term?  $\boxed{\phantom{000}}$

**13** If $k = -3$, what is the value of $k^2 - 4k$?
  A $-3$  B $-21$  C $3$  D $21$

**14** Consider this pattern:
  $2^2 = 0 \times 4 + 4$
  $3^2 = 1 \times 5 + 4$
  $4^2 = 2 \times 6 + 4$
  $5^2 = 3 \times 7 + 4$
  $6^2 = 4 \times 8 + 4$
  Using this pattern, what is the **value** of $98^2$?  $\boxed{\phantom{000}}$

**15** The graph of $y = 3 - 2x$ is to be drawn on this grid.

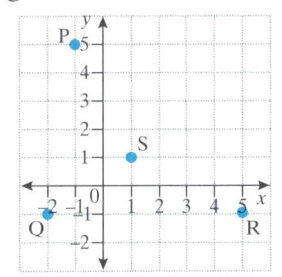

Through which two points will the line pass?
  A P and Q  B Q and R
  C P and S  D Q and S

**16** The rule to change temperatures in degrees Celsius (°C), to temperatures in degrees Fahrenheit (°F) is $F = \frac{9}{5}C + 32$
  The maximum temperature today was 35°C. What is this in degrees Fahrenheit?  $\boxed{\phantom{000}}$ °F

**17** It is known that $\frac{3}{4} > \frac{2}{x}$ where $x$ is a positive whole number. What is the smallest possible value of $x$?  $\boxed{\phantom{000}}$

**18** Which expression is equivalent to $\frac{x^2}{3} + \frac{2x^2}{3}$?
  A $x^2$  B $x^4$  C $\frac{x^2}{2}$  D $\frac{x^4}{2}$

Answers and explanations on pages 116–118

# NON-CALCULATOR — Advanced level questions
## Mini Test 23: Space, Measurement and Data
**20 MIN**

**1** The perimeter of this kite is 160 metres. Each of the shorter sides is 30 metres long. How long is each of the longer sides?
A 45 m   B 50 m   C 65 m   D 100 m 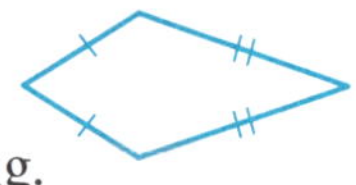

**2** A light on a shop sign turns on for 20 seconds and then off for 5 seconds, on for 20 seconds and off for 5 seconds and so on. What is the probability that when Angela looks at the sign the light will be on?
A 25%   B 40%   C 75%   D 80%

**3** The scores Ned achieved in his first nine tests are 76, 78, 83, 85, 87, 87, 88, 91 and 94. In his tenth test, Ned scores 96. Which is correct?
A The mean increases but the mode and median do not change.
B The mean and median increase but the mode does not change.
C The mean, median and mode all increase.
D The median increases but the mode and mean do not change.

**4** This is the net of a box. (All dimensions are in centimetres.) What is the volume of the box (in cm³)?
A 30   B 38   C 50   D 60

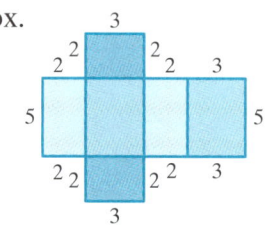

**5** This is a map of Garden Shire. 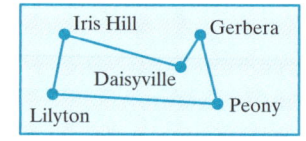
Scale: 1 cm represents 6 km

The distance from Iris Hill to Daisyville on the map is 5 cm. Rosie drives from Iris Hill to Daisyville in half an hour. What is her average speed in kilometres per hour? ☐ km/h

**6** A circular tabletop has diameter of 1.2 metres. The circumference of the tabletop would be closest to 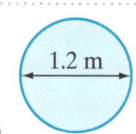
A 2 m   B 4 m   C 6 m   D 8 m

**7** A coin is tossed twice. What is the probability of getting heads both times?
A $\frac{1}{2}$   B $\frac{1}{3}$   C $\frac{1}{4}$   D $\frac{2}{3}$

**8** Boards used to make a deck are 90 mm wide and 4500 mm long. Which calculation will give the number of boards needed for this deck?
A 1.8 × 0.09   B 1.8 × 0.009
C 1.8 ÷ 0.09   D 1.8 ÷ 0.009

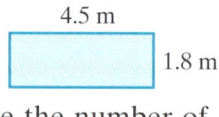

**9** If an isosceles right-angled triangle is cut along its axis of symmetry, what description applies to the two resulting triangles?
A isosceles and right-angled
B isosceles but not right-angled
C right-angled but not isosceles
D neither right-angled nor isosceles

**10** Lucy spun this spinner 30 times. Which table is most likely to show the result?

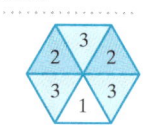

| Number spun | Number of spins |
|---|---|
| 1 | 10 |
| 2 | 10 |
| 3 | 10 |

A

| Number spun | Number of spins |
|---|---|
| 1 | 5 |
| 2 | 10 |
| 3 | 15 |

B

| Number spun | Number of spins |
|---|---|
| 1 | 12 |
| 2 | 6 |
| 3 | 12 |

C

| Number spun | Number of spins |
|---|---|
| 1 | 15 |
| 2 | 10 |
| 3 | 5 |

D

**11** 1200 people were asked if they had read a particular book. The results are shown in the bar chart.

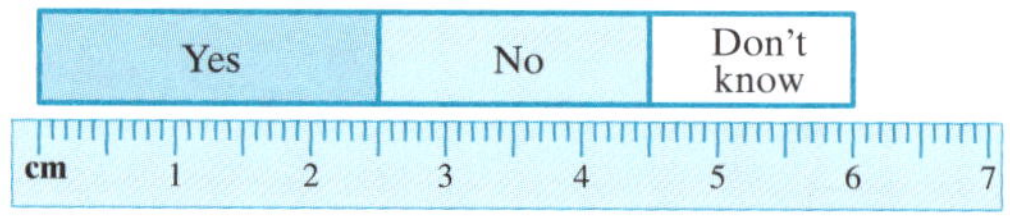

How many people said 'no'? ☐

**12** The table shows the capacity of the fuel tank and the fuel consumption of four different models of a car. Which will travel furthest on a full tank of fuel?

| Model | Capacity | Consumption |
|---|---|---|
| Sedan | 60 L | 8 L per 100 km |
| Coupe | 42 L | 6 L per 100 km |
| Van | 54 L | 9 L per 100 km |
| Wagon | 56 L | 7 L per 100 km |

A sedan   B coupe   C van   D wagon

Answers and explanations on pages 118–120

**CALCULATOR ALLOWED** — **Advanced level questions**

## Mini Test 24: Number

**25 MIN**

1. The value of $\dfrac{43.7 - 19.8}{\sqrt{183 + 79}}$ is closest to
   **A** 1.5   **B** 42.5   **C** 79.1   **D** 121.2

2. There are 70 boys and 80 girls at a particular pre-school. $\dfrac{3}{5}$ of the boys and $\dfrac{3}{4}$ of the girls will start primary school next year. What percentage of the pre-schoolers will start primary school? ☐ %

3. Which is **not** equal to $4\dfrac{3}{5}$?
   **A** $\dfrac{23}{5}$   **B** 4.6   **C** $4\dfrac{9}{25}$   **D** 460%

4. There were 35 pink and white marshmallows in a packet. The ratio of pink to white was 2 to 5. Emma ate 1 pink and 4 white marshmallows. What is the new ratio of pink to white marshmallows?
   **A** 1 to 1   **B** 2 to 5   **C** 3 to 7   **D** 1 to 2

5. Which is **not** a factor of 1001?
   **A** 7   **B** 11   **C** 13   **D** 17

6. $2^4 \times 5^2 =$
   **A** $7^8$   **B** $10^6$   **C** $10^8$   **D** $20^2$

7. In a football season:
   - Joe kicked 7 goals from 12 attempts
   - Harry kicked 8 goals from 15 attempts
   - Tom kicked 12 goals from 19 attempts
   - Rick kicked 15 goals from 26 attempts.
   
   Who had the best percentage success rate?
   **A** Joe   **B** Harry   **C** Tom   **D** Rick

8. What is the smallest number that is a multiple of both 12 and 15? ☐

9. Last year, Luke's total income was $60 000. This year his income has increased by 5%. Luke must pay 30% of his income in tax. How much tax must Luke pay this year? $ ☐

10. Over the last four years the value of a necklace has increased by 40%. The value of the necklace is now $4200. What was the value four years ago?
    **A** $1050   **B** $1680   **C** $2520   **D** $3000

11. Which number is prime?
    **A** 111   **B** 113   **C** 117   **D** 119

12. Kate needed to find the answer to a question, but performed the wrong operations. She was supposed to add 63 and then divide by 1.5, but instead she divided by 63 and added 1.5. Kate's answer was 4.5. What should it have been? ☐

13. A recipe for shortbread uses these ingredients: 3 cups of flour, 1 tablespoon of cornflour, $2\dfrac{1}{2}$ tablespoons of sugar, 240 grams of butter. Elliott wants to make a large batch of shortbread. He uses $7\dfrac{1}{2}$ cups of flour. How many tablespoons of sugar should he use?
    **A** $5\dfrac{1}{2}$   **B** $6\dfrac{1}{4}$   **C** 7   **D** 10

14. There were 120 people at a meeting. The ratio of men to women was 7 to 3. 24 more people joined the meeting. The ratio of men to women was then 11 to 5. How many women were among those 24? ☐

15. A company charges 3.15 cents per copy for printing leaflets. The price for printing 6244 leaflets was found by multiplying 3.15 by 6244 on a calculator. The display on the calculator read 19668.6. What is this cost, to the nearest cent?
    **A** $196.69   **B** $1966.86
    **C** $19 668.06   **D** $19 668.60

16. Two numbers multiply together to give 328 and add to give 49. What are the two numbers? ☐ and ☐

17. Write 3724 as a product of its prime factors.
    ☐

18. Three-fifths of all the members of a club were male. Two-fifths of all the male members were pensioners. What fraction of the members were male pensioners?
    **A** $\dfrac{1}{5}$   **B** $\dfrac{6}{25}$   **C** $\dfrac{1}{10}$   **D** $\dfrac{2}{3}$

**CALCULATOR ALLOWED** — **Advanced level questions** — 25 MIN

## Mini Test 25: Algebra—Patterns, Expressions and Number Plane

**1** Which expression is equivalent to $3(1 - p) - p$?
 **A** $3 - 2p$  **B** $3 - p^2$  **C** $3 - 4p$  **D** $3 + 2p$

**2** Ben used the rule 'multiply by 3 and then add 2' to get the next number in a pattern. The first three numbers are 1, 5 and 17. What is the seventh number in the pattern?

**3** R is the point $(5, -2)$. QR is parallel to the $x$-axis. PQ is parallel to the $y$-axis. PQ = 6 and QR = 8. What are the co-ordinates of P? 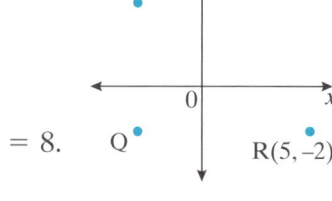
 **A** $(-1, 8)$  **B** $(-3, 4)$  **C** $(-1, 4)$  **D** $(-3, 8)$

**4** $3(5x + 4) + 2(3x - 7) =$
 **A** $21x - 2$  **B** $14x - 2$
 **C** $21x - 3$  **D** $14x - 3$

This pattern is used in questions 5 to 8.

Daniel made this pattern of squares with matches. He then drew up a table:

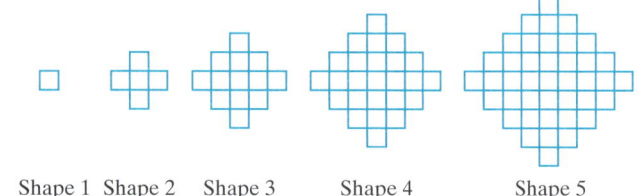

Shape 1  Shape 2  Shape 3  Shape 4  Shape 5

| Shape | 1 | 2 | 3 | 4 | 5 |
|---|---|---|---|---|---|
| Number of squares | 1 | 5 | 13 | 25 | 41 |
| Number of matches | 4 | 16 | 36 | 64 | 100 |

**5** How many squares will there be in Shape 7?

**6** How many matches will Daniel need for Shape 7?

**7** Which rule gives the number of matches needed for each shape?
 **A** $4 \times$ shape number
 **B** $3 \times$ number of squares $+ 1$
 **C** $2 \times$ number of squares $+ 2$
 **D** $(2 \times$ shape number$)^2$

**8** What is the largest number shape that can be made with 500 matches?
 **A** 9  **B** 10  **C** 11  **D** 12

**9** Which expression gives the area of the shaded shape in square centimetres? 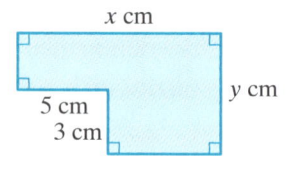
 **A** $5x - 3y$  **B** $3x - 5y$
 **C** $xy - 15$  **D** $xy - 8$

**10** Which rule connects $x$ and $y$?

| $x$ | 1 | 2 | 3 | 4 | 5 |
|---|---|---|---|---|---|
| $y$ | 1 | 13 | 33 | 61 | 97 |

 **A** $y = x^2 + 1$  **B** $y = 2x^2 - 1$
 **C** $y = 3x^2 - 2$  **D** $y = 4x^2 - 3$

**11** Which point will the line $y = 7 - 2x$ pass through? 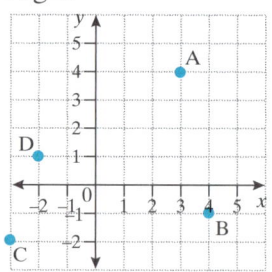
 **A** A  **B** B  **C** C  **D** D

**12** What is the 27th number in this pattern?
 1, 4, 7, 10, 13, …

**13** $3(2x - 1) + 5 + \boxed{?} = 10x + 2$
 What is the missing term?

**14** Which of these points lies on the straight line joining $(1, 3)$ to $(7, 15)$?
 **A** $(2, 4)$  **B** $(3, 8)$  **C** $(4, 10)$  **D** $(5, 11)$

**15** Which expression is equivalent to $4 + x - x^2$?
 **A** $-x^2 + x + 4$  **B** $-x^2 - x + 4$
 **C** $x^2 - x - 4$  **D** $x^2 + x - 4$

**16** What is the next number in this pattern?
 $\dfrac{1}{2}, \dfrac{7}{12}, \dfrac{2}{3}, \dfrac{3}{4}, \dfrac{5}{6}, \ldots$

**CALCULATOR ALLOWED** — **Advanced level questions** — 25 MIN

## Mini Test 26: Algebra—Substitution and Equations

**1** What is the value of $3x - x^2$ when $x = -4$?
A 4    B −5    C −18    D −28

**2** If $a = 3$ and $b = -2$, what is the value of $2ab^2$?
A −24    B −72    C 24    D 72

**3** The volume of a sphere is given by the formula $V = \frac{4}{3}\pi r^3$ where $r$ is the radius of the sphere. When the radius is 8 metres, the volume of the sphere is closest to
A 37 630 m³    B 21 167 m³
C 67 m³    D 2145 m³

**4** $5(2m - 3) = 8m + 7$
The value of $m$ in this equation is    $m = \square$

**5** A rule for $y$ in terms of $x$ is $y = 4 - 5x$. When $x = 1.2$, what is the value of $y$?
A −2    B −2.2    C −1.2    D −0.2

**6** WXYZ is a square. What is the length of each side of the square?    $\square$ cm
(sides labelled $(2m+3)$ cm and $(4m-1)$ cm)

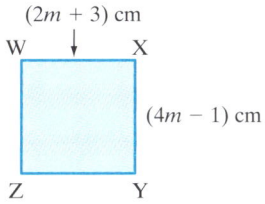

**7** If $t = 6$, what is the value of $2t^2 - 3t$?
A 36    B 54    C 90    D 126

**8** The profit, $P, that Kylie makes when she sells $n$ dolls is given by the rule $P = 8n - 160$. If Kylie makes a profit of $280, how many dolls did she sell?    $\square$

**9** A person of weight $m$ kilograms and height $h$ metres is judged to be overweight if $\frac{m}{h^2} > 25$. A person with which of these measurements would be overweight?
A weight 55 kg, height 1.5 m
B weight 60 kg, height 1.6 m
C weight 75 kg, height 1.7 m
D weight 80 kg, height 1.8 m

**10** If $a = -1$, what is the value of $3 - 2a - a^2$?
A −1    B 4    C 6    D 1

**11** If $c^2 = a^2 + b^2$ and $a = 8$ and $b = 15$, which could be the value of $c$?
A 17    B 23    C 79    D 289

**12** $7x + 8 = 5x - 4$
What is the value of $x$ in the equation?    $x = \square$

**13** The cost, $C, per person for a trip is given by $C = \frac{360}{n}$, where $n$ is the number of people taking the trip. If $C = 9$, what is the value of $n$?    $n = \square$

**14** Which number line shows the solution of $2x - 1 < 5$?
A (closed circle at 3, arrow right)
B (closed circle at 3, arrow left)
C (open circle at 3, arrow left)
D (open circle at 2, arrow left)

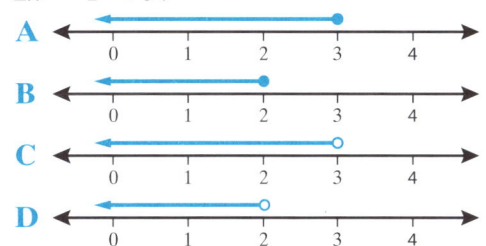

**15** If $y = 5x^2$, what is the value of $y$ when $x = 1.5$?    $\square$

**16** Which value of $x$ will **not** make the inequality $11 - 3x \geq 2$ true?
A $x = -2$    B $x = 0$
C $x = 3$    D $x = 6$

**17** Young's rule is a formula that determines the correct dose of medicine for a child when the adult dose of that medicine and the age of the child are known.
The rule is $C = \frac{nA}{n + 12}$ where $C$ is the child's dose in millilitres, $n$ is the child's age in years and $A$ is the adult dose in millilitres.
What is the correct dose for a four-year-old child when the adult dose is 20 mL?
A 5 mL    B 10 mL    C 12 mL    D 15 mL

**18** It is known that $\frac{3}{8} > \frac{5}{x}$. If $x$ is a positive whole number, what is its smallest possible value?    $\square$

**CALCULATOR ALLOWED** — **Advanced level questions** — 25 MIN

## Mini Test 27: Angles

**1** A regular octagon is cut into three pieces by drawing lines parallel to the top and bottom as shown in the diagram. 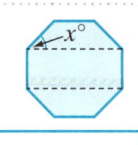
What is the value of $x$?

**2** A polygon has two angles of 90° and its remaining angles are all 135°. What type of polygon is it?
A pentagon  B hexagon
C octagon   D decagon

**3** Lines $l$ and $m$ are parallel. 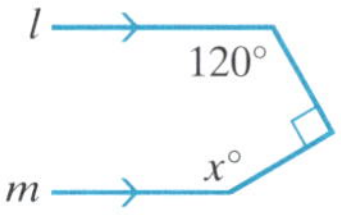
What is the value of $x$?
A 120  B 130
C 140  D 150

**4** A polygon has three angles of 100° and two other equal angles. What size is each of those two remaining angles?

**5** Lines $l$ and $m$ are parallel. 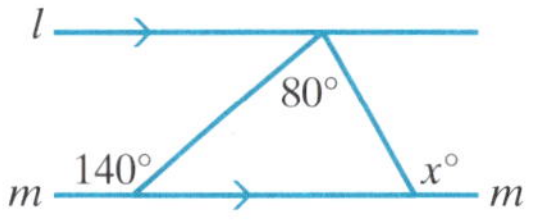
What is the value of $x$?
A 100  B 120  C 140  D 160

**6** The diagram shows a square, an equilateral triangle and an octagon. 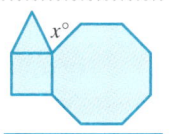
What is the value of $x$?

**7** Lines $m$ and $n$ are parallel.
What is the value of $x$?
A 80  B 90  C 100  D 120

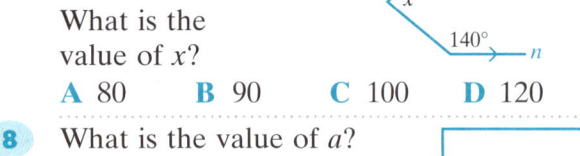

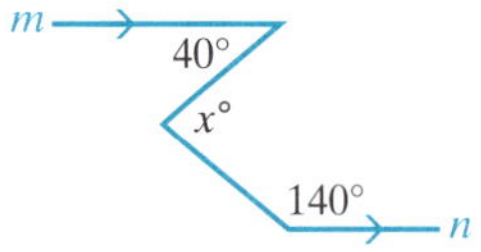

**8** What is the value of $a$?

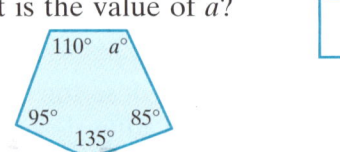

**9** AB = CB
∠ABC = 30°
What is the size of ∠BCD?

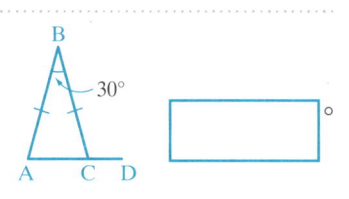

**10** Lines $l$, $m$ and $n$ are all parallel. 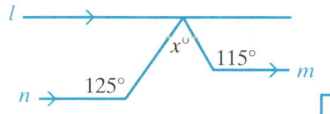
What is the value of $x$?

**11** The clock shows that it is seven o'clock. What is the size of the obtuse angle formed by the hands?

**12** A trapezium is divided into two parts. All the angles are marked.
Which is not necessarily equal to 180? 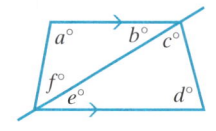
A $a + b + f$    B $a + f + e$
C $a + b + c$    D $b + c + d$

**13** Each of the angles of a regular polygon is 140°.
How many sides does the polygon have?
A 6  B 7  C 8  D 9

**14** AD = BD
BC = DC
BC is parallel to AD.
∠BAD = 50° 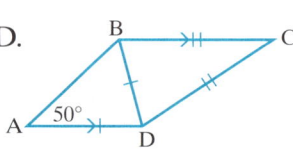
What is the size of ∠BCD?
A 20°  B 30°  C 50°  D 80°

**15** Lines $l$ and $m$ are parallel. 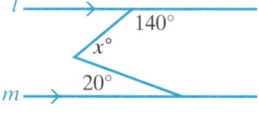
What is the value of $x$?

**16** Which could **not** be placed beside this regular hexagon to fill the space at P? 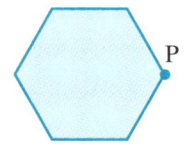
A two regular hexagons
B four equilateral triangles
C two squares and an equilateral triangle
D one regular octagon and one square

Answers and explanations on pages 126–129

**CALCULATOR ALLOWED**    **Advanced level questions**

# Mini Test 28: Measurement

**1** Craig's car uses 8 litres of petrol for every 100 km travelled. He buys $54 worth of petrol at $1.35 per litre. How far will Craig travel on this amount of petrol? ☐ km

**2** The diagram shows a semi-circular garden bed. The curved distance from X to Y is closest to (X to Y = 5 m)
  A 3.9 m   B 7.9 m   C 9.7 m   D 15.7 m

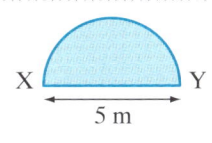

**3** The volume of a cube is 1728 cm³. What is the total area of all the faces of the cube?
  A 144 cm²    B 576 cm²
  C 864 cm²    D 1152 cm²

**4** A bus travelled 336 km at an average speed of 64 kilometres per hour. If the journey began at 8:10 am, what time did it finish?
  A 1:25 pm    B 1:35 pm
  C 3:25 pm    D 3:35 pm

**5** What is the total area of all the surfaces of the triangular prism?
(5 m, 4 m, 2 m, 3 m) ☐ m²

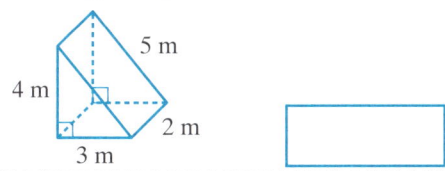

**6** This jug has some juice in it. Marie fills six glasses, each of which hold 125 mL, from the jug. How many millilitres of juice will remain in the jug? ☐ mL

**7** When it is 8:15 am Friday in Melbourne, it is 10:15 pm Thursday in London. When it is 2:30 pm Thursday in Melbourne, it is 11:30 pm Wednesday in New York. What is the time in London when it is 9 am Monday in New York?
  A 4 am Monday    B 4 pm Sunday
  C 2 pm Monday    D 4 pm Monday

**8** The volume of a rectangular prism is 12 m³. A second rectangular prism has its dimensions double those of the first prism. What is the volume of the second prism?
  A 24 m³   B 48 m³   C 72 m³   D 96 m³

**9** A megalitre (ML) is one million litres. The capacity of a dam is 18 ML. How many kilolitres is this?
  A 1800    B 18 000
  C 180 000    D 1 800 000

**10** A truck can carry a maximum load of 25 tonnes. What is the maximum number of containers, each with a total mass of 1200 kg, that the truck can legally carry? ☐

**11** The perimeter of this rectangle is 72 metres. (12 m, not to scale)
What is its area? ☐ m²

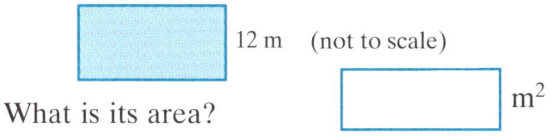

**12** William is 1.8 metres tall and his shadow is 1.5 metres long. At the same time, a tree casts a shadow that is 35 metres long. How tall is the tree? ☐ m
(1.8 m, 1.5 m)

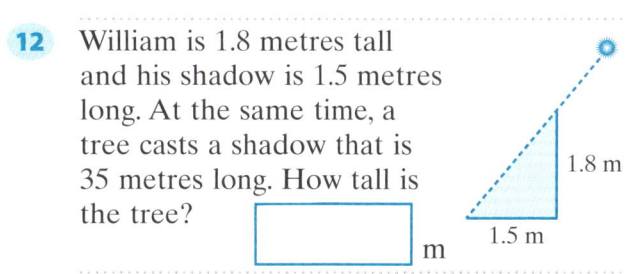

**13** The area of this trapezium is 168 m². What is the area of the shaded rectangle? (15 m, 5 m, 5 m, 5 m, 5 m, 27 m)
  A 84 m²    B 105 m²
  C 108 m²    D 135 m²

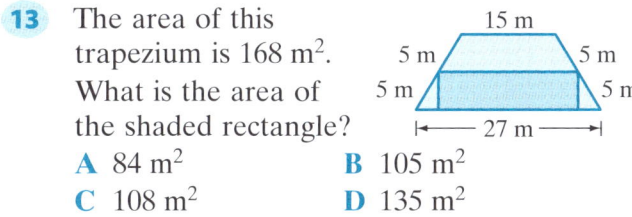

**14** Jenny travels from Brisbane to Mackay passing through first Bundaberg and then Rockhampton. She notices that the distance from Brisbane to Rockhampton is the same as the distance from Bundaberg to Mackay. If Mackay is 1114 km from Brisbane and 398 km from Rockhampton, how far is it from Bundaberg to Rockhampton? ☐ km

**15** Darren and Dane drove 250 km in $3\frac{1}{2}$ hours. Darren drove the first 130 km at an average speed of 65 kilometres per hour. Dane then drove the rest of the way. What was Dane's average speed in kilometres per hour?
  A 65    B 70    C 75    D 80

Answers and explanations on pages 129–131

**CALCULATOR ALLOWED** — **Advanced level questions** — 20 MIN

## Mini Test 29: Plane Figures and Solids—Properties and Measurements

**1** Gemma is tiling a tabletop. She is using small squares of side length 10 cm, rectangles that are twice as long as they are wide and large squares. She has completed one quarter of the tabletop as shown in the diagram. What is the area of the tabletop in square metres? ☐ m²

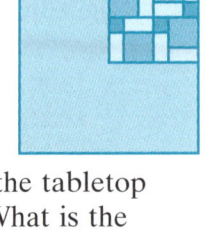

**2** Which of the following properties does **not** mean that a quadrilateral **must** be a parallelogram?
  A  Both pairs of opposite sides are equal.
  B  One pair of opposite sides are equal and parallel.
  C  All four sides are equal.
  D  The diagonals are equal.

**3** Which figure has the most axes of symmetry?
  A  □   B  hexagon   C  cross   D  heptagon

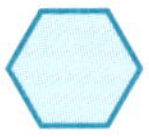

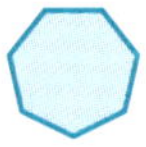

**4** The volume of this rectangular prism is 576 cm². What is its height? ☐ cm
(h m, 8 cm, 12 cm)

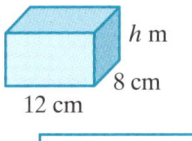

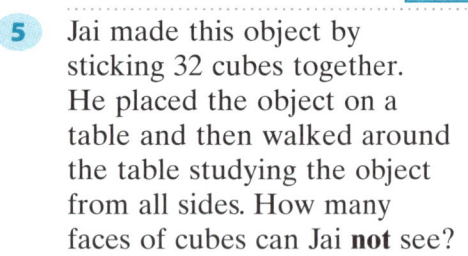

**5** Jai made this object by sticking 32 cubes together. He placed the object on a table and then walked around the table studying the object from all sides. How many faces of cubes can Jai **not** see? 
  A  132   B  92   C  66   D  40

**6** This rectangular prism has a piece of ribbon wrapped right around it in two directions as shown in the diagram. 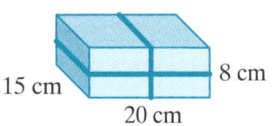
(15 cm, 20 cm, 8 cm)
What is the minimum length of ribbon required? ☐ cm

**7** PQRS is a square. PQTS is a 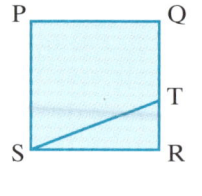
  A  parallelogram
  B  rhombus
  C  trapezium
  D  kite

**8** This object has been made using 12 blocks. It is viewed from the top, front and back, and both sides. Which view cannot be seen? 
  A 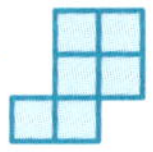    B    C    D

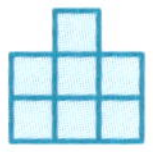

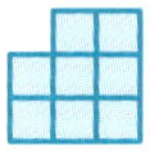

**9** A frame in the shape of a cube has been made from a piece of wire 36 cm long. What is the volume of the cube? ☐ cm³

**10** PQST is a rectangle. The area of triangle PQR is 18 cm² and the area of triangle PTR is 32 cm².
What is the area of triangle TRS? ☐ cm²

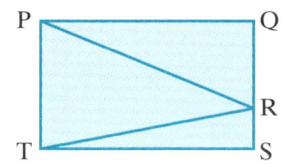

**11** This parallelogram is reflected in the line $m$. What shape is formed by the object and its image?
  A  parallelogram    B  hexagon
  C  rhombus          D  trapezium

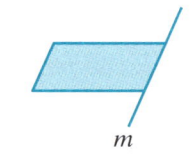

**12** This is the net of a die. 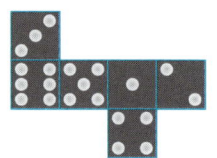
Which could **not** be the die?
  A    B    C    D

**CALCULATOR ALLOWED** — **Advanced level questions** — 20 MIN

# Mini Test 30: Chance and Data

**1** The mean (average) of eight numbers is 56. When one of the numbers was left out, the mean decreased to 54. What number was left out?
**A** 54   **B** 56   **C** 60   **D** 70

**2** Three coins are tossed together. There are eight possible outcomes. What is the probability of getting 2 heads and 1 tail (in any order)?
**A** $\frac{1}{8}$   **B** $\frac{1}{4}$   **C** $\frac{3}{8}$   **D** $\frac{1}{2}$

**3** These are Phoebe's marks in her last seven weekly tests (marked out of 20).

| Week | 1 | 2 | 3 | 4 | 5 | 6 | 7 |
|---|---|---|---|---|---|---|---|
| Mark | 18 | 17 | 19 | 16 | 17 | 15 | 17 |

Which is correct?
**A** mode = median ≠ mean
**B** mode ≠ median = mean
**C** mode = mean ≠ median
**D** mode = mean = median

**4** Members of a tennis club are either seniors or juniors. The average age of the 25 junior members is 15 and the average age of the 15 senior members is 31. What is the average age of the club members?
**A** 20   **B** 21   **C** 22   **D** 23

**5** Sally recorded the colour of the roses on the bushes in a garden.

| Colour | Number of rosebushes |
|---|---|
| Red | 18 |
| Orange | 9 |
| Yellow | 7 |
| White | 12 |
| Pink | 14 |

Sally intended to draw a sector graph to show this information. What size is the angle needed for the red rosebushes? ☐ °

**6** Lulu did a test in which all the questions had to be judged true or false. The table shows her results.

|  | Lulu said true | Lulu said false |
|---|---|---|
| Was True | 36 | 16 |
| Was False | 21 | 27 |

How many questions did Lulu get correct?
**A** 36   **B** 52   **C** 57   **D** 63

**7** Two dice are tossed together. There are 36 possible outcomes. What is the probability of getting a total of 4?
**A** $\frac{1}{36}$   **B** $\frac{1}{18}$   **C** $\frac{1}{12}$   **D** $\frac{1}{9}$

**8** In nine tests, Joe has an average mark of 78%. What would he need to score in his tenth test to increase his average to 80%?
**A** 98%   **B** 96%   **C** 88%   **D** 82%

**9** The graph shows the number of mistakes made by students in a spelling test.

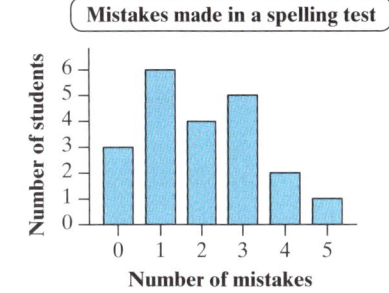

Mistakes made in a spelling test

Which is correct?
**A** mode = median ≠ mean
**B** mode ≠ median = mean
**C** mode = mean ≠ median
**D** mode ≠ mean ≠ median

**10** Consider these scores:
  22  22  22  23  23  24  25
One score can be left out without affecting the mean. Which score is this?
**A** 22   **B** 23   **C** 24   **D** 25

**11** Sheridan recorded the number of movies his friends had seen over the holidays:
  1, 1, 2, 3, 3, 3, 3, 4, 4, 4, 5
One of his friends who said he had seen 3 movies later claimed to have seen 4. Which will **not** increase when Sheridan's record is updated?
**A** median   **B** mode
**C** mean   **D** They will all increase.

**12** The average height of six netball players is 1.75 metres. A seventh player is 1.61 metres tall. What is the average height of the seven players? ☐ m

**NON-CALCULATOR** — **Advanced level questions**

**Mini Test 31:** Mixed Questions

25 min

1. PQRS is a rectangle. PM = MQ. SN is twice NR.

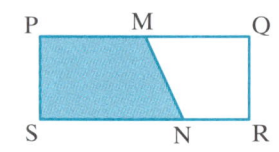

   What fraction of the rectangle is shaded?
   A $\frac{2}{3}$   B $\frac{3}{4}$   C $\frac{5}{6}$   D $\frac{7}{12}$

2. If $a = -1$, what is the value of $5a - 2a^2$?
   A $-7$   B $-3$   C $-9$   D $-1$

3. Which is equal to $3^2 \times 9^3$?
   A $3 \times 2 \times 9 \times 3$
   B $3 \times 3 \times 3 \times 9 \times 9$
   C $9 \times 9 \times 9 \times 9$
   D $3 \times 3 \times 3 \times 3 \times 3 \times 3 \times 3$

4. Which of the following is **not** in order from lowest to highest?
   A $\frac{1}{3}, \frac{2}{5}, \frac{7}{15}$   B $\frac{2}{3}, \frac{3}{4}, \frac{7}{12}$
   C $\frac{3}{5}, \frac{7}{10}, \frac{3}{4}$   D $\frac{5}{8}, \frac{11}{16}, \frac{3}{4}$

5. Lines $l$, $m$ and $n$ are all parallel.

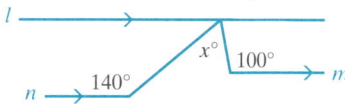

   What is the value of $x$?
   A 40   B 50   C 60   D 70

6. Which of the points $P(-1, 5)$ and $Q(-4, -1)$ lie on the line $y = 2x + 7$?
   A both P and Q   B P only
   C Q only   D neither P nor Q

7. Consider this set of eight scores:
   2, 2, 2, 2, 3, 4, 4, 5
   What will change if the score of 3 is left out?
   A median   B mean   C mode   D range

8. The total number of books for sale at a stall was 600. The ratio of new books to old books was 2 to 3. 30 new books and 10 old books were sold. What is the new ratio of new to old books?
   A 2 to 3   B 1 to 2   C 5 to 8   D 3 to 5

9. $4t^2 - 3t + 5t + t^2 =$
   A $3t^2 + 8t$   B $3t^4 + 2t$
   C $5t^4 - 8t$   D $5t^2 + 2t$

10. In a family of three children, there are eight different possible arrangements of boys and girls. What is the probability that in a family of three children there will be 1 girl and 2 boys?
    A $\frac{1}{8}$   B $\frac{1}{4}$   C $\frac{3}{8}$   D $\frac{5}{8}$

11. Mitchell travels for $2\frac{1}{2}$ hours at an average speed of 60 kilometres per hour. If his car uses fuel at the rate of 8 litres per 100 km travelled, how much fuel will he use on the journey?
    ☐ litres

12. 40% of students at a college are in first year. 30% of first-year students at the college are studying law. Half of the first-year law students are male. What percentage of the college students are males in first year studying law? ☐ %

13. Here are two views of the same cube.

    Which could be the net of the cube?
    A   B   C   D

14. The value of $\sqrt{0.09}$ is ☐

15. $\frac{2}{5} > \frac{a}{b}$
    Which values of $a$ and $b$ will make this inequality true?
    A $a = 1$ and $b = 2$   B $a = 3$ and $b = 8$
    C $a = 4$ and $b = 9$   D $a = 5$ and $b = 12$

16. A rectangular shaped pond is 2.5 metres long and 2 metres wide. It can be filled to a depth of 25 cm. How many litres of water will it hold when full?
    ($1 m^3 = 1000$ L)
    A 125   B 1250   C 12 500   D 125 000

**CALCULATOR ALLOWED** — **Advanced level questions** — 25 MIN

## Mini Test 32: Mixed Questions

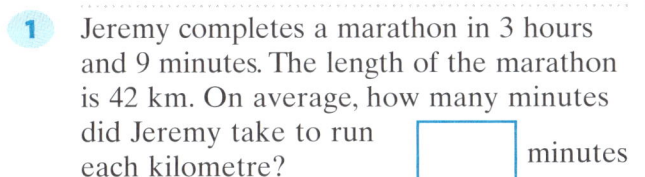

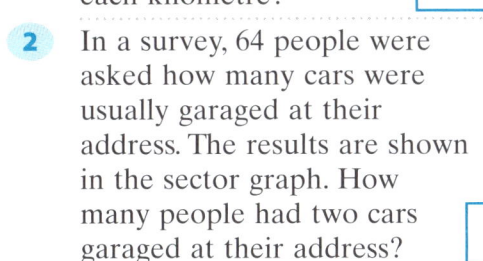

**1** Jeremy completes a marathon in 3 hours and 9 minutes. The length of the marathon is 42 km. On average, how many minutes did Jeremy take to run each kilometre? ☐ minutes

**2** In a survey, 64 people were asked how many cars were usually garaged at their address. The results are shown in the sector graph. How many people had two cars garaged at their address? ☐

**3** If 9 is the mean of 3, 15, 7 and $x$ then $x$ must be
A 2   B 9   C 11   D 12

**4** The formula for finding the area of a trapezium is $A = \dfrac{h}{2}(a + b)$ where $a$ and $b$ are the lengths of the parallel sides and $h$ is the perpendicular height between them. What is the area of this trapezium? ☐ m²

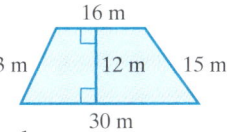

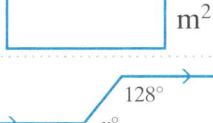

**5** What is the value of $x$?
A 52   B 65
C 115   D 128

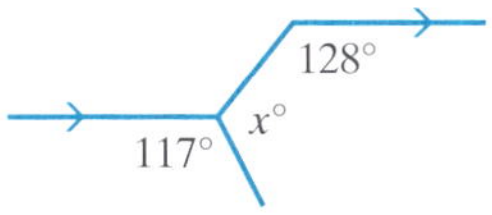

**6** This is a plan of a yard.

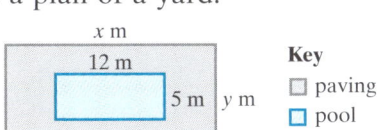

Key: paving, pool

The area of the paving, in square metres, is
A $12x - 5y$    B $12y - 5x$
C $2xy - 60$    D $xy - 60$

**7** What is the value of $2n^2 - 5n + 3$ when $n = -3$?
A 54   B 36   C 6   D 0

**8** A school has just two classes in Year 7. There are 28 students in 7C and 22 students in 7H. The ratio of boys to girls is 3 to 4 in 7C and 5 to 6 in 7H. What percentage of the school's Year 7 students are boys? ☐ %

**9** A garden bed is in the shape of a quarter circle. Jason wants to put a concrete mowing strip around the whole garden. The length of this strip is closest to 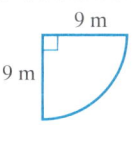
A 32 m   B 64 m   C 25 m   D 46 m

**10** $5(3x + 1) - 7x + \boxed{\phantom{x}} = 8x + 9$
What must be placed in the box so that this equation is true for all values of $x$? ☐

**11** A ramp has been built with a 1-metre high support post 4 metres from the base of the ramp as shown in the diagram. How high is the ramp at its highest point? ☐ m

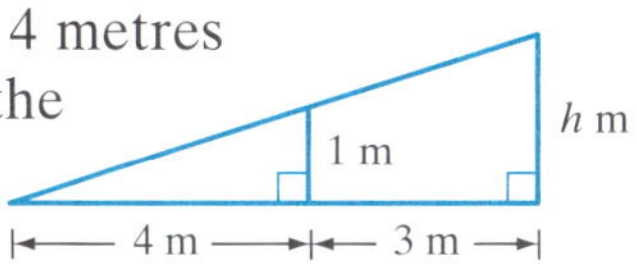

**12** What is the highest prime factor of 1750? ☐

**13** A pentagonal pyramid and a pentagonal prism have identical bases. Those faces are stuck together to form one solid. How many more edges than faces does the new object have?
A 5   B 7   C 9   D 11

**14** This spinner is spun twice and the numbers are added together to get the result. There are 9 different possible outcomes. What is the probability that the result is 4? 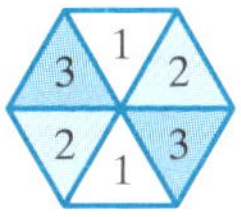
A $\dfrac{1}{3}$   B $\dfrac{1}{4}$   C $\dfrac{1}{9}$   D $\dfrac{4}{9}$

**15** What is the next number in this pattern?
$\dfrac{1}{15}, \dfrac{3}{5}, 1\dfrac{2}{15}, 1\dfrac{2}{3}$
A $1\dfrac{13}{15}$   B $2\dfrac{4}{15}$   C $2\dfrac{1}{3}$   D $2\dfrac{1}{5}$

**16** For the first five games of the netball season, the Wrens' average (mean) number of goals scored per game was 52. For the remaining ten games, the Wrens' average had increased to 67. What was the average number of goals per game for the season?
A 63.5   B 62   C 61   D 59.5

# Year 9 Numeracy  Sample Test 1
## Non-calculator

### Question 1

Which is the best estimate for

29 + 57 × 32 + 78?

- **A**  30 + 60 × 40 + 80
- **B**  30 + 60 × 30 + 70
- **C**  30 + 60 × 30 + 80
- **D**  30 + 50 × 40 + 70

### Question 2

Annabelle folded this net to make a cube.

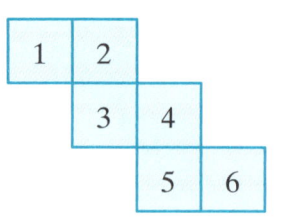

|   |   |   |
|---|---|---|
| 1 | 2 |   |
|   | 3 | 4 |
|   |   | 5 | 6 |

What number is on the face opposite the face numbered 1?

- **A**  3
- **B**  4
- **C**  5
- **D**  6

### Question 3

There are 40 tickets in a hat. 15 are blue and the rest are green. Chad takes a ticket from the hat, without looking. What is the probability that the ticket is blue?

- **A**  $\frac{3}{8}$
- **B**  $\frac{3}{5}$
- **C**  $\frac{2}{5}$
- **D**  $\frac{2}{3}$

### Question 4

Guy has written down the first five numbers in a pattern:

1.2, 2.4, 3.6, 4.8, 6

What is the ninth number in this pattern?

# YEAR 9 NUMERACY SAMPLE TEST 1—NON-CALCULATOR

**Question 5**

1 metre and 35 millimetres is the same as

    **A**  1.35 m      **B**  1.0035 m      **C**  1305 mm      **D**  1035 mm

**Question 6**

Which is the answer to 0.6 ÷ 0.02?

    **A**  0.03      **B**  0.3      **C**  3      **D**  30

**Question 7**

Which shows an obtuse angle?

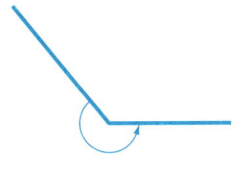

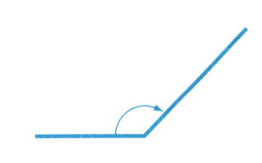

    **A**      **B**      **C**      **D**

**Question 8**

The value of $2 - 3p$ when $p = -4$ is

    **A**  14      **B**  −5      **C**  4      **D**  36

**Question 9**

What fraction has the same value as $3\frac{4}{5}$?

    **A**  $\frac{12}{5}$      **B**  $\frac{17}{5}$      **C**  $\frac{19}{5}$      **D**  $\frac{23}{5}$

Answers and explanations on pages 138–141

# YEAR 9 NUMERACY SAMPLE TEST 1 — NON-CALCULATOR

**Question 10**

Here are a set of seven scores:

4, 4, 6, 6, 6, 7, 9

Which is **not** equal to 6?

- **A** mean
- **B** median
- **C** mode
- **D** range

**Question 11**

The perimeter of this rectangle is 20 metres.

3 m

What is the area of the rectangle? ☐ m²

**Question 12**

Which arrow shows the position of −1.2 on the number line?

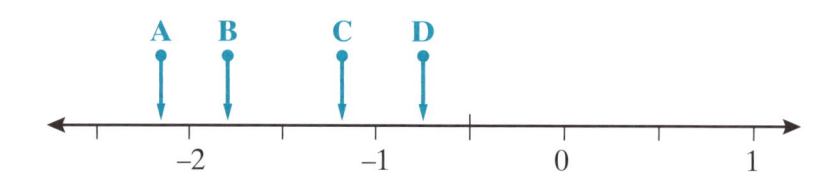

- **A** A
- **B** B
- **C** C
- **D** D

**Question 13**

Which of the following expressions is equivalent to $5 - (2x + 3)$?

- **A** $-2x + 2$
- **B** $-2x + 8$
- **C** $-10x - 15$
- **D** $-10x + 15$

# YEAR 9 NUMERACY SAMPLE TEST 1—NON-CALCULATOR

**Question 14**

The ratio of boys to girls at a party is 3:5. There are 40 children at the party. How many boys are at the party?

    **A** 15      **B** 16      **C** 24      **D** 25

**Question 15**

A train arrived in Perth at a quarter to two in the afternoon after a $6\frac{3}{4}$ hour trip from Kalgoorlie. What time did it leave Kalgoorlie?

    **A** 6:30 am      **B** 6:45 am      **C** 7:00 am      **D** 7:30 am

**Question 16**

Which number is the largest?

    **A** 0.08      **B** 0.4      **C** 0.317      **D** 0.25

**Question 17**

Which property is **not always** true for rhombuses?

    **A** The opposite sides are parallel.
    **B** The opposite sides are equal.
    **C** The adjacent sides are equal.
    **D** The diagonals are equal.

**Question 18**

Which is equivalent to 19 × 36 + 24 × 19?

    **A** 60 × 19      **B** 38 × 60
    **C** 43 × 55      **D** 19 × 60 × 19

# YEAR 9 NUMERACY SAMPLE TEST 1—NON-CALCULATOR

**Question 19**

△ and ○ stand for numbers that are related by a rule.

| △ | 1 | 2 | 3 | 4 | 5 |
|---|---|---|---|---|---|
| ○ | 3 | 12 | 27 | 48 | 75 |

What is the rule?

A  ○ = 3 × △

B  ○ = 9 × △ − 6

C  ○ = △ × △ + 2

D  ○ = 3 × △ × △

**Question 20**

$7x - 3 = 5x + 9$

What is the value of $x$ in this equation?      $x = \boxed{\phantom{xx}}$

**Question 21**

This drum has oil in it. If Evan pours 750 mL of oil into his engine, how much oil (in millilitres) will remain in the drum?

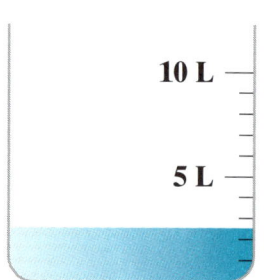

$\boxed{\phantom{xxx}}$ mL

**Question 22**

15% of all cars in the car park are red. $\dfrac{3}{4}$ of all the red cars in the car park are sedans.

If there are 160 cars in the car park, how many are red sedans?

$\boxed{\phantom{xxx}}$

# YEAR 9 NUMERACY SAMPLE TEST 1 — NON-CALCULATOR

**Question 23**

The temperature at 11 pm was −2°C. At 5 am it was 6°C colder than it was at 11 pm. At 9 am it was 9° warmer then it was at 5 am. What was the temperature at 9 am?

☐ °C

**Question 24**

Which is equivalent to $4^2 \times 2^3$?

- **A** $4 \times 2 \times 2 \times 3$
- **B** $4 \times 4 \times 2 \times 2$
- **C** $4 \times 4 \times 4 \times 2$
- **D** $4 \times 2 \times 2 \times 2$

**Question 25**

What is the value of $x$?

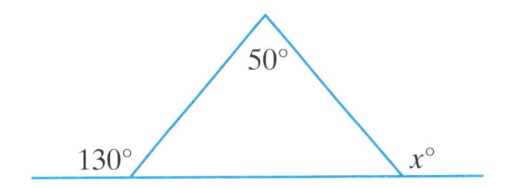

(Triangle with angles 50° at apex, 130° exterior angle on the left, $x°$ exterior angle on the right)

**Question 26**

What number is exactly halfway between $\frac{1}{4}$ and $\frac{1}{6}$?

- **A** $\frac{1}{5}$
- **B** $\frac{5}{24}$
- **C** $\frac{1}{2}$
- **D** $\frac{5}{12}$

**Question 27**

The average (mean) of five numbers is 8. If one of the numbers is left out, the average of the remaining numbers is 7. What number is left out?

- **A** 7
- **B** 8
- **C** 10
- **D** 12

# YEAR 9 NUMERACY SAMPLE TEST 1 — NON-CALCULATOR

**Question 28**

Trish measures the distance from Applegate to Orange on the map and finds it to be 5 cm.

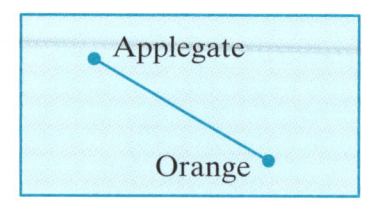

Scale: 1 cm represents 15 km

If Trish rides her bike at an average speed of 25 kilometres per hour, how long will it take to ride from Applegate to Orange?

☐ hours

**Question 29**

The graph of the line $y = 2 - 3x$ will be drawn on this grid.

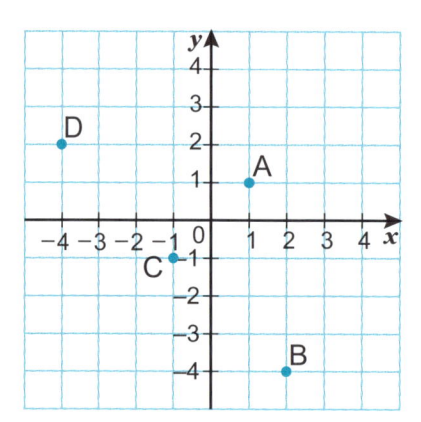

Which point will the line pass through?

**A** A    **B** B    **C** C    **D** D

# YEAR 9 NUMERACY SAMPLE TEST 1—NON-CALCULATOR

**Question 30**

Pippa has US$45.

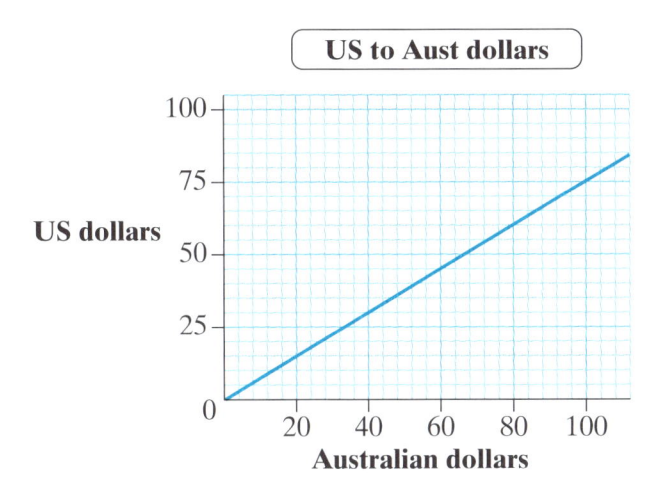

US to Aust dollars

NZ to Aust dollars

How much is this in New Zealand dollars?    NZ$ ☐

---

**Question 31**

On a car trip, Sid travelled for $5\frac{1}{2}$ hours at an average speed of 72 kilometres per hour. His car used petrol at the rate of 8 litres per 100 km travelled. Which calculation will give the amount of fuel (in litres) that Sid's car will have used on the journey?

- **A**  $72 \times 5.5 \div 8 \times 100$
- **B**  $72 \times 5.5 \times 8 \div 100$
- **C**  $72 \div 5.5 \div 8 \times 100$
- **D**  $72 \div 5.5 \times 8 \div 100$

---

**Question 32**

In a certain country, letters can be posted at a cheaper rate provided the length (*l* cm) and height (*h* cm) are such that $l < 3h - 5$ for values of *h* between 6 and 25. The letter with which dimensions could **not** be posted at the cheaper rate?

- **A**  $l = 18, h = 8$
- **B**  $l = 24, h = 9$
- **C**  $l = 12, h = 12$
- **D**  $l = 30, h = 15$

---

## END OF TEST 1—NON-CALCULATOR

# Year 9 Numeracy — Sample Test 1

**Calculator Allowed**

## Question 1

Jess bought 8 apples for $6.80. What was the average price per apple?

$ ____

## Question 2

The diagram shows the floor plan of a shed. What direction is the opening facing?

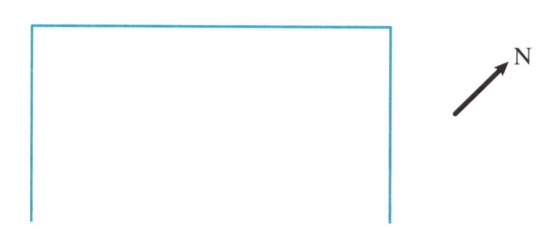

**A** SE  **B** S  **C** SW  **D** W

## Question 3

If $p = -5$, what is the value of $4p^2$?

**A** 100  **B** −100  **C** 400  **D** −400

## Question 4

Jett took 45 minutes to run from his home to the beach. His average speed was 12 kilometres per hour. How far is it from Jett's home to the beach?

____ km

## Question 5

What is the value of $x$?

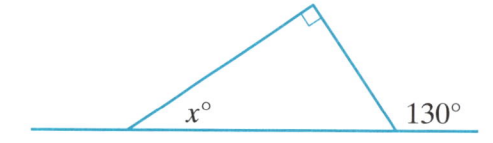

$x°$  130°

# YEAR 9 NUMERACY SAMPLE TEST 1 — CALCULATOR ALLOWED

## Question 6

1 kg and 80 g is the same as

- A  1.8 kg
- B  100 080 g
- C  1080 g
- D  1.008 kg

## Question 7

This graph was drawn to show the number of cars sold by a dealership during the four months of a special promotion.

**Cars sold by Miracle Motors**

Key: represents 8 cars

In which month were 42 cars sold?

- A  March
- B  April
- C  May
- D  June

## Question 8

Which number is the largest?

- A  29%
- B  $\frac{2}{9}$
- C  0.209
- D  0.2009

## Question 9

How many hours and minutes are between 7.25 am and 5.05 pm on the same day?

- A  9 h 20 min
- B  9 h 40 min
- C  10 h 20 min
- D  10 h 40 min

# YEAR 9 NUMERACY SAMPLE TEST 1—CALCULATOR ALLOWED

**Question 10**

Which expression is equivalent to $3(4a - 1)$?

- **A** $7a - 4$
- **B** $12a - 1$
- **C** $12a - 3$
- **D** $9a$

**Question 11**

Carly is making this pattern with pins and string.

Shape 1   Shape 2   Shape 3   Shape 4

What number shape would need 40 pins?

- **A** 10
- **B** 12
- **C** 14
- **D** 16

**Question 12**

Which shape does **not necessarily** have two sides that are equal?

- **A** rhombus
- **B** isosceles triangle
- **C** regular octagon
- **D** trapezium

**Question 13**

The diagram shows the route of a rally that starts and finishes at Cowper and covers a total of 320 km.

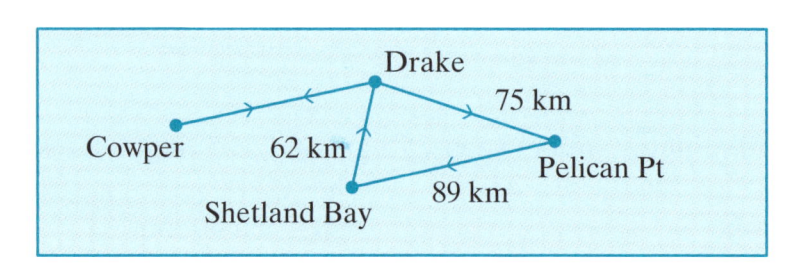

Cowper — 62 km — Shetland Bay — 89 km — Pelican Pt — 75 km — Drake

How far is it from Drake to Cowper? ☐ km

# YEAR 9 NUMERACY SAMPLE TEST 1 — CALCULATOR ALLOWED

## Question 14

The average (mean) age of the male members of a choir is 13 and the average age of female members is 19. There are 20 males and 40 females in the choir. What is the average age of the members of the choir?

A  15      B  16      C  17      D  18

## Question 15

What temperature is shown on this thermometer?

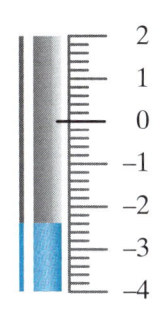

A  $-2.2\,°C$      B  $-2.4\,°C$      C  $-3.4\,°C$      D  $-3.6\,°C$

## Question 16

Which rectangular prism has the greatest volume?

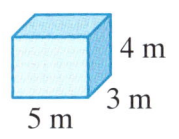

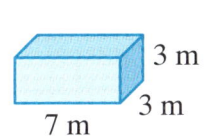

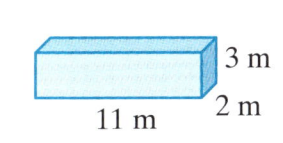

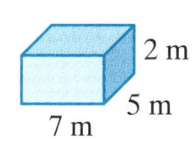

A  (5 m, 3 m, 4 m)      B  (7 m, 3 m, 3 m)      C  (11 m, 2 m, 3 m)      D  (7 m, 5 m, 2 m)

## Question 17

A polygon has four angles that each measure 150° and four other angles that are equal. What size is each of those remaining angles?

☐ °

## Question 18

When two dice are thrown together, there are 36 possible outcomes. What is the probability that the two dice show a total of 8 when tossed together?

A  $\dfrac{1}{36}$      B  $\dfrac{1}{8}$      C  $\dfrac{1}{6}$      D  $\dfrac{5}{36}$

# YEAR 9 NUMERACY SAMPLE TEST 1—CALCULATOR ALLOWED

## Question 19

Mel made a 3D object from identical cubes. She drew a front view and a side view.

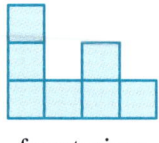

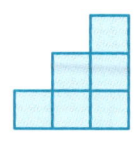

front view         side view

How many of the following could be Mel's object?

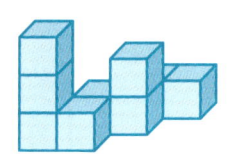

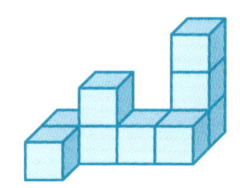

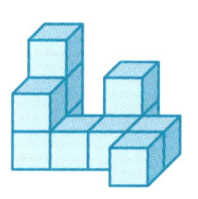

| A | one only | B | exactly two |
| C | exactly three | D | all four |

## Question 20

A photo was originally 12 cm long and 7.5 cm wide. It has been enlarged so that it is now 60 cm wide. How long is the enlarged photo?

☐ cm

## Question 21

Consider this table of values:

| x | 1 | 1.5 | 2 | 3 | 6 |
|---|---|-----|---|---|---|
| y | 6 | 4   | 3 | 2 | 1 |

Which is the correct rule for y in terms of x?

A  $y = 6x$

B  $y = \dfrac{x}{6}$

C  $y = \dfrac{6}{x}$

D  $y = x + 6$

# YEAR 9 NUMERACY SAMPLE TEST 1 — CALCULATOR ALLOWED

**Question 22**

Which is **not** a factor of 6789?

    **A** 31      **B** 53      **C** 73      **D** 93

**Question 23**

When two numbers are added together the result is −5. When the same two numbers are multiplied together the result is 6.

What are the two numbers? ☐ and ☐

**Question 24**

$7a - 15 = 3a + 25$

What is the value of $a$ in this equation?

$a =$ ☐

**Question 25**

The radius of the circle is 5 cm. Which is the best estimate for the shortest distance from P to Q around the outside of the circle?

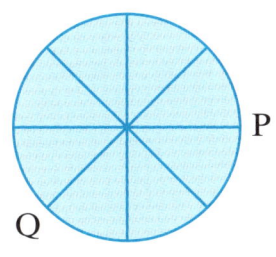

    **A** 9 cm      **B** 10 cm      **C** 11 cm      **D** 12 cm

# YEAR 9 NUMERACY SAMPLE TEST 1—CALCULATOR ALLOWED

**Question 26**

EB is parallel to DC. ∠EAB = 50°.

∠AEB = 60°.

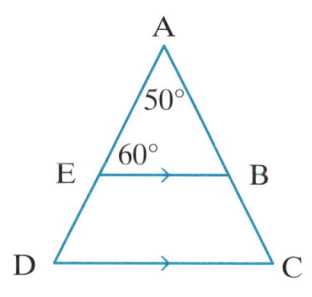

What is the size of ∠ACD?

    **A** 70°      **B** 60°      **C** 55°      **D** 50°

**Question 27**

60 boys and 90 girls were asked if they had seen a particular movie. 40% of boys and 60% of girls had seen the movie. What percentage of the group had seen the movie?

☐ %

**Question 28**

The number of text messages sent from a phone each day was recorded for a week:

    0, 1, 4, 5, 6, 6, 10

Which statement is correct?

    **A** mean < median < mode

    **B** mean < mode < median

    **C** median < mode < mean

    **D** mode < median < mean

**Question 29**

A cricket team needed to score 185 runs from 20 overs to win a game. After 8 overs the team had scored 65 runs. At what rate did the team need to score the rest of the runs?

☐ runs per over

# YEAR 9 NUMERACY SAMPLE TEST 1—CALCULATOR ALLOWED

**Question 30**

A straight line passes through the points (1, 9) and (5, 1). Which of the following points will the line also pass through?

- **A** (2, 8)
- **B** (3, 5)
- **C** (4, 2)
- **D** (6, 0)

**Question 31**

2.7 million seconds would be closest to

- **A** 1 day
- **B** 1 week
- **C** 1 month
- **D** 1 year

**Question 32**

A factory makes garden gnomes. The total cost, $C$, of producing $n$ gnomes is given by $C = 350 + 25n$. The factory receives $35 for each garden gnome. In a week where the factory produces and sells 180 gnomes, how much **profit** will it make?

$ ☐

# END OF TEST 1—CALCULATOR ALLOWED

# Year 9 Numeracy Sample Test 2

## Non-calculator

### Question 1

Donna is driving along Mary Street towards Tulip Road.

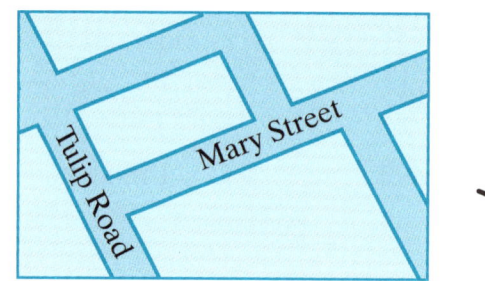

In what direction is she travelling?

- A  north-east
- B  north-west
- C  south-east
- D  south-west

### Question 2

25% of workers at a factory are casual employees and the rest are permanent members of staff. If there are 80 workers altogether, how many are permanent members of staff?

### Question 3

Jon has a standard die. What is the probability that Jon gets a 5 when he throws the die?

- A  $\frac{1}{3}$
- B  $\frac{1}{4}$
- C  $\frac{1}{5}$
- D  $\frac{1}{6}$

### Question 4

The rule for a pattern is 'double the previous number and add 5'. If the first number in this pattern is 2, what is the fourth number?

# YEAR 9 NUMERACY SAMPLE TEST 2—NON-CALCULATOR

## Question 5

This balance shows that 4 blocks have the same mass as 2 balls and a block.

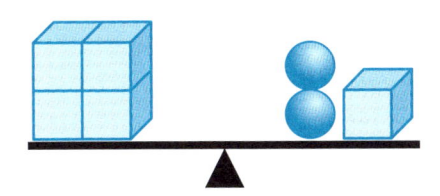

How many blocks would balance 6 balls?

　　A　3　　　　B　7　　　　C　9　　　　D　10

## Question 6

Five girls compared their heights. The diagram shows the results.

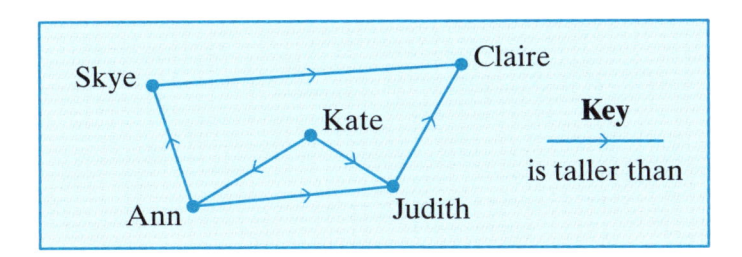

Who is the shortest?

　　A　Ann　　　　B　Kate　　　　C　Claire　　　　D　Judith

## Question 7

Avril arrived at work at 8:50 am and left at 4:15 pm. How long was Avril at work?

　　A　7 h 25 min　　　　B　7 h 35 min
　　C　8 h 25 min　　　　D　8 h 35 min

# YEAR 9 NUMERACY SAMPLE TEST 2—NON-CALCULATOR

## Question 8

This object is made from 12 cubes.

What is the view from the top?

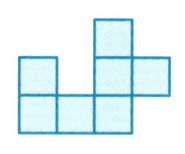

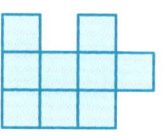

A   B   C   D

## Question 9

What is $12 \div \frac{1}{2}$?

A  6     B  8     C  16     D  24

## Question 10

This sector graph was drawn to show the results when 60 people were asked what their favourite type of movie was. How many people chose sci-fi movies?

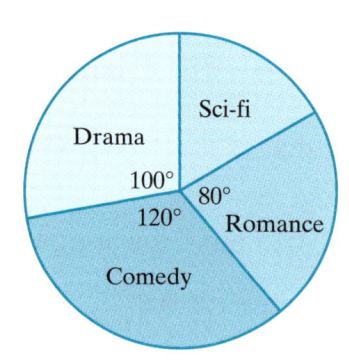

## Question 11

1 m and 85 cm is the same as

A  1850 mm      B  1085 mm
C  1.085 m      D  none of these

54  Answers and explanations on pages 145–148

# YEAR 9 NUMERACY SAMPLE TEST 2—NON-CALCULATOR

**Question 12**

When $a = 2$ and $b = 5$, what is the value of $3ab^2$?

　　A　60　　　　B　150　　　　C　300　　　　D　900

**Question 13**

What is the size of ∠PQR?

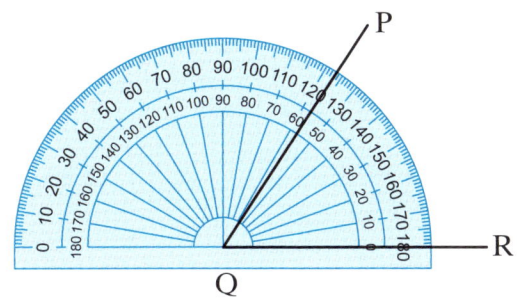

☐ °

**Question 14**

Which of these is not necessarily a parallelogram?

　　A　rectangle　　　　　　　B　rhombus
　　C　square　　　　　　　　D　trapezium

**Question 15**

Which is equivalent to $-x^2 + 5x$?

　　A　$4x^3$　　　B　$x^2 - 5x$　　　C　$5x - x^2$　　　D　$x(x - 5)$

**Question 16**

There are 60 red apples in a box. The ratio of red to green apples in the box is 5 to 3. How many green apples are in the box?

☐

# YEAR 9 NUMERACY SAMPLE TEST 2—NON-CALCULATOR

## Question 17

Which calculation will give the area of the shaded triangle?

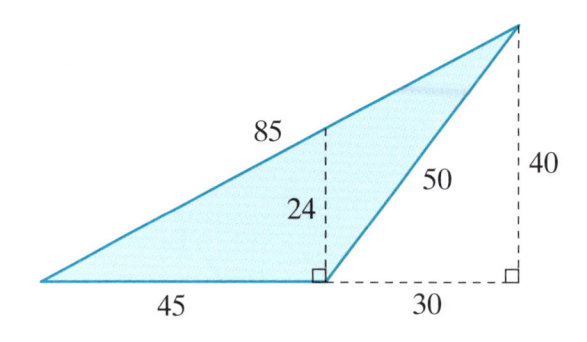

**A** $\frac{1}{2} \times 45 \times 85$  **B** $\frac{1}{2} \times 45 \times 50$

**C** $\frac{1}{2} \times 45 \times 40$  **D** $\frac{1}{2} \times 45 \times 24$

## Question 18

$3(2x + 1) = 9x - 6$

What is the value of $x$ in this equation?

$x = $ ☐

## Question 19

Each of the dimensions of a rectangular prism is three times larger than that of a smaller rectangular prism. How many times larger is the volume of the larger prism than that of the smaller prism?

**A** 27   **B** 9   **C** 6   **D** 3

## Question 20

This graph shows the results when 480 students voted for their year representative.

Selma won with 220 votes.

How many votes did Mary get? ☐

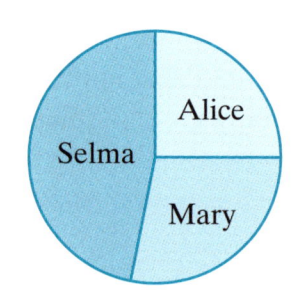

# YEAR 9 NUMERACY SAMPLE TEST 2—NON-CALCULATOR

## Question 21

Which set of fractions is arranged from lowest to highest?

A  $\frac{5}{8}, \frac{2}{3}, \frac{7}{12}, \frac{3}{4}$

B  $\frac{2}{3}, \frac{7}{12}, \frac{5}{8}, \frac{3}{4}$

C  $\frac{2}{3}, \frac{3}{4}, \frac{5}{8}, \frac{7}{12}$

D  $\frac{7}{12}, \frac{5}{8}, \frac{2}{3}, \frac{3}{4}$

## Question 22

Which statement is correct?

A  $0.3 < 0.04$

B  $-0.6 > -0.7$

C  $-0.2 < -0.235$

D  $-2.5 > -1.8$

## Question 23

A pattern has been formed with shapes.

What is the 90th shape in this pattern?

A  (tent)      B  (bird)      C  (waves)      D  (hook)

## Question 24

An isosceles (but not right-angled) triangle is cut along its axis of symmetry. What description applies to the two resulting triangles?

A  equilateral

B  isosceles and right-angled

C  isosceles but not right-angled

D  right-angled but not isosceles

## Question 25

Ray left home at 9:40 am and travelled 315 km, arriving at his destination at 1:10 pm.

What was Ray's average speed for the journey? ☐ km/h

# YEAR 9 NUMERACY SAMPLE TEST 2—NON-CALCULATOR

## Question 26

Hayden is drawing a parallelogram on this grid. He has marked three of the vertices of the parallelogram. Where will the fourth vertex go?

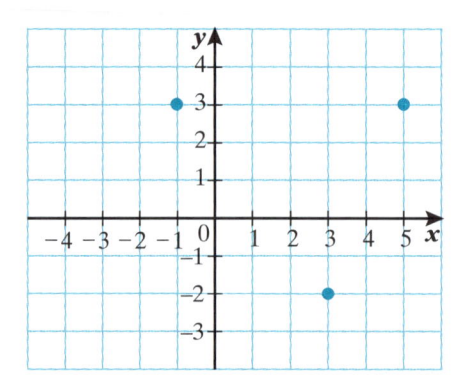

    **A** (−1, −2)      **B** (−3, −2)      **C** (−2, −3)      **D** (−1, −3)

## Question 27

A television was being sold for $560, but the price increased suddenly by 5%. Which calculation gives the new sale price?

    **A** 560 + 5      **B** 560 × 0.5

    **C** 560 × 0.05      **D** 560 × 1.05

## Question 28

Which is equal to $4^3$?

    **A** $2^6$      **B** $2^9$      **C** $3^4$      **D** $3^6$

## Question 29

What is the value of $x$?

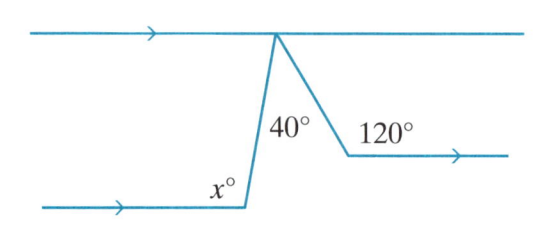

    **A** 80      **B** 100      **C** 120      **D** 140

# YEAR 9 NUMERACY SAMPLE TEST 2—NON-CALCULATOR

**Question 30**

What is the total area of all the surfaces of the prism and what is the volume of the prism?

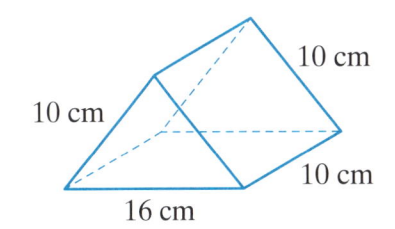

Surface area = ☐ cm² and volume = ☐ cm³

---

**Question 31**

This is a map of Flower Island.

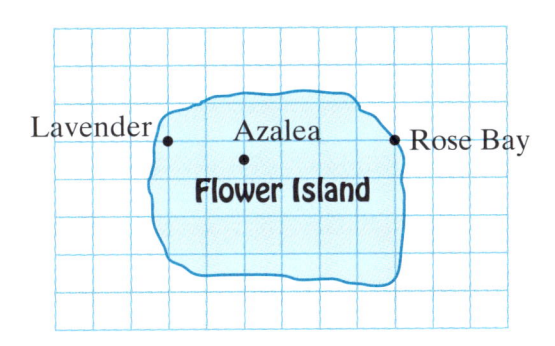

Rose Bay is on the coast, 180 km due south of Lavender.

Begonia is also on the coast. It is due west of Azalea.

Which is the best approximation of the actual distance, in kilometres, from Begonia to Azalea?

    **A** 130      **B** 90      **C** 75      **D** 60

---

**Question 32**

David has a bag of marbles, some of which are blue, some yellow and the rest are green. David knows that if he takes a marble from the bag without looking, there is 1 chance in 4 of selecting a blue marble and 1 chance in 3 of selecting a yellow marble. What is the probability of selecting a green marble?

    **A** $\frac{3}{4}$      **B** $\frac{1}{12}$      **C** $\frac{5}{12}$      **D** $\frac{7}{12}$

## END OF TEST 2—NON–CALCULATOR

# Year 9 Numeracy — Sample Test 2

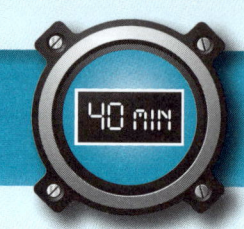

**Calculator Allowed**

## Question 1

The population of a nation is 23 287 564. What is this population to the nearest ten thousand?

- **A** 23 300 000
- **B** 23 290 000
- **C** 23 288 000
- **D** 23 280 000

## Question 2

Which dotted line is an axis of symmetry?

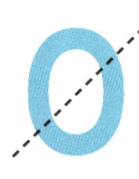

A  Z     B  N     C  M     D  O

## Question 3

Eric is driving south-west in Green Street.

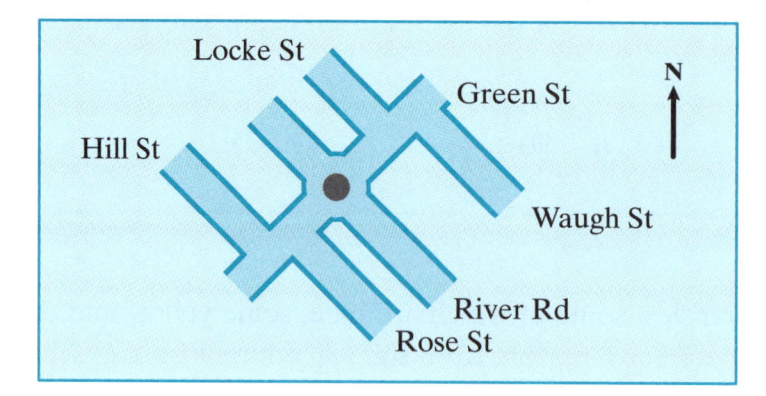

He takes the first street on the right after the roundabout. Into which street does Eric turn?

- **A** Waugh Street
- **B** Locke Street
- **C** Rose Street
- **D** Hill Street

# YEAR 9 NUMERACY SAMPLE TEST 2 — CALCULATOR ALLOWED

## Question 4

When 11 is added to a certain number and the result multiplied by 7 the answer is 203. What is the number?

## Question 5

If $n = 4$, what is the value of $\dfrac{3n}{n-1}$?

A  7.5    B  4    C  3    D  2

## Question 6

There are 60 girls at a dance. The ratio of boys to girls is 3 to 5. How many boys are at the dance?

## Question 7

This stem-and-leaf plot was drawn up to show the scores of students in a test.

**Scores of Class 9P**

| Stem | Leaf |
|------|------|
| 6 | 4 5 6 8 9 |
| 7 | 1 3 5 7 8 |
| 8 | 1 2 2 4 6 9 |
| 9 | 0 3 5 |

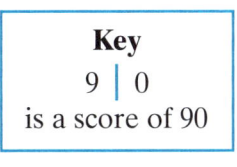

Key: 9 | 0 is a score of 90

What was the median?

A  78    B  71    C  82    D  81

## Question 8

A rectangle has a perimeter of 36 m. The shorter sides are 7 m long. How long are the longer sides?

____ m

# YEAR 9 NUMERACY SAMPLE TEST 2—CALCULATOR ALLOWED

**Question 9**

This jug holds orange juice. Sandi fills two glasses, each holding 250 mL, from the jug.

How many millilitres of juice remain in the jug?

☐ mL

**Question 10**

This pattern is formed by rotating the arrow in a clockwise direction.

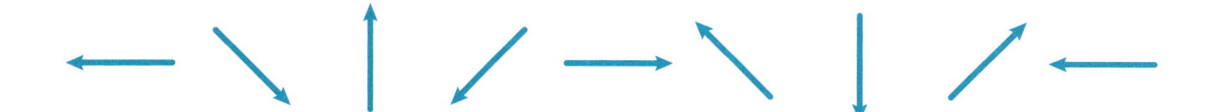

Through how many degrees is the arrow rotated each time? ☐ °

**Question 11**

Which expression is equivalent to $x - x^2$?

    **A**  $-x$        **B**  $x^2 - x$        **C**  $-x^2 - x$        **D**  $-x^2 + x$

**Question 12**

A box holds balls in 4 colours. 15 balls are blue, 12 are green, 18 are white and the rest are red. If a ball is taken from the box without looking, the probability that it is white is $\frac{1}{3}$.

How many red balls are in the box? ☐

# YEAR 9 NUMERACY SAMPLE TEST 2—CALCULATOR ALLOWED

## Question 13

Sam looks at this train timetable.

| Fingal | 7:17 | 7:59 | 8:30 | 9:09 |
| --- | --- | --- | --- | --- |
| Paget | 7:31 | 8:18 | 8:47 | 9:23 |
| Malak | 7:52 | 8:40 | 9:08 | 9:42 |
| City | 8:05 | 8:53 | 9:21 | 9:54 |

What is the latest time that Sam should leave home if it takes him 9 minutes to walk to Paget Station and he needs to be in the city before a quarter past nine?

## Question 14

There are 360 students enrolled at a college. One-quarter are part-time students and the rest full-time. 30% of the full-time students are mature-aged. How many mature-aged full-time students are enrolled at the college?

**A** 27  **B** 72  **C** 81  **D** 90

## Question 15

Sarah bought 6 apples for $4.69. The apples were selling for $4.97 per kilogram. Which is the best approximation for the average mass of each of these apples?

**A** 20 g  **B** 160 g  **C** 180 g  **D** 200 g

## Question 16

Which triangle is **not** isosceles?

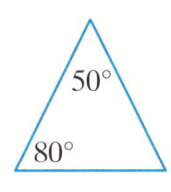

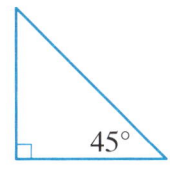

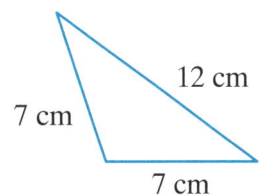

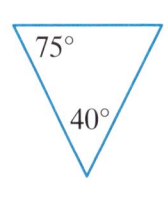

A (50°, 80°)   B (45°, right angle)   C (7 cm, 12 cm, 7 cm)   D (75°, 40°)

# YEAR 9 NUMERACY SAMPLE TEST 2—CALCULATOR ALLOWED

**Question 17**

Caitlin put 7 pens in each of 12 boxes and had 5 pens left over. If she wanted to put 10 pens in each of the boxes, how many more pens would she need?

**Question 18**

A triangle and a parallelogram both have the same perpendicular height and the same area. Which statement is correct?

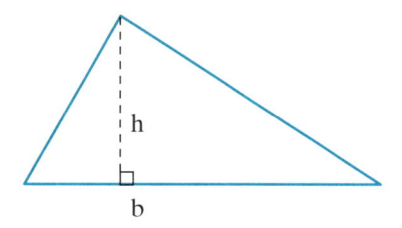

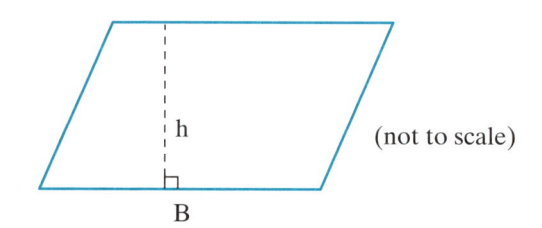

(not to scale)

- **A** The bases are equal in length.
- **B** The base of the triangle is twice that of the parallelogram.
- **C** The base of the triangle is half that of the parallelogram.
- **D** There is not enough information to compare the bases.

**Question 19**

$5x - 2 > 3x$

What value of $x$ will make this inequality true?

- **A** $x = -3$
- **B** $x = 0$
- **C** $x = 1$
- **D** $x = 2$

**Question 20**

Tom's scores in his last five tests were 82, 77, 85, 82 and 79. In his sixth test Tom scores 81. Which of the mean, median and mode will not change?

- **A** none (They will all change.)
- **B** mode only
- **C** mean and mode only
- **D** mean, mode and median

# YEAR 9 NUMERACY SAMPLE TEST 2—CALCULATOR ALLOWED

## Question 21

$y = 5x - 7$
$y = 3x + 5$

What value of *x* satisfies both these equations at the same time?

    **A**  $x = 3$      **B**  $x = 5$      **C**  $x = 6$      **D**  $x = 7$

## Question 22

PQ is parallel to the *x*-axis and QR is parallel to the *y*-axis. The coordinates of R are (9, 4).
PQ = 4, QR = 3 and PR = 5.

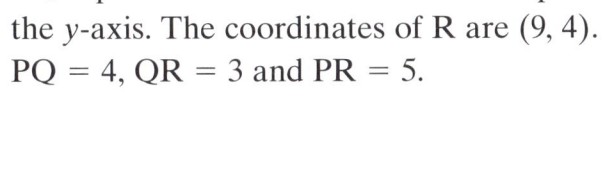

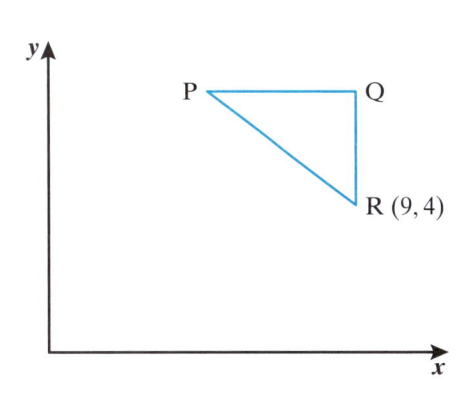

What are the coordinates of P?

    **A**  (5, 7)      **B**  (5, 1)      **C**  (4, 7)      **D**  (4, 1)

## Question 23

Zoe is making a cube from identical blocks. What is the smallest number of extra blocks that Zoe needs to complete her cube (without rearranging any blocks)?

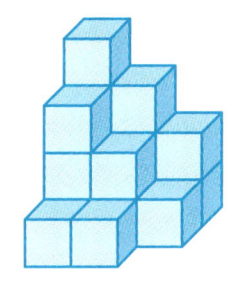

## Question 24

Over the last four years, the value of a ring has increased by 60%. The ring is now valued at $1200. What was the value four years ago?

    **A**  $480      **B**  $720      **C**  $750      **D**  $1000

# YEAR 9 NUMERACY SAMPLE TEST 2—CALCULATOR ALLOWED

**Question 25**

Harry has a container that holds 10 gallons. Approximately how many 3-litre bottles could Harry fill from his full container?

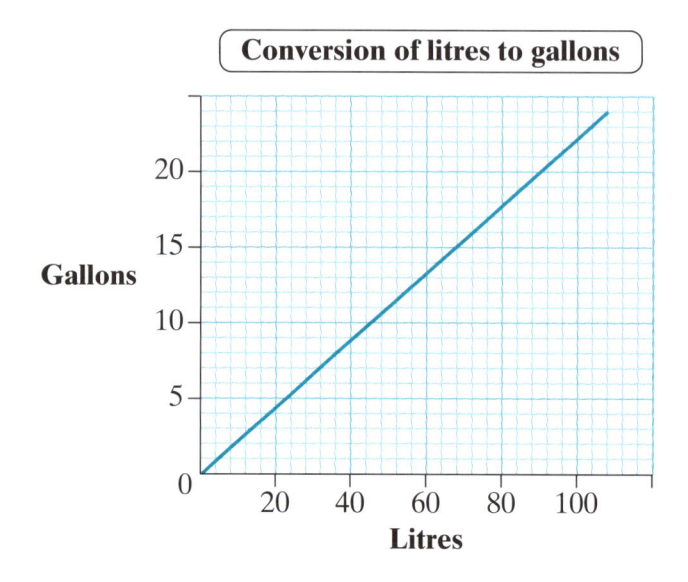

**Conversion of litres to gallons**

A  30     B  15     C  6     D  2

**Question 26**

Liam left home at 7:50 am and drove 175 km at an average speed of 70 kilometres per hour. He then stopped for 40 minutes before setting off again, arriving at his destination at 12:30 pm. If Liam averaged 84 kilometres per hour for the second part of the journey, what was the total length of his journey?

A  301 km     B  329 km     C  359 km     D  392 km

**Question 27**

What is the value of $h$?

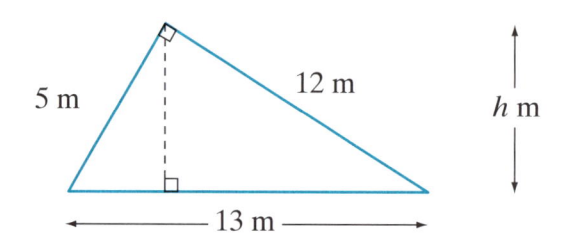

Give the answer correct to one decimal place.

# YEAR 9 NUMERACY SAMPLE TEST 2—CALCULATOR ALLOWED

**Question 28**

The first two numbers in a pattern are 4 and 11. The rule for the pattern is to multiply by 5 and then subtract a certain number. What is the fourth number in this pattern?

**Question 29**

What is the value of $x$ in this diagram?

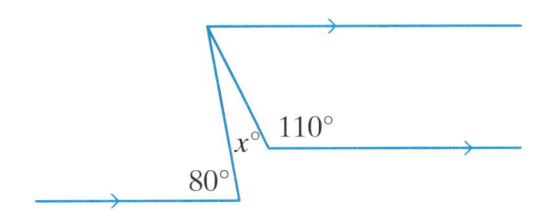

- **A** 10
- **B** 20
- **C** 30
- **D** 40

**Question 30**

Write 595 as a product of its prime factors.

**Question 31**

The average (mean) of eight numbers is 47. Cody left out a number but correctly calculated the average of the remaining numbers to be 43. What number did Cody leave out?

- **A** 43
- **B** 47
- **C** 64
- **D** 75

**Question 32**

$5(2x - 1) + 3(x + 2) - \square = 6x + 1$

What term replaces $\square$ to make this equation true for all values of $x$?

## END OF TEST 2—CALCULATOR ALLOWED

# Year 9 Numeracy Sample Test 3

## Non-calculator

### Question 1

Joanne drew this top view of an object.

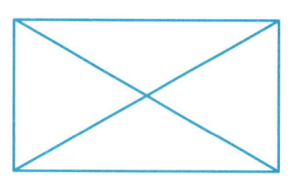

The object could be a

- **A** triangular pyramid.
- **B** triangular prism.
- **C** rectangular prism.
- **D** rectangular pyramid.

### Question 2

48 ÷ 12 = 12 ÷ ☐

☐ = _____

### Question 3

What is the perimeter of this shape?

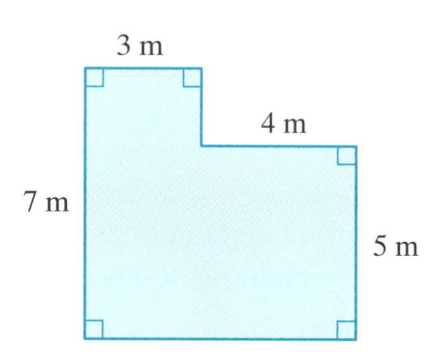

- **A** 19 m
- **B** 26 m
- **C** 28 m
- **D** 38 m

### Question 4

This spinner is to be spun 60 times. Which colour would you expect to get 5 times?

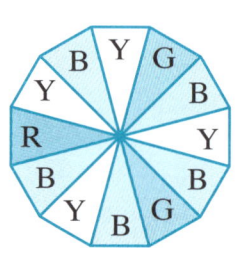

- **A** red
- **B** blue
- **C** green
- **D** yellow

# YEAR 9 NUMERACY SAMPLE TEST 3—NON-CALCULATOR

**Question 5**

$2x - 3 + x + 5 =$

    **A**   $2x^2 - 8$      **B**   $x - 8$      **C**   $x + 2$      **D**   $3x + 2$

**Question 6**

Last year 300 accidents were reported in a region. This year the number of reported accidents in the region is 240. What percentage decrease is this?

    **A**   20%      **B**   25%      **C**   75%      **D**   80%

**Question 7**

A bag holds 12 blue, 15 yellow, 8 green and 25 white pegs. If a peg is taken from the bag without looking, the probability that it is blue is

    **A**   $\frac{1}{6}$      **B**   $\frac{1}{5}$      **C**   $\frac{1}{4}$      **D**   $\frac{1}{3}$

**Question 8**

8.4, 7.6, 6.8, 6, …

What is the eleventh number in this pattern?

**Question 9**

What is the value of $x$?

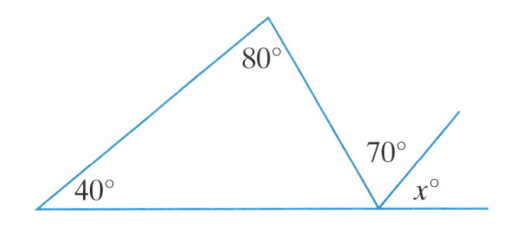

    **A**   40      **B**   50      **C**   60      **D**   70

# YEAR 9 NUMERACY SAMPLE TEST 3—NON-CALCULATOR

## Question 10

Which paddock has an area of six hectares?

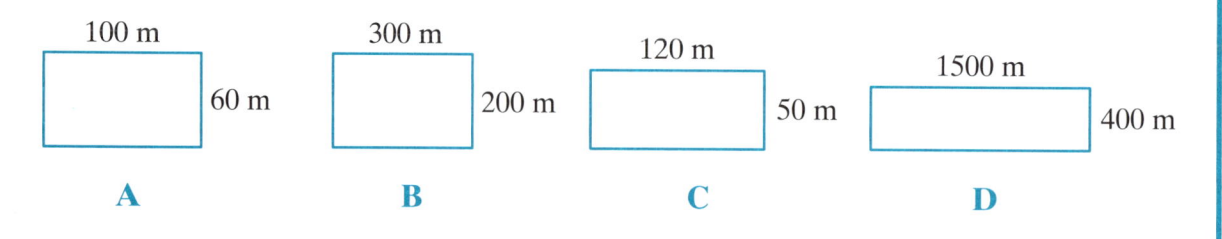

A: 100 m × 60 m
B: 300 m × 200 m
C: 120 m × 50 m
D: 1500 m × 400 m

## Question 11

Dan drove for 40 minutes at an average speed of 30 kilometres per hour. How far did he travel?

☐ km

## Question 12

The arrow points to a position on the number line.

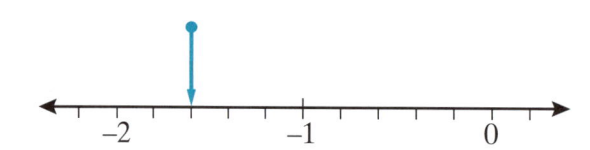

(arrow points between −2 and −1, at −1.5, on a number line showing −2, −1, 0)

What number is at this position?  ☐

## Question 13

When $t = -3$, what is the value of $2t^2$?

    **A**  −18    **B**  −36    **C**  18    **D**  36

## Question 14

$\sqrt{250}$ is about

    **A**  16    **B**  24    **C**  50    **D**  125

# YEAR 9 NUMERACY SAMPLE TEST 3—NON-CALCULATOR

**Question 15**

Which fraction is equal to $2\frac{5}{7}$?

- **A** $\frac{16}{7}$
- **B** $\frac{17}{7}$
- **C** $\frac{18}{7}$
- **D** $\frac{19}{7}$

**Question 16**

Which expression is equivalent to $3(2n + 1)$?

- **A** $5n + 1$
- **B** $5n + 3$
- **C** $6n + 1$
- **D** $6n + 3$

**Question 17**

PQRS is a square. Triangle TRS is equilateral.

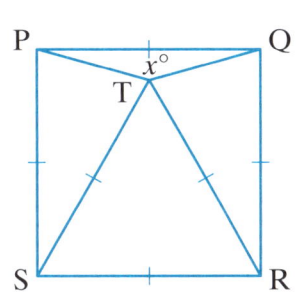

What is the value of $x$?

**Question 18**

What is $0.03 \div 0.5$?

- **A** 0.006
- **B** 0.06
- **C** 0.6
- **D** 6

**Question 19**

Here are some steps in a pattern:

$4^2 = 1 \times 7 + 9$
$5^2 = 2 \times 8 + 9$
$6^2 = 3 \times 9 + 9$
$7^2 = 4 \times 10 + 9$
$8^2 = 5 \times 11 + 9$

Using the pattern, the **value** of $97^2$ is?

# YEAR 9 NUMERACY SAMPLE TEST 3—NON-CALCULATOR

**Question 20**

The area of a square is 100 cm$^2$. What is the perimeter of the square?

☐ cm

**Question 21**

Jackson knows that 56 × 73 = 4088. What is 5.6 × 7.3?

    **A** 0.4088      **B** 4.088      **C** 40.88      **D** 408.8

**Question 22**

The four sides of this rectangle were divided into three equal parts as shown in the diagram.

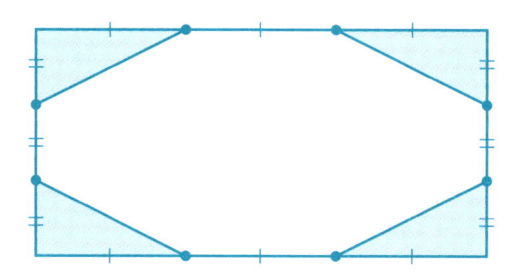

What fraction of the rectangle is shaded?

    **A** $\frac{1}{4}$      **B** $\frac{1}{3}$      **C** $\frac{2}{9}$      **D** $\frac{4}{9}$

**Question 23**

rectangle      parallelogram      rhombus

Which of these shapes have the same number of axes of symmetry?

    **A** parallelogram and rectangle      **B** parallelogram and rhombus

    **C** rectangle and rhombus      **D** none of them

# YEAR 9 NUMERACY SAMPLE TEST 3—NON-CALCULATOR

**Question 24**

If the minute hand on this clock turns through another 240°, what will be the time?

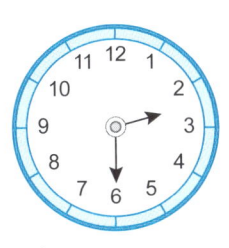

    **A**  2:40     **B**  2:50     **C**  3:10     **D**  6:50

**Question 25**

A car uses 7 litres of petrol for every 100 km travelled. The capacity of the car's fuel tank is 56 litres. How far will the car travel on a full tank of fuel?

    [      ] km

**Question 26**

Which is equivalent to $\frac{17}{100} + \frac{3}{10}$?

    **A**  0.173     **B**  0.317     **C**  0.2     **D**  0.47

**Question 27**

$n$ is the smallest number in a set of four consecutive whole numbers. What is the largest number in the set?

    **A**  $n + 3$     **B**  $n + 4$     **C**  $n + 5$     **D**  $q$

**Question 28**

The ratio of boys to girls enrolled in a course was 3 to 4. Three more boys enrolled in the course bringing the number of boys to 18. What is the ratio of boys to girls now?

    **A**  3 to 2     **B**  3 to 4     **C**  6 to 7     **D**  9 to 10

Answers and explanations on pages 152–155

# YEAR 9 NUMERACY SAMPLE TEST 3—NON-CALCULATOR

**Question 29**

Dominic counted the number of each colour in a packet of 25 balloons. He placed the results in a table, but the number of orange balloons cannot be read.

| Colour | Number |
|---|---|
| Red | 7 |
| White | 4 |
| Blue | 6 |
| Green | 5 |
| Orange | |

What percentage of the balloons is orange?  ☐ %

**Question 30**

Julie needs to travel from Seascape to Hilltop, along Coast Road and Hilltop Road, and wants to arrive at Hilltop at about 10 am. Julie knows she can average around 70 kilometres per hour on the trip.

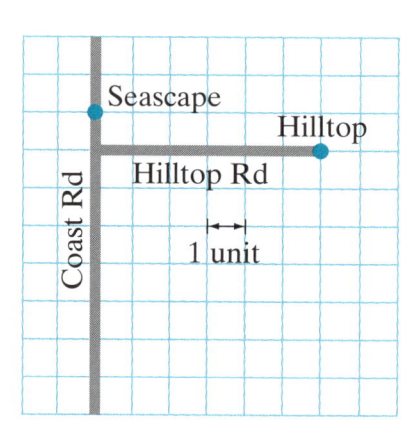

Scale: 1 unit represents 20 km

What time should Julie leave Seascape?

   **A** 7 am     **B** 8 am     **C** 9 am     **D** 9:30 am

# YEAR 9 NUMERACY SAMPLE TEST 3—NON-CALCULATOR

**Question 31**

$\frac{3}{10} > \frac{5}{x}$ where $x$ is a positive whole number. What is the smallest possible value of $x$?

**Question 32**

Line $l$ passes through $(1, 3)$ and $(-1, -1)$.

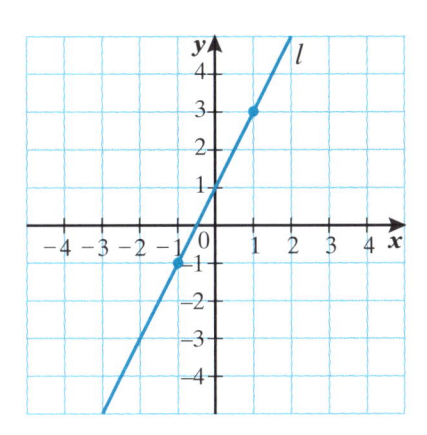

What is the equation of line $l$?

    **A**   $y = 2x + 1$      **B**   $y = x + 2$      **C**   $y = 3x$      **D**   $y = -x + 2$

## END OF TEST 3—NON–CALCULATOR

# Year 9 Numeracy — Sample Test 3

**Calculator Allowed**

## Question 1

Gavin folded this net to make a cube.

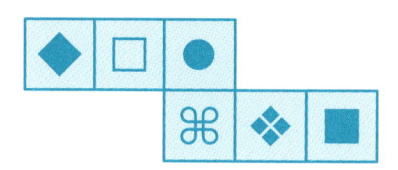

What symbol is on the face opposite the face showing ●?

A ◆   B ⌘   C ❖   D ■

## Question 2

Valerie wrote down the first six numbers in a pattern:

　　1, 2, 4, 7, 11, 16

What is the tenth number in this pattern?

## Question 3

What is $8^2 + 15^2$?

A $17^2$   B $19^2$   C $21^2$   D $23^2$

## Question 4

A car uses petrol at the rate of 6.5 litres per 100 kilometres travelled. Which is the best approximation for the number of litres it will use to travel 750 km?

A 40   B 50   C 60   D 70

# YEAR 9 NUMERACY SAMPLE TEST 3—CALCULATOR ALLOWED

**Question 5**

This table shows the amount of time Ricky spent at the gym after school this week.

| Day | Time |
| --- | --- |
| Monday | 20 min |
| Tuesday | 1 h 10 min |
| Wednesday | 45 min |
| Thursday | 1 h 15 min |
| Friday | 40 min |

What is the average amount of time that Ricky spent at the gym each afternoon?

☐ min

**Question 6**

$\frac{2}{3}$ of a number is 72. What is $\frac{3}{4}$ of the number?

- **A** 36
- **B** 64
- **C** 81
- **D** 96

**Question 7**

1 tonne and 80 kilograms is the same as

- **A** 100 080 kg
- **B** 1 000 080 kg
- **C** 1.008 t
- **D** 1.08 t

**Question 8**

If $x = 6$, what is the value of $2x - x^2$?

- **A** −24
- **B** −10
- **C** 24
- **D** 36

# YEAR 9 NUMERACY SAMPLE TEST 3—CALCULATOR ALLOWED

## Question 9

What is the value of *x* in this diagram?

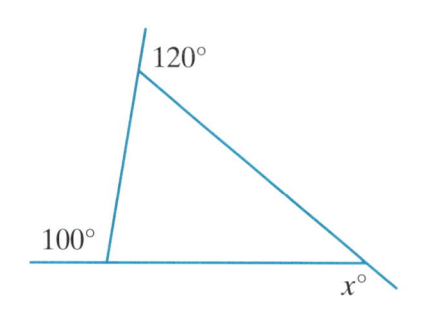

- A  100
- B  110
- C  120
- D  140

## Question 10

A bag holds 10 red, 15 blue and 25 green marbles. Without looking, Joy takes a marble from the bag. What is the chance that the marble is blue?

- A  15%
- B  20%
- C  25%
- D  30%

## Question 11

Here is a table of values for *x* and *y*.

| x | 0 | 1 | 2 | 3 | 4 |
|---|---|---|---|---|---|
| y | 2 | 3 | 6 | 11 | 18 |

What is the correct rule for *y* in terms of *x*?

- A  $y = x + 2$
- B  $y = x^2 + 2$
- C  $y = 2x^2$
- D  $y = 2x^2 + 2$

## Question 12

Both diagonals of which special type of quadrilateral will always be equal?

- A  rhombus
- B  rectangle
- C  kite
- D  trapezium

# YEAR 9 NUMERACY SAMPLE TEST 3—CALCULATOR ALLOWED

**Question 13**

A vertical cut is made through a cone as shown in the diagram.

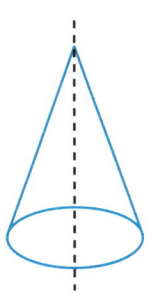

Which diagram shows the shape of the cross-section made by the cut?

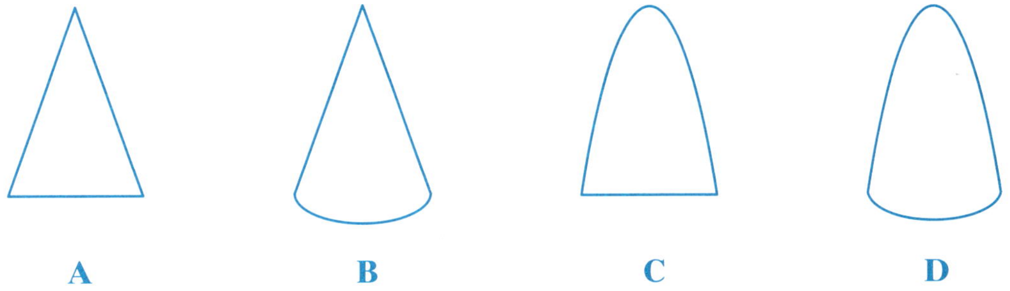

A　　　　B　　　　C　　　　D

**Question 14**

Which expression is equivalent to $-5p + p^2$?

A　$-p^2 + 5p$ 　　　　　B　$p^2 - 5p$

C　$-p + 5p^2$ 　　　　　D　$5p - p^2$

**Question 15**

This is a scale drawing of a tabletop.

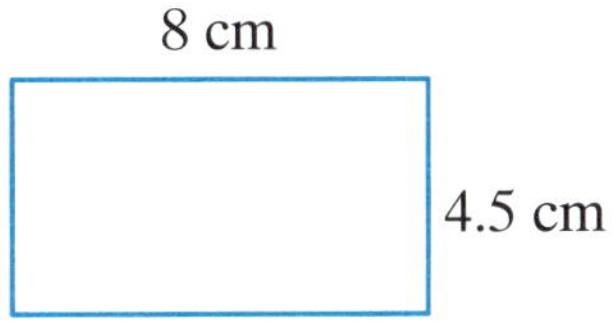

8 cm
4.5 cm

The table is actually 1.6 m long.

How wide is the table in centimetres? ▢ cm

Answers and explanations on pages 155–158

# YEAR 9 NUMERACY SAMPLE TEST 3—CALCULATOR ALLOWED

**Question 16**

What is the value of *x*?

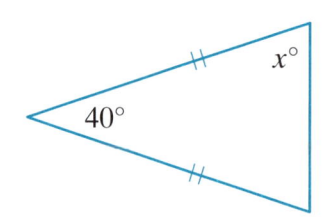

**Question 17**

What number is exactly halfway between 0.12 and 0.4?

    **A** 0.8      **B** 0.28      **C** 0.26      **D** 0.08

**Question 18**

The graph shows the cost of certain holiday tours and their length (in days). Which two tours can be used to show that 'the higher the cost the longer the tour' is not always correct?

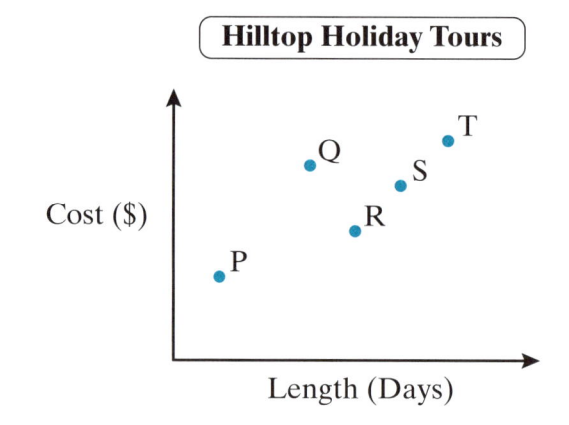

    **A** P and T      **B** R and S      **C** S and P      **D** R and Q

**Question 19**

The diagram shows a plan of the fence around the pool in Jim's yard. The fenced section is made up of a square and a semi-circle. Which is the best approximation for the length of the fence?

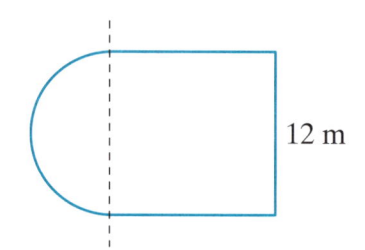

    **A** 55 m      **B** 48 m      **C** 74 m      **D** 67 m

# YEAR 9 NUMERACY SAMPLE TEST 3—CALCULATOR ALLOWED

**Question 20**

John bought a computer that was on sale at $17\frac{1}{2}$% off the marked price. The marked price was $640. How much did John pay?

- **A** $112
- **B** $544
- **C** $528
- **D** $622.50

**Question 21**

How many square metres are in 2 square kilometres?

- **A** 2000
- **B** 4000
- **C** 2 000 000
- **D** 4 000 000

**Question 22**

Sand is tipped from a truck and forms a pile in the shape of a cone. The height of the cone, $h$ metres, is given by $h = \dfrac{3V}{\pi r^2}$ where $V$ is the volume of sand (in m³) and $r$ (m) is the radius of the cone. When $V = 1.5$ and $r = 0.8$, the height of the cone is closest to

- **A** 0.7 m
- **B** 0.9 m
- **C** 1.9 m
- **D** 2.2 m

**Question 23**

Shelly has two objects, both made by joining together four identical cubes.

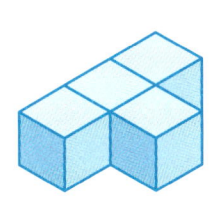

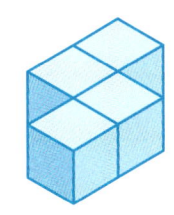

Which of these cannot be made by joining Shelley's two objects together?

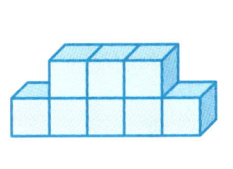

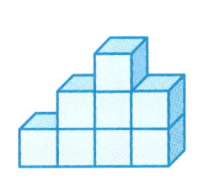

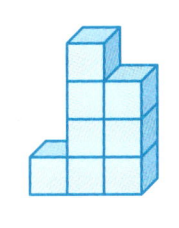

A    B    C    D

# YEAR 9 NUMERACY SAMPLE TEST 3—CALCULATOR ALLOWED

## Question 24

When it is 5 pm in Melbourne it is 7 am in London (on the same day). What time and day is it in Melbourne when it is 5 pm Monday in London?

- **A** 3 am Tuesday
- **B** 3 am Monday
- **C** 7 am Tuesday
- **D** 7 am Monday

## Question 25

Corinne travelled 90 km at an average speed of 72 kilometres per hour. How long did the journey take?

- **A** 48 min
- **B** 1 h 15 min
- **C** 1 h 20 min
- **D** 1 h 25 min

## Question 26

The total area of all the faces of a cube is 24 m². What is the volume of the cube?

- **A** 8 m³
- **B** 36 m³
- **C** 64 m³
- **D** 216 m³

## Question 27

$3^3 \times 9^2 =$

- **A** $3 \times 3 \times 9 \times 2$
- **B** $3 \times 3 \times 3 \times 9 \times 2$
- **C** $3 \times 3 \times 3 \times 3 \times 9$
- **D** $3 \times 3 \times 3 \times 3 \times 3 \times 9$

## Question 28

What is the value of $x$ in this diagram?

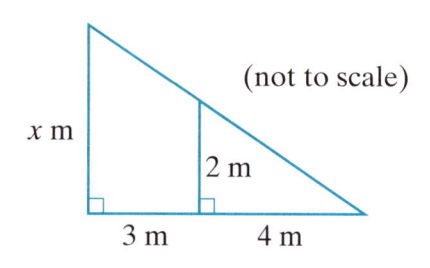

(not to scale)

$x$ m, 2 m, 3 m, 4 m

- **A** 1.5
- **B** 3.5
- **C** 5
- **D** 6

# YEAR 9 NUMERACY SAMPLE TEST 3—CALCULATOR ALLOWED

## Question 29

$$\frac{a}{5} > \frac{b}{3}$$

Which values of *a* and *b* make this inequality true?

- **A** $a = 3$ and $b = 2$
- **B** $a = 4$ and $b = 3$
- **C** $a = 7$ and $b = 4$
- **D** $a = 8$ and $b = 5$

## Question 30

A polygon has three angles of 150° and its other angles each measure 126°. What type of polygon is it?

- **A** pentagon
- **B** hexagon
- **C** octagon
- **D** decagon

## Question 31

The other 24 students in Callum's class sat for a test. The average (mean) mark was 73%. Callum was away on the day of the test and did it the next day. When Callum's mark was included the average increased to 74%. What was Callum's mark?

☐ %

## Question 32

There were 36 people at a barbecue. The ratio of adults to children was 4:5. Two more adults and four more children arrived at the barbecue. What was the new ratio of adults to children?

☐ : ☐

## END OF TEST 3—CALCULATOR ALLOWED

# Year 9 Numeracy — Mini Test Answers

**ANSWERS TO MINI TESTS**

Note: Units that are given in the question are repeated in the answer. For example, if the question says _____ m (where the number to be written on the space is 78) the answer will say 78 m.

## Basic level questions

**Mini Test 1:** Basic Numbers .................... Page 4

1 A  2 5  3 $320  4 D  5 C  6 B  7 57 000 km$^2$
8 A  9 B  10 4  11 B  12 27  13 $0.55  14 100
15 32  16 C  17 B  18 1500  19 D  20 0.45  21 A
22 300  23 D  24 D

1  $18 \times 37 - 26 \times 18$
   $= 18 \times 37 - 18 \times 26$
   $= 18 \times (37 - 26)$
   $= 18 \times 11$

2  The answer was 17.
   Before 8 was subtracted the answer was 17 + 8 or 25.
   After the number was multiplied by itself the answer was 25.
   The number was $\sqrt{25}$ or 5.

3  25% is one-quarter.
   Weekly rent = $1280 ÷ 4
                = $320

4  $87 + 43 \times 28 - 19$
   Rounding each number to the nearest ten:
   87 is closest to 90, 43 is closest to 40, 28 is closest to 30 and 19 is closest to 20.
   The best estimate is $90 + 40 \times 30 - 20$.

5  Add numbers to the number line:

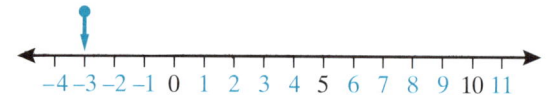

   ←—|—|—|—|—|—|—|—|—|—|—|—|—|→
   −4 −3 −2 −1  0  1  2  3  4  5  6  7  8  9 10 11

   The arrow is pointing to −3.

6  Consider each option:
   $2 + 3 \times 6 = 2 + 18$
                  $= 20$
   $4 + 6 \times 2 = 4 + 12$
                  $= 16$

   $2 \times 5 \times 2 = 10 \times 2$
                       $= 20$
   $14 - 3 + 9 = 11 + 9$
              $= 20$
   The expression that is not equal to 20 is $4 + 6 \times 2$.

7  The area = 56 823 km$^2$
   To the nearest thousand square kilometres the area = 57 000 km$^2$
   [It is between 56 000 and 57 000 and closer to 57 000.]

8  20% is one-fifth.
   Number of students in Year 9 = 150 ÷ 5
                                = 30

9  $2.49 is about $2\frac{1}{2}$ dollars.
   Approximate cost = $$2\frac{1}{2} \times 6$
                    = $(2 \times 6 + \frac{1}{2} \times 6)$
                    = $(12 + 3)$
                    = $15

10  $36 \div 12 = 12 \div \square$
    Now $36 \div 12 = 3$
    So $12 \div \square = 3$
    This means that $\square = 4$ because $12 \div 4 = 3$.

11  $3^4 = 3 \times 3 \times 3 \times 3$
    [The index (4) tells us how many factors of 3 are multiplied together.]

12  10% of 180 = 180 ÷ 10
              = 18
    5% of 180 = 18 ÷ 2
             = 9
    So 15% of 180 = 18 + 9
                 = 27

13  Price per pen = $1.65 ÷ 3
                 = $0.55

14  234 ÷ 100 = 2.34
    The number Paris divided by was 100.
    [When dividing by powers of ten, the decimal point moves one place to the left for each zero.]

15  $\frac{3}{4}$ of the number = 24
    $\frac{1}{4}$ of the number = 24 ÷ 3
                               = 8
    The number = 8 × 4
               = 32

84

# YEAR 9 NUMERACY MINI TEST ANSWERS

**16** $632 \times 35 = 22\,120$
$6.32 \times 3.5 = 22.120$
[There must be the same number of places after the decimal point in the answer as there were (in total) in the question.
Or use estimation. The answer must be about $6 \times 4 = 24$.]

**17** For every 3 wet days there were 2 sunny days.
12 wet days = $4 \times 3$ wet days
Number of sunny days = $4 \times 2$
$= 8$

**18** 20% is one-fifth.
Number of shares = $300 \times 5$
$= 1500$

**19** [Write each decimal with the same number of places after the decimal point.]
0.2006
0.1080
0.0390
0.2700
In order, from smallest to largest, the numbers are 0.039, 0.108, 0.2006 and 0.27.
The largest number is 0.27.

**20** [The number halfway between two others is the average.]
$0.2 + 0.7 = 0.9$
$0.9 \div 2 = 0.45$
The number halfway between 0.2 and 0.7 is 0.45.

**21** $\dfrac{7}{10} + \dfrac{13}{100} = 0.7 + 0.13$
$= 0.83$

$\quad\;\; 0.70$
$+\,0.13$
$\overline{\quad\;\; 0.83}$

**22** $\dfrac{1}{6}$ of the people = 60
Number of people = $6 \times 60$
$= 360$
Number of adults = $360 - 60$
$= 300$

**23** $12 + 1.2 + 0.12 = 12.00 + 1.20 + 0.12$
$= 13.32$

$\quad 12.00$
$\quad\;\; 1.20$
$+\,\;\; 0.12$
$\overline{\quad 13.32}$

**24** $8^2 = 64$
$9^2 = 81$
Now 70 is between 64 and 81.
So $\sqrt{70}$ is between 8 and 9.

## Basic level questions

**Mini Test 2:** Basic Algebra ............ Page 5

**1** B  **2** 63  **3** C  **4** B  **5** 29  **6** 5  **7** 74  **8** A  **9** D
**10** A  **11** A  **12** D  **13** C  **14** C  **15** B  **16** D
**17** 29  **18** C  **19** B  **20** 26

**1** [$3k$ means $3 \times k$.]
If $k = 5$, $3k = 3 \times 5$
$= 15$

**2** 1, 3, 7, 15, 31, ...
The differences between the numbers are 2, then 4, then 8, then 16. The differences are doubling each time. The next difference will be 32.
Next number = $31 + 32$
$= 63$
[Or use the rule 'to find the next number, double the previous number and add 1'.]

**3**

| □ | 1 | 3 | 5  | 7  | 9  | 11 |
|---|---|---|----|----|----|----|
| ○ | 3 | 7 | 11 |    | 19 | 23 |

The rule is ○ = $2 \times$ □ $+ 1$.
So when □ = 7,
○ = $2 \times 7 + 1$
$= 14 + 1$
$= 15$

**4** [$pq$ means $p \times q$.]
When $p = 3$ and $q = 4$,
$pq = 3 \times 4$
$= 12$

**5** The first number is 1.
The second number = $2 \times 1 + 3$
$= 2 + 3$
$= 5$
The third number = $2 \times 5 + 3$
$= 10 + 3$
$= 13$
The fourth number = $2 \times 13 + 3$
$= 26 + 3$
$= 29$

# YEAR 9 NUMERACY MINI TEST ANSWERS

**6** 2, 2.6, 3.2, 3.8, 4.4
Now 2.6 − 2 = 0.6
3.2 − 2.6 = 0.6
The numbers are increasing by 0.6 each time.
Next number = 4.4 + 0.6
= 5.0
The next number is 5.

**7**

The number of pins
= 6 × number of octagons + 2
When there are 12 octagons:
The number of pins = 6 × 12 + 2
= 72 + 2
= 74

**8** $y = 4x + 3$
When $x = 2$,
$y = 4 × 2 + 3$
= 8 + 3
= 11

**9**

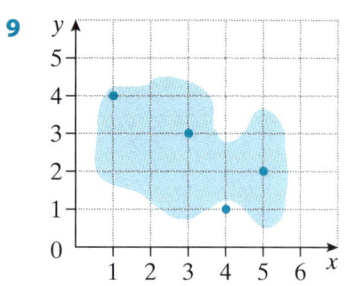

Of the choices, (3, 3), (1, 4) and (5, 2) lie in the shaded region.
The point that does not lie in the shaded region is (4, 1).

**10** $3t + 2t + 4t = 9t$
[Of the $t$'s there are 3 plus 2 plus 4 so altogether there are 9.]

**11** 4.3, 3.6, 2.9, …
4.3 − 3.6 = 0.7
3.6 − 2.9 = 0.7
The rule is to decrease by 0.7.

**12** ⊗ + ◇ = △ + △
Now △ = 4,
so △ + △ = 4 + 4
= 8
This means that ⊗ + ◇ = 8.

But ⊗ = 3
So 3 + ◇ = 8
So ◇ = 5 because 3 + 5 = 8.

**13** 3, 6, 9, 12, 15, …
The first number is 3 × 1.
The second number is 3 × 2.
The third number is 3 × 3.
The numbers are the multiples of 3.
Of the options, the only number not divisible by 3 is 67.
So 67 is not a number in the pattern.

**14**

| $x$ | 1 | 2 | 3 | 4 | 5 |
|---|---|---|---|---|---|
| $y$ | 3 | 7 | 11 | 15 | 19 |

[The $x$-values increase by 1 each time.
The $y$-values increase by 4 each time.
So try the option that involves multiplying by 4.]
Try $y = 4 × x − 1$
When $x = 1$,
$y = 4 × 1 − 1$
= 4 − 1
= 3
When $x = 2$,
$y = 4 × 2 − 1$
= 8 − 1
= 7
When $x = 3$,
$y = 4 × 3 − 1$
= 12 − 1
= 11
When $x = 4$,
$y = 4 × 4 − 1$
= 16 − 1
= 15
When $x = 5$,
$y = 4 × 5 − 1$
= 20 − 1
= 19
The rule is $y = 4 × x − 1$.

**15** 2, 7, 12, 17, 22, …
The numbers increase by 5 each time.
The first number is 5 × 1 − 3.
The second number is 5 × 2 − 3.
The third number is 5 × 3 − 3.
The fourth number is 5 × 4 − 3.
The fifth number is 5 × 5 − 3.

# YEAR 9 NUMERACY MINI TEST ANSWERS

Using this pattern:
the 21st number = $5 \times 21 - 3$
$= 105 - 3$
$= 102$

**16** If $a = 6$ and $b = 5$,
$ab - b = 6 \times 5 - 5$
$= 30 - 5$
$= 25$

**17** 2, 5, 8, 11, 14, …
The numbers are increasing by 3 each time.
Continue the pattern:
2, 5, 8, 11, 14, 17, 20, 23, 26, 29, 32, 35, …
The tenth number is 29.

**18** $2x + 1 = 25$
[Subtract 1 from both sides.]
$2x = 24$
[Divide both sides by 2.]
$x = 12$

**19** ♦♥♣♠♦♥♣♠♦♥♣♠♦♥♣♠…
There are four symbols that are being repeated.
So every fourth symbol will be ♠.
So the 48th symbol will be ♠.
The 49th symbol will be ♦ and the 50th symbol will be ♥.

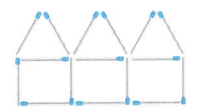

**20** First shape  Second shape  Third shape

[Draw up a table showing the number of matches needed for each shape.]

| Shape | 1 | 2 | 3 |
|---|---|---|---|
| Number of matches | 6 | 11 | 16 |

The number of matches increases by 5 each time.
So $16 + 5 = 21$ matches will be needed for the fourth shape.
For the fifth shape,
number of matches = $21 + 5$
$= 26$

## Basic level questions

**Mini Test 3:** Basic Space .................. Page 6

**1** D  **2** B  **3** C  **4** C  **5** D  **6** D  **7** A  **8** B  **9** B  **10** C
**11** A  **12** A  **13** A  **14** C  **15** D  **16** B

**1** The view from the top does not depend on how high the cubes are stacked. There will be three rows of cubes. The front row has two cubes (on the far left and middle left), the middle row has four cubes and the back row has just one cube on the far right.
The view from the top is D.

**2** A reflex angle is larger than 180° but less than 360°. Of the choices, only B is larger than 180° so it is the reflex angle.

**3** Sandra is facing south-west.

**4** The net of a cube cannot be  .
Three faces meet at any vertex of a cube, whereas this net has four faces meeting at a point.

**5** The top part of the octagon is a trapezium.
It is a quadrilateral with one pair of parallel sides.
[A rectangle, a parallelogram and a rhombus all have two pairs of parallel sides.]

**6** An isosceles triangle has two equal sides and two equal angles.
Of the options, A has no equal angles, B has no equal sides and C has no equal angles.
Only the triangle in D has two equal angles and is isosceles.

**7** All four objects can be made from Wayne's two objects.

87

# YEAR 9 NUMERACY MINI TEST ANSWERS

**8** A line of symmetry is a line along which the item could be folded and the two halves match exactly.
Only in B will the two halves match exactly.

**9** The solid is a square pyramid.

When viewed from the top the square base will be seen with a dot in the centre for the top vertex and lines to all the corners of the square from this dot being the edges that join the top vertex to the base.

**10** Angles in a straight line add to 180°.
So $x + 40 = 180$
$x = 180 - 40$
$= 140$

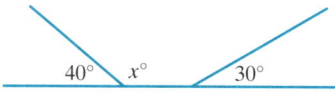

[The angle of 30° has no effect on the size of $x$.]

**11** 90° is a right angle. 270° is three right angles or three-quarters of a turn.
Clockwise is in the same direction as the hands of a clock turn.
The correct option is A.

**12**

The card will look the same as it did originally.
The correct option is A.

**13** Edward turned into John Street.

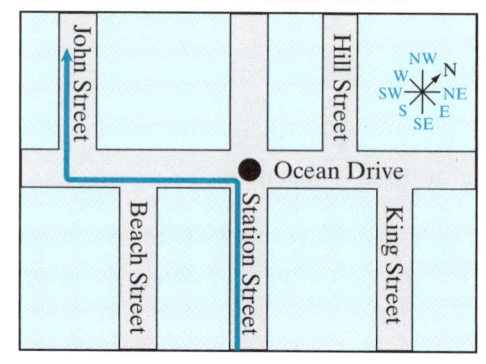

**14** A rectangular prism has 6 faces, 8 vertices and 12 edges.
The correct option is C.

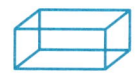

**15** A reflection in a vertical line will move P to P¹.

**16** An angle of 190° is larger than 180° but less than 360°. An angle that is larger than 180° but less than 360° is reflex. An angle of 190° is a reflex angle.

## Basic level questions

**Mini Test 4:** Basic Numbers ................... Page 7

**1** $0.85  **2** A  **3** A  **4** B  **5** $1.50  **6** 79  **7** C  **8** A
**9** A  **10** 18  **11** D  **12** D  **13** $40.50  **14** C
**15** 3 and 6  **16** B  **17** B  **18** C  **19** $3.25
**20** $3060  **21** D  **22** C

**1** One dozen is twelve.
Price per orange = $10.20 ÷ 12
= $0.85

**2** 24 out of 36 = $\frac{24}{36}$
= $\frac{2}{3}$

**3** $\sqrt{36 + 64} = \sqrt{100}$
= 10

**4** Number with licence = 15% of 120
= $\frac{15}{100} \times 120$
= 18

**5** Cost of 4 hamburgers = 4 × $2.50
= $10.00
Cost of 3 drinks = $14.50 − $10.00
= $4.50
Cost of each drink = $4.50 ÷ 3
= $1.50

**6** 2686 ÷ 34 = 79
So 2686 ÷ 79 = 34
The number was 79.

**7** $15^2 = 225$
$16^2 = 256$
So numbers between $15^2$ and $16^2$ are between 225 and 256.
Of the choices, the number that is between $15^2$ and $16^2$ is 250.

# YEAR 9 NUMERACY MINI TEST ANSWERS

**8** Increase = $315 − $300
         = $15
Percentage increase = $\frac{\$15}{\$300} \times 100\%$
                    = 5%

**9** Fraction that is black and white = $\frac{28}{70}$
                                      = $\frac{2}{5}$

**10** 25% is one-quarter.
Number eaten = 24 ÷ 4
             = 6
Number remaining = 24 − 6
                 = 18

**11** For every 4 parts of the length there are 3 parts for the width.
Now 84 ÷ 4 = 21
So there are 21 lots of 4 parts in the length.
Now 21 × 3 = 63
So the width is 63 cm.

**12** $\frac{63.2 + 16.8}{4 - 1.5} = \frac{80}{2.5}$
                                  = 32

**13** Cost per ticket = $108 ÷ 8
                      = $13.50
Cost of 3 tickets = 3 × $13.50
                  = $40.50

**14** Temperature at 5 am = (13.7 − 4.2)°C
                          = 9.5°C
Temperature at 9 am = (9.5 + 9.8)°C
                    = 19.3°C

**15** 6 × 3 = 18
6 + 3 = 9
The numbers are 6 and 3.

**16** $-3\frac{1}{3}$ lies between −3 and −4. It must be closer to −3 than −4.

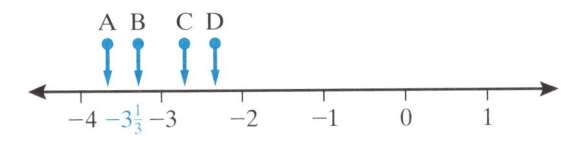

A B C D
−4 $-3\frac{1}{3}$ −3 −2 −1 0 1

The arrow that is pointing to the position of $-3\frac{1}{3}$ is B.

**17** 36 × ☐ = 27
☐ = 27 ÷ 36
  = $\frac{27}{36}$
  = $\frac{3}{4}$

[Or simply multiply each of the options by 36 to see which gives an answer of 27.]

**18** Total balloons = 20 + 5
                    = 25
Percentage inflated = $\frac{5}{25} \times 100\%$
                   = 20%

**19** Cost of 5 daily tickets = 5 × $3.75
                             = $18.75
Saving = $18.75 − $15.50
       = $3.25

**20** Takings on Saturday = $2375 + $685
                         = $3060
[The takings on Monday were less than those on Saturday. You needed to add.]

**21** 20% is one-fifth.
So $500 is $\frac{1}{5}$ of the bill.
Bill = 5 × $500
     = $2500

**22** Round each option to the nearest million.
8 512 782 is 9 000 000 to the nearest million.
7 216 928 is 7 000 000 to the nearest million.
7 658 107 is 8 000 000 to the nearest million.
7 040 315 is 7 000 000 to the nearest million.

The only option that rounds to 8 million is option C.

Of the options, the only possible population is 7 658 107.

## Basic level questions

**Mini Test 5:** Basic Measurement ............... Page 8

**1** B  **2** D  **3** D  **4** B  **5** C  **6** A  **7** D  **8** 750 km
**9** 179 km  **10** A  **11** C  **12** B  **13** 16 m  **14** C
**15** A  **16** 8 m

**1** Speed = 300 km in 4 hours
           = 75 km in 1 hour
           = 75 km/h

**2** 1 cm represents 15 km.
So 8.6 cm represents 8.6 × 15 km or 129 km.

# YEAR 9 NUMERACY MINI TEST ANSWERS

**3** Show 500 mL on each jug.

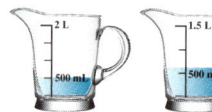

Only the last jug has more than 500 mL.
The jug that contains the most juice is D.

**4** From 2:38 pm until 3:00 pm is 22 minutes.
From 3:00 pm until 3:11 pm is 11 minutes.
Total time = (22 + 11) minutes
= 33 minutes

**5** Find the area of each rectangle.
A: Area = (19 × 8) m²
= 152 m²

B: Area = (16 × 9) m²
= 144 m²

C: Area = (13 × 13) m²
= 169 m²

D: Area = (35 × 4) m²
= 140 m²

The largest area is that of rectangle C.
[It is a square, but it is still a rectangle.]

**6** 1 km = 1000 m
1 km + 50 m = (1000 + 50) m
= 1050 m
= 1.05 km

**7** Remove 2 boxes and 1 drum from each side of the balance.
So 2 drums balance 1 box.
So 8 drums would balance 4 boxes.

**8** 60 litres is (60 ÷ 8) lots of 8 litres or 7.5 lots of 8 litres.
So the car will travel 7.5 lots of 100 km or 750 km.

**9** Distance to Sunshine = 453 km
Distance to Red Hill = (453 − 87) km
= 366 km
Distance from Acacia to Red Hill
= (366 − 187) km
= 179 km

**10** The base of the triangle is 28 units.
The height is 48 units.

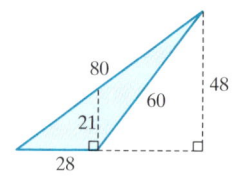

Area = $\frac{1}{2}$ × base × height
= $\frac{1}{2}$ × 28 × 48

**11** The total top side = 5 m + 7 m
= 12 m
So the bottom side will also be 12 metres.
The left side is 8 metres so the total right side will also be 8 metres.

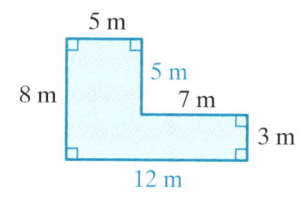

Perimeter = 2 × (12 m + 8 m)
= 2 × 20 m
= 40 m

**12** 1 cm = 10 mm
The nail extends from 10 mm until 46 mm.
Length = (46 − 10) mm
= 36 mm

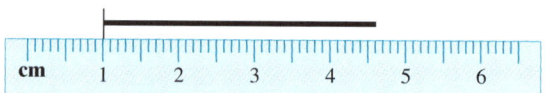

**13** A square has four equal sides.
Each side = (64 ÷ 4) m
= 16 m

**14** Speed = 5 km in 20 minutes
= 15 km in 60 minutes
= 15 km/h

**15** 3 hours after 10:20 am is 1:20 pm.
$\frac{3}{4}$ hour = 45 minutes
40 minutes after 1:20 pm is 2:00 pm.
Another 5 minutes after that is 2:05 pm.

**16** Perimeter = 26 m
Length + width = (26 ÷ 2) m
= 13 m
But the width is 5 m.
Length = (13 − 5) m
= 8 m

90

# YEAR 9 NUMERACY MINI TEST ANSWERS

### Basic level questions

**Mini Test 6:** Basic Chance and Data ............... Page 9

**1** D  **2** 40 min  **3** 17  **4** 37  **5** A  **6** 21  **7** C  **8** B
**9** B  **10** C  **11** 27  **12** A

**1** There are 6 possible results, (1, 2, 3, 4, 5 or 6).
There is just one possible result of 5.
Chance of 5 = $\frac{1}{6}$

**2** Total time
= (25 + 35 + 45 + 40 + 55) minutes
= 200 minutes
Average time = (200 ÷ 5) minutes
= 40 minutes

**3** Number in the club = 60
Number shown in table = 8 + 22 + 13
= 43
Number remaining = 60 − 43
= 17
So 17 seniors had unpaid fees.

**4** 
**Computers in houses**

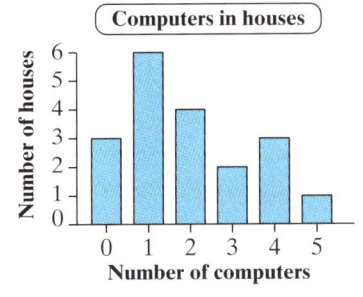

3 houses had no computers, 6 houses had 1 computer, 4 houses had 2 computers, 2 houses had 3 computers, 3 houses had 4 computers and 1 house had 5 computers.
Total computers = 3 × 0 + 6 × 1 + 4 × 2 + 2 × 3 + 3 × 4 + 1 × 5
= 0 + 6 + 8 + 6 + 12 + 5
= 37

**5** Total number of jelly beans
= 5 + 6 + 4 + 3
= 18
6 jelly beans are yellow.
Chance of yellow jelly bean = $\frac{6}{18}$
= $\frac{1}{3}$

**6** Total points = 6 × 3.5
= 21

**7** **Cars at Jim's Autos**

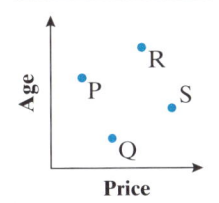

Consider each statement:
'Car Q is younger and cheaper than car P.'
This statement is not correct. Car Q is younger but is more expensive than car P.
'Car R is younger and cheaper than car S.'
This statement is not correct. Car R is cheaper but is older than car S.
'Car P is younger and cheaper than car R.'
This statement is correct.
'Car S is younger and cheaper than car Q.'
This statement is not correct. Car S is older and more expensive than car Q.
The correct statement is 'Car P is younger and cheaper than car R'.

**8** 0, 1, 2, 2, 4, 5, 7, 7, 7, 8, 8, 9
There are 12 scores.
The median is the average of the sixth and seventh scores.
Median = $\frac{5 + 7}{2}$
= 6

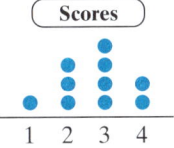

**9** **Scores**

[The mode is the score with the highest frequency. It is the score that occurs the most often.]
Mode = 3

**10** Bucket A has 5 balls, 1 being white.
The chance of choosing a white ball is $\frac{1}{5}$.
Bucket B has 6 balls, 1 being white.
The chance of choosing a white ball is $\frac{1}{6}$.
Bucket C has 8 balls, 2 being white.
The chance of choosing a white ball is $\frac{2}{8}$ or $\frac{1}{4}$.
Bucket D has 8 balls, 4 being white.
The chance of choosing a white ball is $\frac{4}{8}$ or $\frac{1}{2}$.

# YEAR 9 NUMERACY MINI TEST ANSWERS

The bucket where the chance of choosing a white ball is one in four is bucket C.

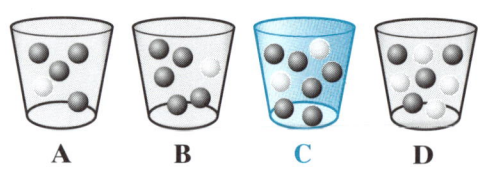

A   B   C   D

**11** 16, 17, 17, 19, 20, 23, 28, 31, 35, 41

**Ages of surf students**

| 1 | 6 7 7 9 |
|---|---|
| 2 | 0 3 7 8 |
| 3 | 1 5 |
| 4 | 1 |

**Key**
4 | 1 = Age of 41

The stem-and-leaf plot shows an age of 27. There is no 27 in the list of ages so 27 must be the age of the 11th person.

**12** 18 of the 30 apples are red.

Number of green apples = 30 − 18
= 12

Chance of choosing green apple = $\frac{12}{30}$
= $\frac{2}{5}$

## Basic level questions

**Mini Test 7:** Mixed Questions................... Page 10

**1** 999 **2** 16 **3** D **4** D **5** B **6** A **7** A **8** 375
**9** D **10** B **11** 33 **12** C **13** A **14** B **15** $325
**16** C

**1** 1007, 1005, 1003, 1001, …
The numbers are decreasing by 2 each time.
Next number = 1001 − 2
= 999

**2** 12 × 8 = 6 × ☐
12 × 8 = 96
So 6 × ☐ = 96
☐ = 96 ÷ 6
= 16

[The first number in the first product halved so the second number in the first product must be doubled.]

**3** 4 × 7 = 28
Now consider the options:
3 × 9 + 1 = 27 + 1
= 28

5 × 5 + 3 = 25 + 3
= 28
10 × 3 − 2 = 30 − 2
= 28
2 × 12 + 5 = 24 + 5
= 29

Of the options, 2 × 12 + 5 is not equal to 28.

**4** Objects south of the shed are the pond, the bridge and the statue. Items east of the statue are the gazebo and the pond. The item that is both south of the shed and east of the statue is the pond.

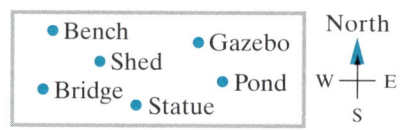

• Bench    • Gazebo
  • Shed
• Bridge      • Pond
     • Statue

N / W-E / S

**5** Average speed = (350 ÷ 5) km/h
= 70 km/h

**6** Angle A is reflex.

[B and C are obtuse. D is acute.]

**7** 15:30 is expressed in 24-hour time.
Now 15 − 12 = 3
So 15:30 is 3:30 pm.

**8** 25% is one-quarter.
Number not sold = 500 ÷ 4
= 125
Number sold = 500 − 125
= 375

**9** Find the area of each rectangle:
A: Area = 9 m × 4 m
= 36 m²

B: Area = 6 m × 6 m
= 36 m²

C: Area = 12 m × 3 m
= 36 m²

D: Area = 8 m × 5 m
= 40 m²

The area that is not the same as the others is the area of rectangle D.

**10** 87 × 42 = 3654
8.7 × 0.42 = 3.654
[There are 3 places (in total) after the decimal point in the question, so there must be 3 places after the decimal point in the answer.]

# YEAR 9 NUMERACY MINI TEST ANSWERS

**11** 

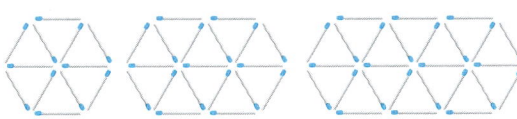

| Shape | 1 | 2 | 3 |
|---|---|---|---|
| Number of matches | 12 | 19 | 26 |

The number of matches is increasing by 7 each time.
Number of matches needed for fourth shape
= 26 + 7
= 33

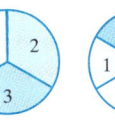

**12** Consider each option:
A has three sections, one of which shows 2.
The chance of 2 is 1 in 3.
B has six sections, one of which shows 2.
The chance of 2 is 1 in 6.
C has eight sections, two of which show 2.
The chance of 2 is 2 in 8 or 1 in 4.
This is the correct option.
D has 12 sections, four of which show 2.
The chance of 2 is 4 in 12 or 1 in 3.

**13** 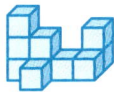 When viewed from the front, the rows of cubes are three deep. The front row has just one cube, the middle row has cubes three high and the back row has cubes two high.
The view from the right side is

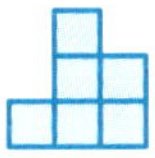

**14** $20^2 = 20 \times 20$
       $= 400$
So $\sqrt{400} = 20$
$30^2 = 30 \times 30$
       $= 900$
So $\sqrt{900} = 30$
Now 500 lies between 400 and 900 (and is closer to 400).
So $\sqrt{500}$ will lie between 20 and 30 (and will be closer to 20).
Of the options, the closest number to $\sqrt{500}$ must be 22.

**15**

| Name | Amount |
|---|---|
| Adam | $350 |
| Brian | $250 |
| Sarah | $400 |
| Louise | $300 |

Total amount raised
= $(350 + 250 + 400 + 300)
= $1300
Average amount = $1300 ÷ 4
              = $325

**16** 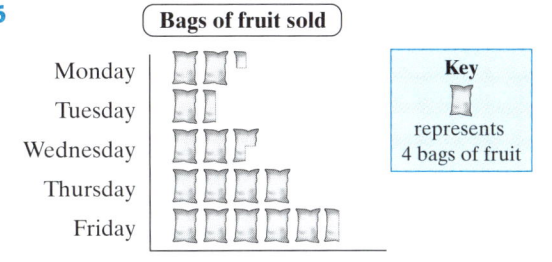 Each symbol represents 4 bags of fruit.
On Tuesday there are $1\frac{1}{2}$ symbols.
$\frac{1}{2}$ symbol represents 2 bags of fruit.
So, on Tuesday, 6 bags of fruit were sold.
If 10 more bags are sold another day, then 16 bags would be sold.
Now 16 = 4 × 4
So 16 bags will be represented by 4 symbols.
The day that has 4 symbols is Thursday so Thursday is the day on which 10 more bags of fruit were sold than on Tuesday.

### Basic level questions

**Mini Test 8:** Mixed Questions ............... Page 11

**1** A  **2** B  **3** $960  **4** B  **5** D  **6** B  **7** C  **8** A
**9** 32  **10** D  **11** C  **12** 740 000 km²  **13** 63
**14** 110 km/h  **15** C  **16** D

**1**  Saxon is north-east of Portland.

# YEAR 9 NUMERACY MINI TEST ANSWERS

**2** From 8:40 am until 1:40 pm is 5 hours.
From 1:40 pm until 2:15 pm is 35 minutes.
Total time = 5 h 35 min

**3** Savings = 20% of $1200
$= \frac{20}{100} \times \$1200$
= $240
Price paid = $1200 − $240
= $960

**4** [4t means 4 × t.]
When t = 3,
4t = 4 × 3
= 12

**5** Total number of buttons
= 9 + 5 + 7 + 19
= 40
Probability of blue = $\frac{5}{40}$
$= \frac{1}{8}$

**6** −1.4 is between −1 and −1.5.

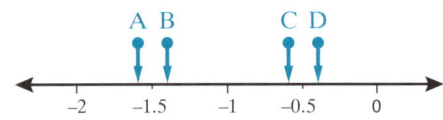

The correct arrow is B.

**7** 1 cm represents 20 km.
So 5.6 cm represents 5.6 × 20 km or 112 km.

**8** [Find the area of each rectangle.]
I: Area = (25 × 8) cm²
= 200 cm²
II: Area = (20 × 10) cm²
= 200 cm²
III: Area = (15 × 12) cm²
= 180 cm²
Only the areas of I and II are the same.

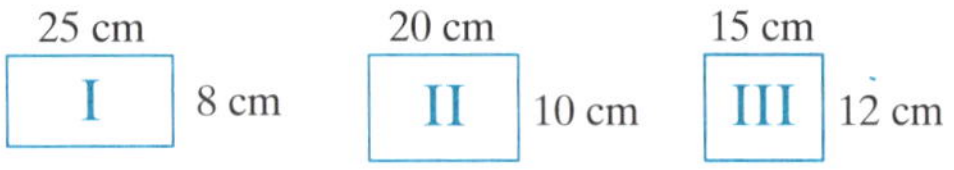

**9** Sum = 23 + 25 + 48
= 96
Average = 96 ÷ 3
= 32

**10** The prism is a triangular prism.
It has two triangular faces and three rectangular faces. 
So option A is not correct.
The triangular faces must be opposite each other.
So options B and C are not correct.
The correct option is option D.

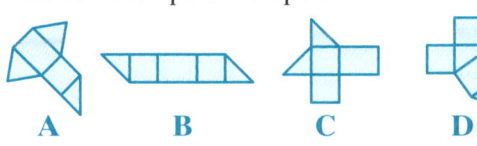

**11** For every 5 cows there are 2 horses.
Now 350 ÷ 5 = 70
So there are 70 lots of 5 cows on the property.
Now 70 × 2 = 140
So there are 140 horses.

**12** The area of Western Australia is 2 526 000 km².
Combined area of NSW and South Australia
= (802 000 + 984 000) km²
= 1 786 000 km²
Difference = (2 526 000 − 1 786 000) km²
= 740 000 km²

| State | Area (km²) |
|---|---|
| NSW | 802 000 |
| Vic | 228 000 |
| Qld | 1 727 000 |
| SA | 984 000 |
| WA | 2 526 000 |
| Tas | 68 000 |
| NT | 1 346 000 |
| ACT | 2000 |

**13** First number = 3
Second number = 2 × 3 + 1
= 6 + 1
= 7
Third number = 2 × 7 + 1
= 14 + 1
= 15
Fourth number = 2 × 15 + 1
= 30 + 1
= 31
Fifth number = 2 × 31 + 1
= 62 + 1
= 63

**14** Average speed = $(275 \div 2\frac{1}{2})$ km/h
= 110 km/h

# YEAR 9 NUMERACY MINI TEST ANSWERS

**15**

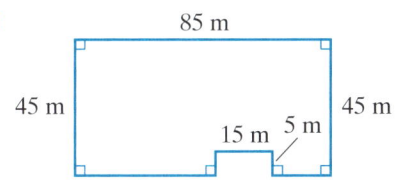

The top is 85 metres so the entire bottom adds to 85 metres.
Perimeter = 2 × (85 + 45 + 5) m
= 2 × 135 m
= 270 m

**16** A rotation of 90° is a quarter turn.
Anticlockwise is the opposite direction to that in which the hands of a clock turn.

The correct option is D.

## Intermediate level questions

**Mini Test 9:** Numbers .................................................. Page 12

> **1** D  **2** 32  **3** B  **4** D  **5** C  **6** A  **7** B  **8** C  **9** D
> **10** 35%  **11** C  **12** C  **13** A  **14** D  **15** 2.65
> **16** B  **17** A  **18** A  **19** 16%  **20** B

**1**  4.2 ÷ 0.2 = 42 ÷ 2
= 21

**2**  $\frac{3}{4}$ of a number is 36.

$\frac{1}{4}$ of the number = 36 ÷ 3
= 12

The number = 12 × 4
= 48

Now $\frac{1}{3}$ of 48 = 48 ÷ 3
= 16

So $\frac{2}{3}$ of 48 = 16 × 2
= 32

**3**  Increase = $100 − $80
= $20

Percentage increase = $\frac{\$20}{\$80} \times 100\%$
= $\frac{1}{4} \times 100\%$
= 25%

**4**  $12 \div \frac{1}{2}$ = 12 × 2
= 24

[If 12 was divided into halves how many would there be? There are two halves in every one, so there are 24 halves in 12.]

**5**  [Equivalent fractions are formed by multiplying both the numerator and denominator by the same number, or by dividing the numerator and denominator by the same number. Adding a number to both the numerator and denominator, subtracting a number from both the numerator and denominator or squaring both the numerator and denominator will not produce equivalent fractions.]

The fraction that is equivalent to $\frac{5}{8}$ is $\frac{5 \times 2}{8 \times 2}$

**6**  [Write each decimal with the same number of places after the decimal point.]
0.300
0.050
0.006
0.123
The largest number is 0.300 (or 0.3).

**7**  $4\frac{2}{5} = \frac{4 \times 5 + 2}{5}$
$= \frac{22}{5}$

**8**  Number of boys = 80 − 50
= 30
Ratio of girls to boys = 50 to 30
= 5 to 3

**9**  At midnight the temperature was 3° below zero. It was 5°C colder at 6 am. So it was a further 5° below zero.
So the temperature at 6 am was 8° below zero.
At 9 am it was 7°C warmer.
So the number of degrees below zero
= 8 − 7
= 1
The temperature at 9 am was −1°C.

**10**  Amount slashed on Tuesday = 30%
Amount remaining = (100 − 30)%
= 70%
The amount slashed on Wednesday was 50% (or half) of the amount remaining.
Half of 70% = 35%
The remaining half was slashed on Thursday.
So percentage slashed on Thursday = 35%.

# YEAR 9 NUMERACY MINI TEST ANSWERS

**11** $10^2 = 100$
and $20^2 = 20 \times 20$
$\phantom{and 20^2} = 400$
So $\sqrt{100} = 10$ and $\sqrt{400} = 20$
So $\sqrt{300}$ lies between 10 and 20.
$17^2 = 17 \times 17$
$\phantom{17^2} = 10 \times 17 + 7 \times 17$
$\phantom{17^2} = 170 + 119$
$\phantom{17^2} = 289$
So $\sqrt{300}$ lies between 17 and 20.

**12** 1 dozen scones require $\frac{3}{4}$ cup water.
The number of cups for 2 dozen scones
$= 2 \times \frac{3}{4}$ cups
$= \frac{6}{4}$ cups
$= 1\frac{1}{2}$ cups

**13** $\frac{4 + 12}{2 \times 4} = \frac{16}{8}$
$\phantom{\frac{4+12}{2 \times 4}} = 2$

**14** Cost of 2 loaves = $11.00 − $3.00
$\phantom{Cost of 2 loaves} = $8.00
Cost of 1 loaf = $8.00 ÷ 2
$\phantom{Cost of 1 loaf} = $4.00
Cost of 3 loaves = 3 × $4.00
$\phantom{Cost of 3 loaves} = $12.00
Cost of 2 juices = 2 × $3.00
$\phantom{Cost of 2 juices} = $6.00
Total cost = $12.00 + $6.00
$\phantom{Total cost} = $18.00

**15** [The number halfway between two others is the average.]
1.84 + 3.46 = 5.30
5.30 ÷ 2 = 2.65
So the number halfway between 1.84 and 3.46 is 2.65.

**16** $3 - 1\frac{1}{5} = 2 - \frac{1}{5}$
$\phantom{3 - 1\frac{1}{5}} = 1\frac{4}{5}$

[Or $3 - 1\frac{1}{5} = \frac{3}{1} - 1\frac{1}{5}$
$\phantom{Or 3 - 1\frac{1}{5}} = \frac{15}{5} - \frac{6}{5}$
$\phantom{Or 3 - 1\frac{1}{5}} = \frac{9}{5}$
$\phantom{Or 3 - 1\frac{1}{5}} = 1\frac{4}{5}$]

**17** $20 \times \square = 12$
$\square = 12 \div 20$
$\phantom{\square} = \frac{12}{20}$
$\phantom{\square} = \frac{3}{5}$
[Or simply multiply each of the options by 20 to see which gives an answer of 12.]

**18** Fraction of red and black $= \frac{3}{5} + \frac{1}{4}$
$\phantom{Fraction of red and black} = \frac{12 + 5}{20}$
$\phantom{Fraction of red and black} = \frac{17}{20}$

Fraction of yellow $= 1 - \frac{17}{20}$
$\phantom{Fraction of yellow} = \frac{3}{20}$

**19** There are 50 animals altogether.

| Animal | Cow | Horse | Pig | Goat | Sheep |
|---|---|---|---|---|---|
| Number | 16 | 13 | | 7 | 6 |

Total in table = 16 + 13 + 7 + 6
$\phantom{Total in table} = 42$
Number of pigs = 50 − 42
$\phantom{Number of pigs} = 8$
Fraction that are pigs $= \frac{8}{50}$
$\phantom{Fraction that are pigs} = \frac{16}{100}$
So 16% were pigs.

**20** The competitors are made up of 5 parts men, 3 parts women and 4 parts children.
Total parts = 5 + 3 + 4
$\phantom{Total parts} = 12$
Each part = 120 ÷ 12
$\phantom{Each part} = 10$
Number of men = 5 × 10
$\phantom{Number of men} = 50$
Number of women = 3 × 10
$\phantom{Number of women} = 30$
Difference = 50 − 30
$\phantom{Difference} = 20$

# YEAR 9 NUMERACY MINI TEST ANSWERS

**Intermediate level questions**

Mini Test 10: Algebra .................................... Page 13

**1** C **2** A **3** C **4** C **5** 60 **6** D **7** A **8** D **9** C
**10** 100 **11** B **12** B **13** B **14** D **15** D **16** A

**1** When $k = -5$,
$4k = 4 \times -5$
$\phantom{4k} = -20$

**2** $3x + 5 + 2x = (3x + 2x) + 5$
$\phantom{3x + 5 + 2x} = 5x + 5$

**3**

| Triangles | 1 | 2 | 3 | 4 | 5 | 6 | 7 |
|---|---|---|---|---|---|---|---|
| Matches | 3 | 5 | 7 | 9 | 11 | 13 | 15 |

The number of matches is one more than double the number of triangles.
The rule is '2 × number of triangles + 1'.

**4** The number 2 less than $x$ is $x - 2$.
[If unsure, use numbers to see what happens. The number 2 less than 6, for example, is 4 (6 − 2). The number 2 less than 9 is 7 (9 − 2).]

**5**

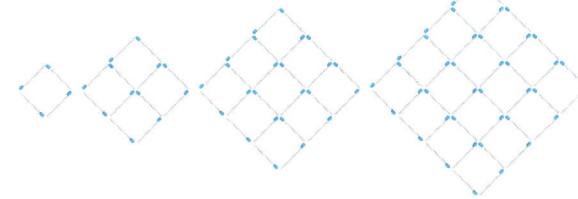

| | First | Second | Third | Fourth |
|---|---|---|---|---|
| Shape | 1 | 2 | 3 | 4 |
| Number of matches | 4 | 12 | 24 | 40 |

The number of extra matches needed for each shape is 8, then 12, then 16.
So the number of extra matches increases by 4 each time.
The next number of extra matches will be 20.
Number of matches for the fifth shape
$= 40 + 20$
$= 60$

**6** $y = 2x - 3$
$y = x + 5$
[If a value of $x$ satisfies both equations it will also satisfy the equation $2x - 3 = x + 5$.]
$2x - 3 = x + 5$
[Subtract $x$ from both sides.]
$x - 3 = 5$
[Add 3 to both sides.]
$x = 5 + 3$
$x = 8$
[Or substitute each value of $x$ to see which gives the same value of $y$ for both equations.]

**7** [Divide the shape into two rectangles.]

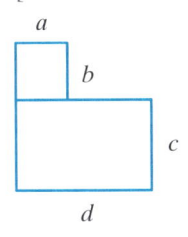

Area $= (a \times b) + (c \times d)$

**8** $2x - 3 \leq 8$
Try each option:
If $x = -4$,
$2x - 3 = 2 \times -4 - 3$
$\phantom{2x - 3} = -8 - 3$
$\phantom{2x - 3} = -11$
Now $-11 < 8$, so $x = -4$ satisfies the inequality.
If $x = 0$,
$2x - 3 = 2 \times 0 - 3$
$\phantom{2x - 3} = 0 - 3$
$\phantom{2x - 3} = -3$
Now $-3 < 8$, so $x = 0$ satisfies the inequality.
If $x = 5\frac{1}{2}$,
$2x - 3 = 2 \times 5\frac{1}{2} - 3$
$\phantom{2x - 3} = 11 - 3$
$\phantom{2x - 3} = 8$
Now $8 = 8$, so $x = 5\frac{1}{2}$ satisfies the inequality.
If $x = 7$,
$2x - 3 = 2 \times 7 - 3$
$\phantom{2x - 3} = 14 - 3$
$\phantom{2x - 3} = 11$
Now $11 > 8$, so $x = 7$ does not satisfy the inequality.

**9**

| $x$ | 1 | 2 | 3 | 4 | 5 |
|---|---|---|---|---|---|
| $y$ | 1 | 4 | 7 | 10 | 13 |

[The $x$-values increase by 1.
The $y$-values increase by 3.
So try the rule that involves multiplying by 3.]

97

# YEAR 9 NUMERACY MINI TEST ANSWERS

Try $y = 3x - 2$

When $x = 1$,
$y = 3 \times 1 - 2$
$= 3 - 2$
$= 1$ ✓

When $x = 2$,
$y = 3 \times 2 - 2$
$= 6 - 2$
$= 4$ ✓

When $x = 3$,
$y = 3 \times 3 - 2$
$= 9 - 2$
$= 7$ ✓

When $x = 4$,
$y = 3 \times 4 - 2$
$= 12 - 2$
$= 10$ ✓

When $x = 5$,
$y = 3 \times 5 - 2$
$= 15 - 2$
$= 13$ ✓

The rule is $y = 3x - 2$.

**10** 1, 4, 9, 16, 25

The numbers in the pattern are perfect squares.

[The first number = $1 \times 1$
$= 1$
The second number = $2 \times 2$
$= 4$
The third number = $3 \times 3$
$= 9$
and so on.]

The tenth number = $10 \times 10$
$= 100$

**11** $y = 4x - 7$

When $x = 2\frac{1}{2}$,
$y = 4 \times 2\frac{1}{2} - 7$
$= 10 - 7$
$= 3$

**12** $3(p + 5) = 3 \times p + 3 \times 5$
$= 3p + 15$

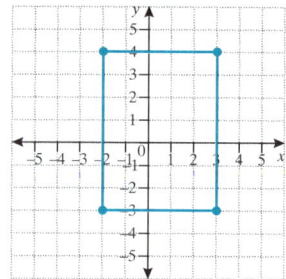

**13**

The fourth point lies at $(-2, 4)$.

**14** $3x - 7 = x + 3$
[Subtract $x$ from both sides.]
$2x - 7 = 3$
[Add 7 to both sides.]
$2x = 10$
[Divide both sides by 2.]
$x = 5$
[Or substitute each value of $x$ to see which satisfies the equation.]

**15** $m^2 = m \times m$
[The index, 2, tells us how many factors of $m$ are multiplied together.]

**16**

| Number of octagons | 1 | 2 | 3 | 4 |
| Number of matches | 8 | 15 | 22 | 29 |

[The number of octagons increases by 1 each time while the number of matches increases by 7.]

The rule involves multiplying by 7.

When there is 1 octagon, the number of matches = $7 \times 1 + 1$.

When there are 2 octagons, the number of matches = $7 \times 2 + 1$.

So, when there are $n$ octagons, the number of matches = $7 \times n + 1$.

### Intermediate level questions

**Mini Test 11:** Plane Figures and Solids .......... Page 14

**1** B **2** D **3** B **4** B **5** A **6** C **7** D **8** B **9** D **10** C
**11** 64 **12** A

**1** The cut is made parallel to the base. The cross-section is a circle.

# YEAR 9 NUMERACY MINI TEST ANSWERS

**2** A rectangle, a rhombus and a square are all parallelograms. The opposite sides of a parallelogram are always equal.

A trapezium might not have opposite sides that are equal. For example, PQRS is a trapezium but PQ does not equal SR and PS does not equal QR.

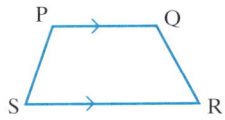

[If a trapezium has opposite sides that are equal, it must be a parallelogram.]

**3** The net in B is not the net of a standard die.

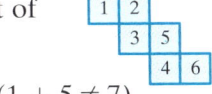

This net has 1 opposite 5 ($1 + 5 \neq 7$), 2 opposite 4 ($2 + 4 \neq 7$) and 3 opposite 6 ($3 + 6 \neq 7$).

**4** [By drawing the axes of symmetry, the rectangle is divided into four smaller rectangles. The diagonals of the original rectangle divide each of these new rectangles in half. So the rectangle has been divided into eight equal pieces. Two of these have been shaded.]

Fraction shaded = $\dfrac{2}{8}$
= $\dfrac{1}{4}$

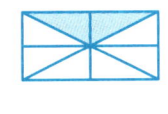

**5** [Find the number of faces, edges and vertices for each solid.]

A triangular prism has 5 faces, 9 edges and 6 vertices.

The number of edges plus the number of vertices = 9 + 6
= 15

Now $15 = 3 \times 5$

So the answer is a triangular prism.

[A triangular pyramid has 4 faces, 6 edges and 4 vertices.

Now $6 + 4 \neq 3 \times 4$

So the solid is not a triangular pyramid.

A rectangular prism has 6 faces, 12 edges and 8 vertices.

Now $12 + 8 \neq 3 \times 6$

So the solid is not a rectangular prism.

A rectangular pyramid has 5 faces, 8 edges and 5 vertices.

Now $8 + 5 \neq 3 \times 5$

So the solid is not a rectangular pyramid.]

**6** Consider each statement:

'The adjacent sides of a rhombus are always equal.' This statement is correct.

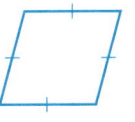

'The opposite sides of a parallelogram are always equal.' This statement is correct.

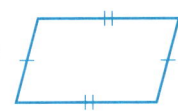

'The diagonals of a parallelogram are always equal.' This statement is not correct.

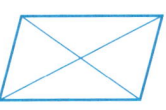

'The diagonals of a square always meet at right angles.' This statement is correct.

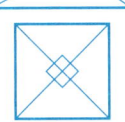

The incorrect statement is 'The diagonals of a parallelogram are always equal.'

**7** [Perpendicular means at right angles.]

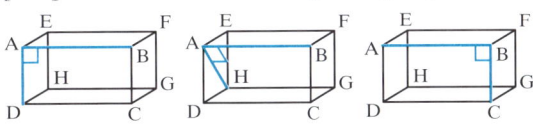

AD, AH and BC are all at right angles to AB.

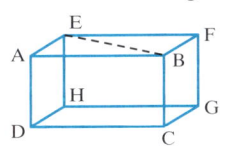

∠ABE is not a right angle so BE is not perpendicular to AB.

**8** There are two cubes from the front face that have just one face painted. There will also be two from the back face.

There are two from the right side face so there will also be two from the left side.

There are four from the top face so there will be four from the bottom face.

Total cubes with one face painted
= $2 \times (2 + 2 + 4)$
= $2 \times 8$
= 16

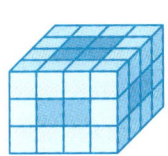

**9** If an equilateral triangle is cut along an axis of symmetry it divides the original triangle into two new ones. Each of these triangles will be right-angled. The three sides of each triangle will be different lengths so each triangle will be right-angled and scalene.

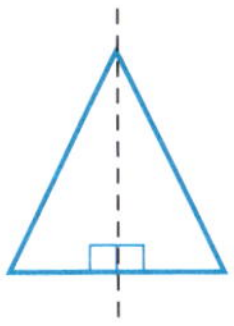

**10** From the front view you can see that the object is four cubes wide. So the view from

# YEAR 9 NUMERACY MINI TEST ANSWERS

the top must show four cubes in one direction.
The view from the top cannot be C.
[The other views could be:

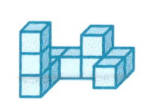

View B is shown from the back.]

**11** There are four tiles shown in a larger pattern. 16 of these larger patterns will fit onto the square.

Total tiles = 4 × 16
= 64

**12**

The face with the small dot appears in both views. The symbol not shown in either view (the triangle) must be on the face opposite the small dot.

So the cross and the large dot must be opposite (in some order) the circle and square.

In the first view of the cube, the large dot must be on the bottom and the cross on the left side.

The symbol that is opposite the large dot is the circle.

## Intermediate level questions

**Mini Test 12:** Measurement and Data ............ Page 15

**1** 17 cm **2** D **3** 24 **4** D **5** B **6** 100 km **7** A
**8** D **9** 7 m **10** B **11** C **12** C **13** A **14** 50 L
**15** A

**1**   85 cm²   5 cm

Area = length × width
85 cm² = length × 5 cm
length = (85 ÷ 5) cm
= 17 cm

**2** Total marbles = 12 + 15 + 9 + 6
= 42
Number of green marbles = 6

Chance of green marble = $\frac{6}{42}$
= $\frac{1}{7}$

**3** **Vehicles passing Glenda's house**

| Motorbikes | Cycles | Trucks | Cars |

3 divisions represent motorbikes.
There were 18 motorbikes.
So 3 divisions represent 18 vehicles.
This means 1 division represents 6 vehicles.
There are 4 divisions for trucks.
Number of trucks = 4 × 6
= 24

**4** 1 kg = 1000 g
So 1500 g = 1.5 kg
1.2 kg + 1500 g = 1.2 kg + 1.5 kg
= 2.7 kg

**5** Mean after 7 tests is 8.
Total marks from 7 tests = 7 × 8
= 56
Total marks from 8 tests = 56 + 10
= 66
Mean after 8 tests = 66 ÷ 8
= 8.25
Of the options, the closest to the mean is 8.3.

**6** Distance travelled in first 2 hours
= 2 × 70 km
= 140 km

Distance travelled in last $1\frac{1}{2}$ hours
= (240 − 140) km
= 100 km

**7**      •  •  •      100 m          •   (not to scale)
         ├─┤
         5 m

Number of gaps between posts
= 100 ÷ 5
= 20
But there will be one more gap than posts needed.
[The first post is at the end of the first gap, but the last post is at the beginning of the last gap.]
Number of posts = 19

**8** 4, 2, 6, 4, 4
In order the scores are 2, 4, 4, 4, 6.
Mode = 4

100

# YEAR 9 NUMERACY MINI TEST ANSWERS

Range = 6 − 2
    = 4
Sum of the scores = 2 + 3 × 4 + 6
    = 20
Mean = 20 ÷ 5
    = 4
Median = 4
The mean, mode, median and range are all 4.

**9** Perimeter = 24 m
2 × (length + width) = 24 m
length + width = 12 m
The width is 5 metres.
The length = (12 − 5) m
    = 7 m

**10**

←———— 60 km ————→   (not to scale)
● X   ● Y              ● Z

Distance from X to Z = 60 km
Distance from Y to Z is three times the distance from X to Y.
So the distance from X to Y is one-quarter of the distance from X to Z.
Distance from X to Y = 60 km ÷ 4
    = 15 km

**11** Amount shown on the scales is about 900 g.
Required amount = 1.5 kg
    = 1500 g
Extra needed = (1500 − 900) g
    = 600 g

**12** Number of green pegs = 40 − 15
    = 25
Probability of green = $\frac{25}{40}$
    = $\frac{5}{8}$

**13** 3, 5, 5, 8, 12
Mode = 5
Median = 5
Range = 12 − 3
    = 9
Sum of scores = 3 + 5 + 5 + 8 + 12
    = 33
Mean = 33 ÷ 5
    = 6.6
If 8 is removed: 3, 5, 5, 12
Mode = 5

Median = $\frac{5 + 5}{2}$
    = 5
Range = 12 − 3
    = 9
Sum of scores = 3 + 5 + 5 + 12
    = 25
Mean = 25 ÷ 4
    = 6.25
Only the mean will change.
[Because the number being removed was different to the mean, the mean must have changed. It was not necessary to find the new mean.]

**14** The car uses 8 litres for 100 km.
So it will use 6 × 8 litres for 600 km.
It will use 48 litres to travel 600 km.
25 km is one-quarter of 100 km.
So the car will use one-quarter of 8 litres or 2 litres to travel 25 km.
Total litres = 48 + 2
    = 50

**15** The plane left Brisbane $3\frac{3}{4}$ hours before 1:20 pm.
3 hours before 1:20 pm is 10:20 am.
45 minutes before this is 25 minutes before 10 am or 9:35 am.

### Intermediate level questions

**Mini Test 13:** Number Operations and Ratios ................................. Page 16

**1** 93  **2** 672  **3** C  **4** 1 and 12  **5** A  **6** D  **7** A
**8** $66.90  **9** D  **10** C  **11** $0.48  **12** B  **13** D
**14** $3.00  **15** C  **16** 16  **17** B  **18** A  **19** A
**20** $2640

**1** [The number was squared, so to find the number you need to take the square root.]
Number = $\sqrt{8649}$
    = 93

**2** After subtracting 17 Isabel's answer was 1008.
Before subtracting 17 it must have been 1008 + 17 = 1025.
So, after multiplying by 25 Isabel's answer was 1025. Before multiplying by 25 the number must have been 1025 ÷ 25 = 41.

# YEAR 9 NUMERACY MINI TEST ANSWERS

Now 41 should have been multiplied by 17.
$41 \times 17 = 697$
Then 25 should have been subtracted.
$697 - 25 = 672$
The answer should have been 672.

**3** The traffic was made up of 7 parts cars and 2 parts trucks.
For every 7 cars there were 2 trucks.
Number of cars = 126
Now $126 \div 7 = 18$
So there were 18 lots of 7 cars.
Number of trucks = $18 \times 2$
$= 36$
Total cars and trucks = $126 + 36$
$= 162$

**4** $1 \times 12 = 12$
$1 + 12 = 13$
The numbers are 1 and 12 [or 12 and 1].

**5** $12^2 + 16^2 = 144 + 256$
$= 400$
Now $20^2 = 400$
So $12^2 + 16^2 = 20^2$

**6** There were 30 medals altogether.
Number of gold and silver = $9 + 6$
$= 15$
Number of bronze = $30 - 15$
$= 15$
Ratio of gold to silver to bronze = 9:6:15
$= 3:2:5$

**7** $87 \div 3 = 29$
$111 \div 3 = 37$
So 87 and 111 are both divisible by 3.
3 is a factor of both 87 and 111.

**8** Pia could buy six packets of two hinges.
Cost = $6 \times \$11.90$
$= \$71.40$
Or Pia could buy two packets of five hinges and one packet of two hinges.
Cost = $2 \times \$27.50 + \$11.90$
$= \$55.00 + \$11.90$
$= \$66.90$
The least amount that Pia could pay is $66.90.

**9** $4^3 = 4 \times 4 \times 4$
But $4 = 2 \times 2$
So $4^3 = 2 \times 2 \times 2 \times 2 \times 2 \times 2$

**10** Consider each option:
$40 \div 8 \times 4 = 5 \times 4$
$= 20$
$3 \times 8 - 2 \times 2 = 24 - 4$
$= 20$
$3 + 7 \times 2 = 3 + 14$
$= 17$
$32 - 3 \times 4 = 32 - 12$
$= 20$
So $3 + 7 \times 2$ is the only expression not equal to 20.

**11** Cost of ten daily tickets = $10 \times \$2.60$
$= \$26.00$
Total saving = $\$26.00 - \$21.20$
$= \$4.80$
Daily saving = $\$4.80 \div 10$
$= \$0.48$

**12**

| Town | Maximum (°C) | Minimum (°C) |
|---|---|---|
| Sullivan | 15 | −1 |
| Lotus | 12 | −5 |
| Paxton | 7 | −8 |
| Kenton | −1 | −12 |

Sullivan: Difference = $15 - (-1)$
$= 15 + 1$
$= 16$
Lotus: Difference = $12 - (-5)$
$= 12 + 5$
$= 17$
Paxton: Difference = $7 - (-8)$
$= 7 + 8$
$= 15$
Kenton: Difference = $-1 - (-12)$
$= -1 + 12$
$= 11$
Lotus had the biggest difference between its minimum and maximum temperatures.

**13** For every 7 men there were 5 women present at the meeting.
So 7 out of 12 people present were men.
Number of men = $\frac{7}{12}$ of 120
$= 70$
Number of women = $120 - 70$
$= 50$
Difference = $70 - 50$
$= 20$

# YEAR 9 NUMERACY MINI TEST ANSWERS

**14** The bread cost $0.50 more than the biscuits. So subtracting $0.50 from the total cost will give the price of two packets of biscuits.
Now $5.50 − $0.50 = $5.00
$5.00 ÷ 2 = $2.50
So the biscuits cost $2.50 and the bread $3.00.

**15** To find the cost per kilogram, Neil needs to divide $8.60 by 2.5.
Then to find the cost of 7 kg he needs to multiply the answer by 7.
The correct calculation is $8.60 ÷ 2.5 × 7.

**16** Number of sweets = 3 × 9 + 5
= 27 + 5
= 32
Total number needed = 4 × 12
= 48
Extra sweets needed = 48 − 32
= 16

**17** [Mark the position of all the numbers on a number line.]

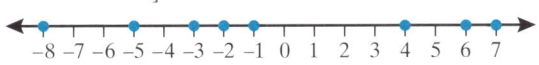

So consider the options:
4 ≤ 7 This is correct.
−5 < −8 This is not correct. −5 > −8
−2 > −3 This is correct.
6 ≥ −1 This is correct.
The incorrect statement is −5 < −8.

**18** Jess gets 5 parts and Jo gets 4 parts of $3600.
Total parts = 5 + 4
= 9
Each part = $3600 ÷ 9
= $400
Jo's share = 4 × $400
= $1600

**19** $\sqrt{1600 + 81} = \sqrt{1681}$
= 41

**20** 2 years = 2 × 12 months
= 24 months
Total monthly payments = 24 × $360
= $8640
Total amount paid = $2000 + $8640
= $10 640
Cash price = $8000
Difference = $10 640 − $8000
= $2640

## Intermediate level questions

**Mini Test 14:** Fractions, Decimals and Percentages ........... Page 17

**1** C **2** C **3** A **4** B **5** $360 **6** B **7** A **8** D
**9** $3750 **10** B **11** C **12** D **13** 0.49 **14** B
**15** A **16** D

**1** The number halfway between $2\frac{3}{4}$ and $4\frac{1}{4}$ is the number halfway between 3 and 4 (after adding $\frac{1}{4}$ to $2\frac{3}{4}$ and subtracting $\frac{1}{4}$ from $4\frac{1}{4}$).
It is $3\frac{1}{2}$.
[Or find the average.]

**2** Saving = 40% of $120
$= \frac{40}{100} \times \$120$
= $48
Price paid = $120 − $48
= $72

**3** $\frac{18.4 - 6.8}{4 \div 0.2} = \frac{11.6}{20}$
= 0.58

**4** Percentage eaten on Saturday = 40%
Remaining percentage = (100 − 40)%
= 60%
Percentage of whole pie eaten on Sunday
= 40% of 60%
= 24%
Percentage eaten on Saturday and Sunday
= 40% + 24%
= 64%
Percentage remaining = (100 − 64)%
= 36%

**5** $225 is $\frac{1}{4}$ of Liam's income.
Total income = $225 × 4
= $900
Rent = $\frac{2}{5}$ of $900
= $360

**6** English mark = $\frac{37}{50} \times 100\%$
= 74%
Maths mark = $\frac{51}{60} \times 100\%$
= 85%

# YEAR 9 NUMERACY MINI TEST ANSWERS

Science mark $= \dfrac{56}{70} \times 100\%$
$= 80\%$

History mark $= \dfrac{19}{25} \times 100\%$
$= 76\%$

The Maths result was the best.

**7** Increase $= 30 - 25$
$= 5$

Percentage increase $= \dfrac{5}{25} \times 100\%$
$= 20\%$

**8** [Write each decimal with the same number of places after the decimal point.]
0.300
0.050
0.048
0.107

In order the numbers are 0.048, 0.050, 0.107, 0.300.

So the order is 0.048, 0.05, 0.107, 0.3.

**9** 12% = $3000
1% = $3000 ÷ 12
$= \$250$
15% = 15 × $250
$= \$3750$

**10** [Write each number as a decimal.]
0.56
$\dfrac{5}{6} = 0.8333\ldots$
65% = 0.65
$\dfrac{4}{5} = 0.8$

The largest decimal is 0.8333…
The largest number is $\dfrac{5}{6}$.

**11** 3.2185 is closer to 3.2 than 3.3.
7.462 is closer to 7.5 than 7.4.

When rounded off to one decimal place 3.2185 and 7.462 become 3.2 and 7.5.

**12** Number of sheep = 200 ÷ 5
$= 40$
Number of cattle = 200 − 40
$= 160$

Number of calves = 40% of 160
$= \dfrac{40}{100} \times 160$
$= 64$

**13** 0.35 + 0.63 = 0.98
Now 0.98 ÷ 2 = 0.49
So the number halfway between 0.35 and 0.63 is 0.49.

**14** 4 dozen = 4 × 12
$= 48$
Now 48 ÷ 16 = 3
So Jamie wants to make 3 times the quantity of biscuits in the recipe.

Amount of honey $= 3 \times \dfrac{3}{4}$ cups
$= 2\dfrac{1}{4}$ cups

**15**

| Event | Number |
|---|---|
| Discus | 37 |
| Javelin | 29 |
| Shot-put | 36 |
| High jump | |
| Long jump | 48 |

Total in table = 37 + 29 + 36 + 48
$= 150$

Number who preferred high jump
= 200 − 150
= 50

Percentage who preferred high jump
$= \dfrac{50}{200} \times 100\%$
$= 25\%$

**16** $\dfrac{\frac{3}{4} - \frac{1}{2}}{8} = \dfrac{\frac{1}{4}}{8}$
$= \dfrac{1}{32}$

### Intermediate level questions

**Mini Test 15:** Angles .................................................... Page 18

**1** 73° **2** 130 **3** C **4** B **5** 60 **6** 50 **7** 25 **8** 135
**9** 100 **10** 150 **11** 70° **12** A **13** D **14** 170
**15** C **16** 60

# YEAR 9 NUMERACY MINI TEST ANSWERS

**1** ∠PQR = 73°

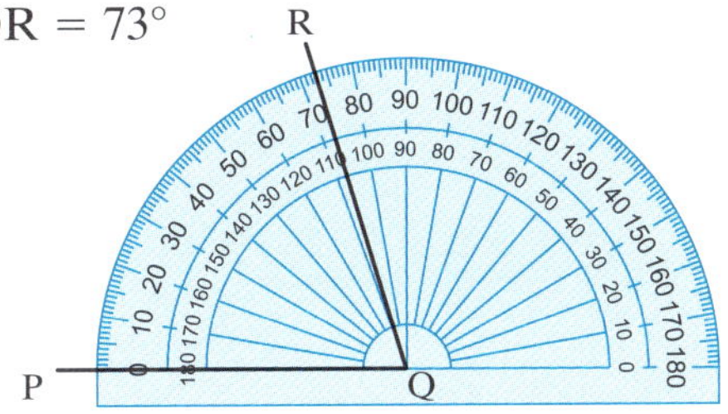

[The angle 'begins' at P so the scale used on the protractor must be the one where 0 is on the left side.]

**2** [The exterior angle of a triangle is equal to the sum of the interior opposite angles.]

$y = 60 + 70$
$\phantom{y} = 130$

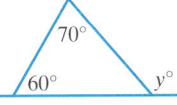

**3** The best estimate for the size of the angle is 140°.

[The angle is larger than a right angle so is bigger than 90°. Of the options, 110° is a little bigger than a right angle and 170° is a little smaller than a straight angle. 140° is about halfway between a right angle and a straight angle.]

**4** The angle sum of a triangle is 180°.
[Find the size of the remaining angle in each triangle.]

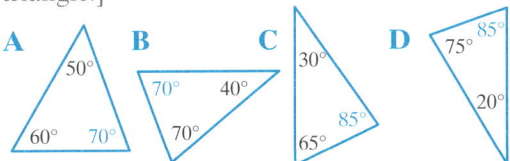

Triangle B has two equal angles.
So triangle B is isosceles.

**5** Angle sum of a hexagon = $(6 - 2) \times 180°$
$\phantom{Angle sum of a hexagon } = 4 \times 180°$
$\phantom{Angle sum of a hexagon } = 720°$

Each angle of a regular hexagon
$= 720° \div 6$
$= 120°$

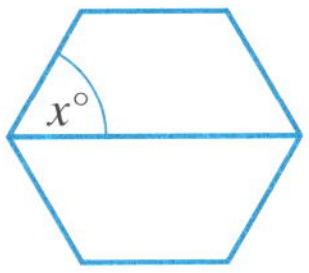

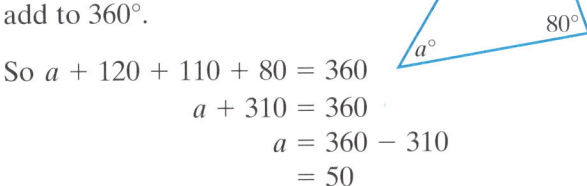

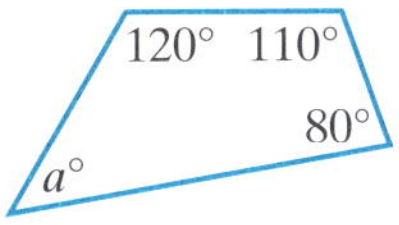

Now $x = 120 \div 2$
$\phantom{Now x } = 60$

[The hexagon was divided into two equal trapeziums, so the angle was divided in two.]

**6** The angles of a quadrilateral add to 360°.

So $a + 120 + 110 + 80 = 360$
$a + 310 = 360$
$a = 360 - 310$
$\phantom{a} = 50$

**7** The triangle is isosceles so two angles are equal.

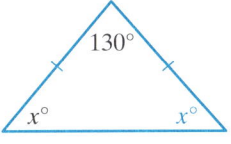

The angles of a triangle add to 180°.

So $2x + 130 = 180$
$2x = 50$
$x = 25$

**8** Angle sum of a pentagon
$= (5 - 2) \times 180°$
$= 3 \times 180°$
$= 540°$

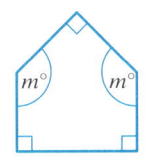

Three angles of the pentagon are right angles.
So $2m + 3 \times 90 = 540$
$2m + 270 = 540$
$2m = 540 - 270$
$2m = 270$
$m = 270 \div 2$
$\phantom{m} = 135$

**9** Angles in a straight line add to 180°.

So the angle adjacent to the angle of 120° must be 60°.

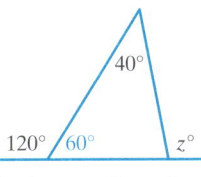

The exterior angle of a triangle is equal to the sum of the interior opposite angles.

So $z = 60 + 40$
$z = 100$

**10** Each angle of a rectangle is 90°.
Each angle of an equilateral triangle is 60°.

So $x = 90 + 60$
$\phantom{x} = 150$

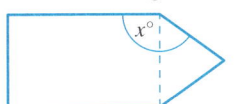

**11** A trapezium is a quadrilateral.
The angle sum of a quadrilateral is 360°.
Now two angles are 110°.
So they total 220°.
Total of remaining angles $= 360° - 220°$
$= 140°$

A trapezium has four angles so two remain.
Each remaining angle $= 140° \div 2$
$= 70°$

**12** Angles in a straight line add to 180°.

So the angle adjacent to the angle of 130° is 50° and the angle adjacent to the angle of 100° is 80°.

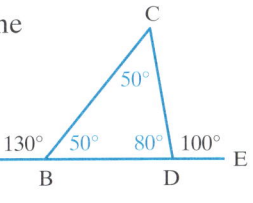

105

# YEAR 9 NUMERACY MINI TEST ANSWERS

Now the angle sum of a triangle is 180°.
So the remaining angle is 50°.
All of the angles of the triangle are less than 90°, so it is an acute-angled triangle.
Two of the angles are equal, so the triangle is isosceles.
The triangle is acute-angled and isosceles.

13  The angle sum of a triangle is 180°.
[Find the remaining angle for each triangle.]

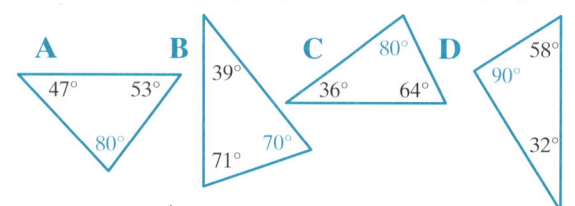

A  47°, 53°, 80°
B  39°, 71°, 70°
C  80°, 36°, 64°
D  58°, 90°, 32°

The only triangle with an angle of 90° is triangle D.

14  The angle sum of a quadrilateral is 360°.
Sum of the given angles = 100° + 30° + 40°
 = 170°
Remaining angle = 360° − 170°
 = 190°
Angles at a point add to 360°.
So $a$ = 360 − 190
 = 170

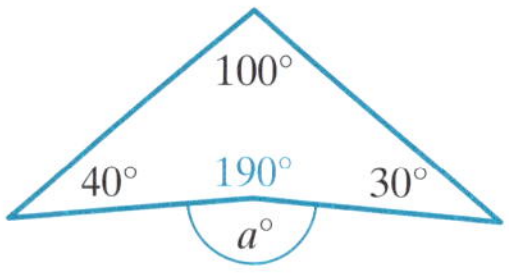

15  Angles in a straight line add to 180°.
So ∠AGB + ∠BGC + ∠CGE = 180°
70° + ∠BGC + 30° = 180°
∠BGC + 100° = 180°
∠BGC = 180° − 100°
 = 80°

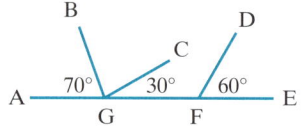

16  Angles at a point add to 360°.
$x$ = 360 ÷ 6
 = 60

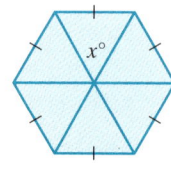

[Because the hexagon is regular, all the triangles are equilateral.]

### Intermediate level questions

**Mini Test 16:** Rates and Measurements ......... Page 19

1 B  2 1.6 km  3 B  4 D  5 B  6 A  7 D  8 D  9 C
10 1450 mL  11 B  12 C  13 A  14 30
15 8 L/100 km  16 C

1  1 kL = 1000 L
So 9.75 kL = 9750 litres

2  Total distance = 21 km
Total distances shown in diagram
 = (5.9 + 4.3 + 7.6) km
 = 17.8 km
Remaining distance = (21 − 17.8) km
 = 3.2 km
This is twice the distance from the start to A.
Distance from the start to A = 3.2 km ÷ 2
 = 1.6 km

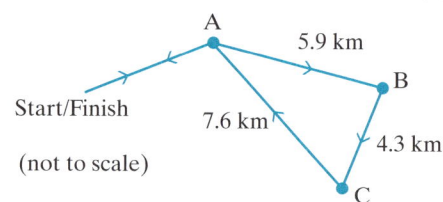

3  Time = (21 ÷ 9) h
 = $2\frac{1}{3}$ h
 = 2 h 20 min

4  1 kg = 1000 g
1 kg + 75 g = (1000 + 75) g
 = 1075 g
 = 1.075 kg

5  For each 100 km the car uses 7.5 litres of petrol.
Now 750 km = 7.5 lots of 100 km
Petrol used = 7.5 × 7.5 L
 = 56.25 L
 = 60 L to the nearest 10 L

6  Flow rate = 7.2 L in 1 hour
 = 7200 mL in 60 minutes
 = 120 mL in 1 minute
 = 120 mL in 60 seconds
 = 2 mL in 1 second
 = 2 mL/s

# YEAR 9 NUMERACY MINI TEST ANSWERS

**7** When it is 7:30 am in London, it is 3:30 pm in Perth.
So Perth is 8 hours ahead of London time.
London is 8 hours behind Perth time.
When it is 7:30 am Monday in Perth, in London it will be 11:30 pm Sunday.

**8** 3 hours and 15 minutes = (3 × 60 + 15) min
        = 195 min
[So options A and B are not correct.]
15 minutes is a quarter of an hour.
3 hours and 15 minutes = $3\frac{1}{4}$ h
        = 3.25 h

**9** 5.6 m (not to scale)
5.6 m = 5600 mm
Each 20-cent piece is 28 mm across.
Number of 20-cent pieces = 5600 ÷ 28
        = 200
Value = 200 × 20 cents
     = 4000 cents
     = $40.00

**10** Amount of juice in bottle = 2.2 L
        = 2200 mL
Amount taken out = 3 × 250 mL
        = 750 mL
Amount remaining = (2200 − 750) mL
        = 1450 mL

**11** Distance = 108 km
Time from 9:30 until 11:00 is $1\frac{1}{2}$ hours.
Speed = (108 ÷ $1\frac{1}{2}$) km/h
     = 72 km/h

**12** Time taken = (330 ÷ 60) hours
        = $5\frac{1}{2}$ hours
$\frac{1}{2}$ hour after 10:30 am is 11:00 am.
5 hours after 11:00 am is 4:00 pm
The bus trip finished at 4 pm.

**13** 4 kilometres and 80 metres
= 4000 m + 80 m
= 4080 m
= 4.08 km

**14** In the pattern, a group of three tiles are repeating. The length of this pattern piece is 40 cm + 20 cm or 60 cm.

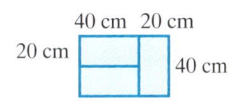

Required length = 6 m
        = 600 cm
Number of patterns = 600 ÷ 60
        = 10
Number of tiles = 10 × 3
        = 30

**15** Fuel consumption = 50 L on 625 km
        = 50 L on (6.25 × 100) km
        = (50 ÷ 6.25) L on 100 km
        = 8 L on 100 km
        = 8 L/100 km

**16** 1 cm = 10 mm
So 9 cm = 90 mm
9 cm + 15 mm = 90 mm + 15 mm
        = 105 mm
        = 10.5 cm

## Intermediate level questions

**Mini Test 17:** Perimeter, Area and Volume .... Page 20

**1** A  **2** D  **3** 14 cm  **4** C  **5** 24 cm  **6** B  **7** A  **8** A
**9** 4.5 cm  **10** D  **11** C  **12** B  **13** 5 m
**14** 1060 cm²  **15** 56 m²  **16** D

**1** Perimeter = 4 m
Each side = 4 m ÷ 4
        = 1 m
Area = 1 m × 1 m
     = 1 m²

**2** Each dimension of the larger prism is two times greater than the corresponding dimension of the smaller prism.
Number of times that the volume is greater
= 2 × 2 × 2
= 8

**3** Area = 84 cm²
So length × width = 84 cm²
    length × 6 cm = 84 cm²
        length = (84 ÷ 6) cm
            = 14 cm

# YEAR 9 NUMERACY MINI TEST ANSWERS

**4** Area of each face = 7 cm × 7 cm
= 49 cm$^2$

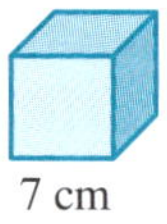

Area of all six faces = 6 × 49 cm$^2$
= 294 cm$^2$

**5** Area = 36 cm$^2$
Each side = $\sqrt{36}$ cm
= 6 cm 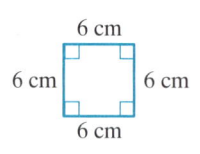
Perimeter = 4 × 6 cm
= 24 cm

**6** [Divide the shape into two rectangles by drawing a vertical line.]

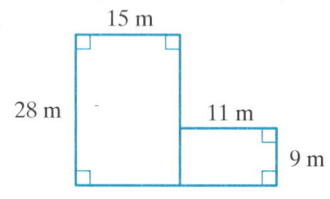

Area = 28 m × 15 m + 11 m × 9 m
= 420 m$^2$ + 99 m$^2$
= 519 m$^2$

[The shape could have been divided into two rectangles with a horizontal line, but then more work would have needed to be done to find the dimensions of those rectangles.]

**7** Circumference = π × diameter
= π × 48 cm
= 150.7964… cm

Of the options, the best answer is 150 cm.

**8** Area = $\frac{1}{2}$ × base × height
= $\frac{1}{2}$ × 12 m × 5 m
= 30 m$^2$

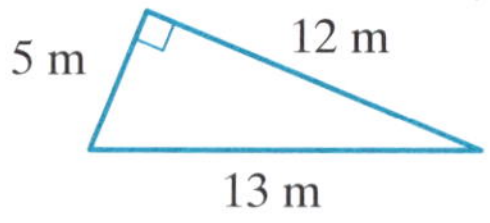

[The height must be perpendicular (at right angles) to the base. So the base and height must be the two dimensions (in either order) found each side of the right angle.]

**9** A regular hexagon has six equal sides.
Length of wire = 6 × 3 cm
= 18 cm
A square has four equal sides.
Length of each side = (18 ÷ 4) cm
= 4.5 cm

**10** Volume = length × width × height
[Find the volume of each prism.]

Volume = (7 × 4 × 3) m$^3$
= 84 m$^3$

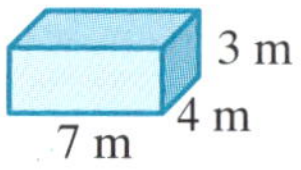

Volume = (9 × 3 × 3) m$^3$
= 81 m$^3$

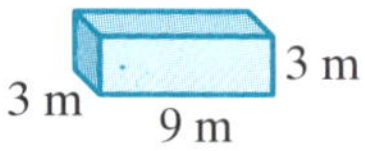

Volume = (8 × 5 × 2) m$^3$
= 80 m$^3$

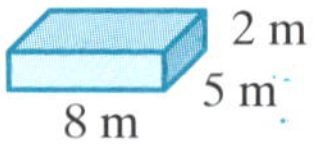

Volume = (11 × 4 × 2) m$^3$
= 88 m$^3$

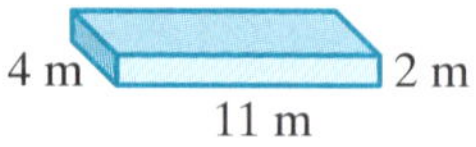

The prism with the greatest volume is prism D.

**11** [Because the conversion to litres has been given in cubic metres, first change the dimensions to metres.]

The fish tank is 0.5 m long, 0.3 m wide and 0.2 m high.

Volume = (0.5 × 0.3 × 0.2) m$^3$
= 0.03 m$^3$

Now 1 m$^3$ = 1000 L
so 0.03 m$^3$ = 0.03 × 1000 L
= 30 L

**12** [The length and width must be in the same units.]

The rectangle is 2 m long and 0.9 m wide.

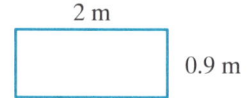

Area = 2 m × 0.9 m
= 1.8 m$^2$

**13** Volume = 480 m$^3$

The length is 12 m and the width 8 m.

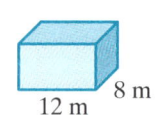

Let the height be $h$ metres.
So 12 × 8 × $h$ = 480
96 × $h$ = 480
$h$ = 480 ÷ 96
= 5

The height is 5 metres.

**14** The prism has two hexagonal faces and 6 rectangular faces.
Total area of hexagonal faces
= 2 × 260 cm$^2$
= 520 cm$^2$

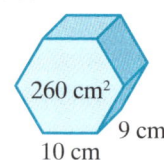

# YEAR 9 NUMERACY MINI TEST ANSWERS

Area of each rectangular face
= 10 cm × 9 cm
= 90 cm²
Total area of rectangular faces = 6 × 90 cm²
= 540 cm²
Total area = (520 + 540) cm²
= 1060 cm²

**15** The wall is made up of a rectangle and triangle:

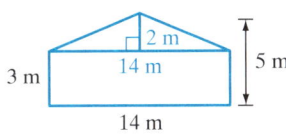

Area of rectangle = length × width
= 14 m × 3 m
= 42 m²

Area of triangle = $\frac{1}{2}$ × base × height
= $\frac{1}{2}$ × 14 m × 2 m
= 14 m²

Total area = (42 + 14) m²
= 56 m²

**16** The pool has a path of width 1 metre on all sides. So the outer rectangle is 20 metres long and 17 metres wide.

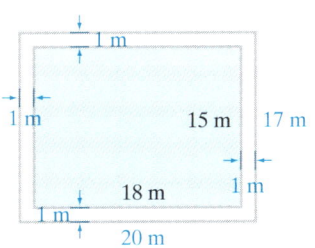

Area of outer rectangle = 20 m × 17 m
= 340 m²
Area of inner rectangle = 18 m × 15 m
= 270 m²
Area to be paved = (340 − 270) m²
= 70 m²

## Intermediate level questions

**Mini Test 18:** Chance and Data ............ Page 21

**1** C  **2** C  **3** D  **4** 44  **5** D  **6** 41  **7** 69  **8** 74
**9** B  **10** B  **11** 35 British pounds  **12** $48
**13** NZ$50  **14** $800  **15** A  **16** A

**1** Number of tickets = 5 + 4 + 3
= 12
Chance of white ticket = $\frac{3}{12}$
= $\frac{1}{4}$

**2** Ways of getting 6:
1 on first die and 5 on second
2 on first die and 4 on second
3 on both dice
4 on first die and 2 on second
5 on first die and 1 on second
There are 5 ways of getting 6.

**3** The spinner has ten equal sections. So you would expect to land on each section once in ten spins, or three times in 30 spins.
So if you would expect a number to be landed on six times, it would need to appear in two sections.
The number is 1.

**4** 168 children are from the city and 85 of those are boys.
Number of girls from city = 168 − 85
= 83
Total number of girls = 250 − 123
= 127
Girls from country = 127 − 83
= 44

|  | City | Country | Total |
|---|---|---|---|
| Boys | 85 | 38 | 123 |
| Girls | 83 | 44 | 127 |
| Total | 168 | 82 | 250 |

**5** The sector graph is divided into 12 equal sectors. Five of those sectors show the number of women.

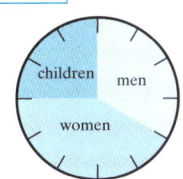

Number of women = $\frac{5}{12}$ of 300
= 125

Of the choices, the number of women is closest to 130.

**6** **Marks for Class 9P**

```
5 | 7 9
6 | 0 2 4 5 8 9 9 9
7 | 1 3 4 6 6 7 8
8 | 0 2 5 5 7 9
9 | 3 8
```

Key
9 | 3 is a score of 93

The highest score is 98.
The lowest score is 57.
Range = 98 − 57
= 41

**7** The score that occurs the most often is 69.
The mode is 69.

109

# YEAR 9 NUMERACY MINI TEST ANSWERS

**8** There are 25 scores altogether.
The middle score is the 13th score.
The median is 74.

**9** The score left out must have been equal to the mean.
The sum of the scores
= 2 + 7 + 9 + 10 + 11 + 12 + 14 + 15
= 80
There are eight scores.
Mean = 80 ÷ 8
= 10
So, the score that Ellen left out must have been 10.

**10**

| Colour | Red | Black | Blue | Green | Pink |
|---|---|---|---|---|---|
| Number | 23 | 8 | 16 | 6 | 11 |

Total number of bicycles
= 23 + 8 + 16 + 6 + 11
= 64
Probability of blue = $\frac{16}{64}$
= $\frac{1}{4}$

**11** [On the vertical scale, five divisions is 25 units so one division is 5 units.]
$80 Australian = 35 British pounds

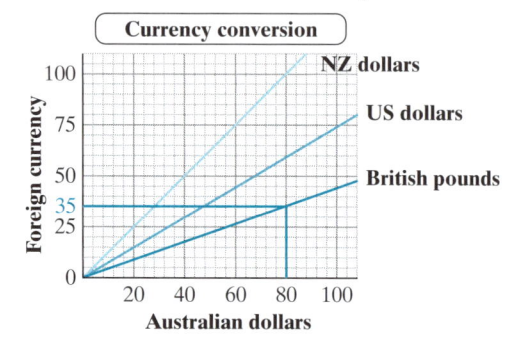

**12** [On the horizontal scale, five divisions is $20 so one division is $4.]
NZ$60 = $48 Australian

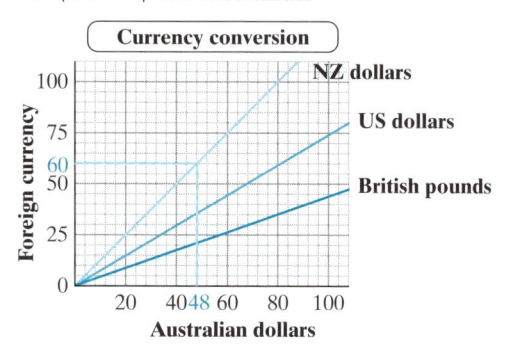

**13** US$30 = NZ$50

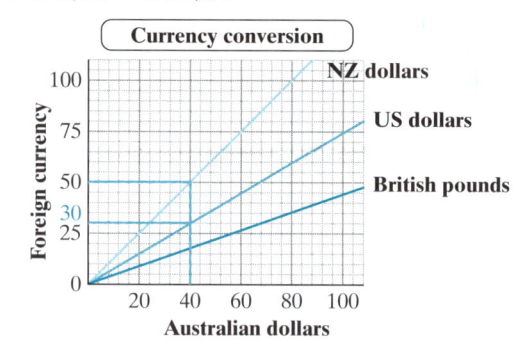

**14** Total raised = 40 × $20
= $800

**15** Number who didn't come by bus
= 200 − 120
= 80
Probability of not coming by bus = $\frac{80}{200}$
= $\frac{2}{5}$

**16** 5, 8, 8, 11, 13
Range = 13 − 5
= 8
Mode = 8
Median = 8
Mean = (5 + 8 + 8 + 11 + 13) ÷ 5
= 45 ÷ 5
= 9
The mean is not equal to 8.

## Intermediate level questions

**Mini Test 19:** Mixed Questions .................... Page 22

**1** D **2** A **3** 50 cm **4** A **5** D **6** A **7** D **8** D
**9** $h$ = 8 **10** C **11** B **12** B **13** 60 **14** C **15** C
**16** B

**1** $3\frac{2}{5} = \frac{3 \times 5 + 2}{5}$
$= \frac{17}{5}$

**2** Angles at a point add to 360°.

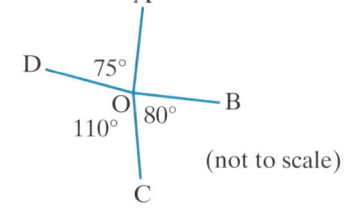

(not to scale)

Sum of known angles = 80° + 110° + 75°
= 265°
∠AOB = 360° − 265°
= 95°
So ∠AOB is obtuse.

# YEAR 9 NUMERACY MINI TEST ANSWERS

**3** The photo was 8 cm wide and is now 40 cm wide.
Number of times larger = 40 ÷ 8
= 5
New length = 5 × 10 cm
= 50 cm

**4** When $x = -2$ and $y = 4$
$3xy = 3 \times -2 \times 4$
$= -24$

**5** The average of five scores is 7.
Sum of scores = 5 × 7
= 35
The average of six scores is 8.
Sum of those scores = 6 × 8
= 48
Difference between sums = 48 − 35
= 13
The score that was added must have been 13.

**6** $56 \times 17 - 12 \times 56 = 56 \times 17 - 56 \times 12$
$= 56 \times (17 - 12)$
$= 56 \times 5$

**7** $0.2 \div 0.04 = 20 \div 4$
$= 5$
[Move the decimal point to the right (the same number of places in both parts of the question), so that you divide by a whole number.]

**8** Number of balls = 8 + 12 + 4
= 24
Probability of white ball = $\frac{4}{24}$
= $\frac{1}{6}$

**9** $2h + 7 = 23$
$2h = 23 - 7$
$= 16$
$h = 16 \div 2$
$= 8$

**10** For every 5 boys there are 4 girls.
So 5 out of 9 students are boys.
Number of boys = $\frac{5}{9}$ of 27
= 15
Number of girls = 27 − 15
= 12
Difference = 15 − 12
= 3
There are 3 more boys than girls.

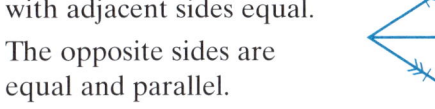

**11** A rhombus is a parallelogram with adjacent sides equal. 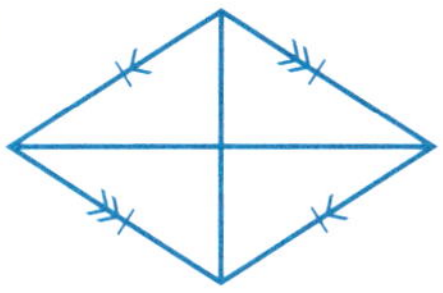
The opposite sides are equal and parallel.
The diagonals of a rhombus are not always equal.

**12** Liz has plotted the points (2, −3), (−2, 3) and (−3, 2).

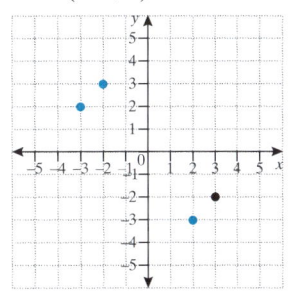

She still needs to plot the point (3, −2).

**13** Original number = 12 000
Number at first audition = 30% of 12 000
= $\frac{30}{100} \times 12\,000$
= 3600
Number at second audition = 3600 ÷ 4
= 900
Number interviewed = 20% of 900
= $\frac{20}{100} \times 900$
= 180
Number chosen = 180 ÷ 3
= 60

**14** $m + n = 4$
$m - n = -6$
Try each option:
$m = 1$ and $n = 3$
$1 + 3 = 4$ ✓
$1 - 3 = -2$ ✗ (not −6)
This is not the correct option.
$m = 2$ and $n = 2$
$2 + 2 = 4$ ✓
$2 - 2 = 0$ ✗ (not −6)
This is not the correct option.
$m = -1$ and $n = 5$
$-1 + 5 = 4$ ✓
$-1 - 5 = -6$ ✓
This is the correct option.

# YEAR 9 NUMERACY MINI TEST ANSWERS

$m = -2$ and $n = 4$
$-2 + 4 = 2$ ✗ (not 4)
This is not the correct option.

The values of $m$ and $n$ that satisfy both equations are $m = -1$ and $n = 5$.

**15** Area = 20 m²
Width = 4 m
So length × 4 m = 20 m²
length = (20 ÷ 4) m
= 5 m
Perimeter = 2 × (length + width)
= 2 × (5 + 4) m
= 18 m

**16** Consider each statement:

'No cubes have no painted faces.'

This statement is correct. All of the cubes have at least one painted face.

'8 cubes have exactly one painted face.'

This statement is not correct. 3 cubes at the front and 3 at the back will have exactly one painted face. The number of cubes with exactly one painted face is 6.

The incorrect statement is '8 cubes have exactly one painted face.'

## Intermediate level questions

**Mini Test 20:** Mixed Questions .................... Page 23

**1** D  **2** 164°  **3** 72  **4** A  **5** −1.7  **6** B  **7** C  **8** D
**9** A  **10** 150  **11** 45  **12** B  **13** $200 000  **14** B
**15** C  **16** D

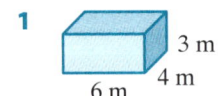

**1**
There are two faces 6 m by 4 m, two faces 4 m by 3 m and two faces 6 m by 3 m.
Total area = 2 × (6 × 4 + 4 × 3 + 6 × 3) m²
= 2 × (24 + 12 + 18) m²
= 2 × 54 m²
= 108 m²

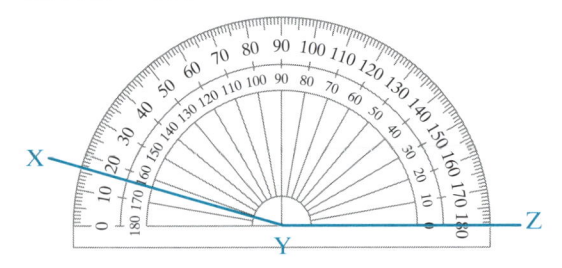

**2** ∠XYZ = 164°

[The angle 'begins' at Z so use the scale that has 0° at Z—the inside scale.]

**3** Three parts of the books are paperbacks and one part is hardcover books.
So one-quarter are hardcover.
Number of hardcover books = 96 ÷ 4
= 24
Number of paperbacks = 3 × 24
= 72

**4** From 6:42 am until 7:00 am is 18 minutes.
From 7 am until 3 pm is 8 hours.
From 3 pm until 3:24 pm is 24 minutes.
Total time = 8 h and (18 + 24) min
= 8 h 42 min

**5** [Fill in the numbers on the number line.]

The arrow is pointing to the number halfway between −1.6 and −1.8. It is pointing to −1.7.

**6** The solid has 9 faces and 16 edges.
Difference = 16 − 9
= 7
The solid has 7 more edges than faces.

**7** Opposite sides of a rectangle are equal.

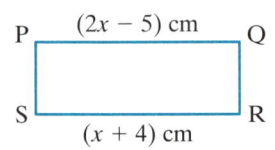

So $2x − 5 = x + 4$
[Add 5 to both sides.]
$2x = x + 9$
[Take $x$ from both sides.]
$x = 9$

# YEAR 9 NUMERACY MINI TEST ANSWERS

**8** | Number of pets | 0, 0, 1, 1, 1, 2, 2, 3, 5 |

Sum of scores
$= 2 \times 0 + 3 \times 1 + 2 \times 2 + 3 + 5$
$= 15$
Mean $= \dfrac{15}{9}$
$= 1\dfrac{2}{3}$
Mode $= 1$
Median $= 1$
Range $= 5 - 0$
$= 5$
The range is the greatest.

**9** For every 2 boys in 9K there are 5 girls.
So 5 out of 7 students are girls.
Number of girls $= \dfrac{5}{7} \times 28$
$= 20$
Number of boys $= 28 - 20$
$= 8$
In 9Y, for every 7 boys there are 3 girls.
Now $21 \div 7 = 3$
So there are 3 lots of 7 boys.
Number of girls $= 3 \times 3$
$= 9$
Total number of boys $= 8 + 21$
$= 29$
Total number of girls $= 20 + 9$
$= 29$
There are the same number of boys and girls in the two classes.

**10** Each angle of a rectangle $= 90°$
Each angle of an equilateral triangle $= 60°$
Angles at a point add to $360°$.
So $x + 60 + 90 + 60 = 360$
$x + 210 = 360$
$x = 360 - 210$
$= 150$

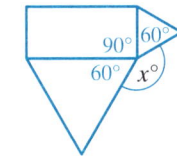

**11** $\dfrac{2}{5}$ are blue and $\dfrac{1}{3}$ are black.
Fraction that is blue and black $= \dfrac{2}{5} + \dfrac{1}{3}$
$= \dfrac{11}{15}$

Fraction that is red $= 1 - \dfrac{11}{15}$
$= \dfrac{4}{15}$
But 12 pens are red.
So $\dfrac{4}{15}$ of the pens $= 12$
$\dfrac{1}{15}$ of the pens $= 12 \div 4$
$= 3$
The number of pens $= 3 \times 15$
$= 45$

**12**

| $x$ | 1 | 3 | 5 | 7 | 9 |
|---|---|---|---|---|---|
| $y$ | 1 | 2 | 3 | 4 | 5 |

Try each option:
$y = \dfrac{1}{2}x + 1$
When $x = 1$,
$y = \dfrac{1}{2} \times 1 + 1$
$= 1\dfrac{1}{2}$
This is not the option.
$y = \dfrac{1}{2}(x + 1)$
When $x = 1$,
$y = \dfrac{1}{2} \times 2$
$= 1$
When $x = 3$,
$y = \dfrac{1}{2} \times 4$
$= 2$
When $x = 5$,
$y = \dfrac{1}{2} \times 6$
$= 3$
When $x = 7$,
$y = \dfrac{1}{2} \times 8$
$= 4$
When $x = 9$,
$y = \dfrac{1}{2} \times 10$
$= 5$
This is the option.
The rule is $y = \dfrac{1}{2}(x + 1)$.

# YEAR 9 NUMERACY MINI TEST ANSWERS

**13** If the value six years ago was 100%, the value is now 160% of what it was.
So 160% = $320 000
1% = $320 000 ÷ 160
= $2000
100% = 100 × $2000
= $200 000

**14** Dave is older than Paul and Kim.
Mary is older than Dave.
So Mary is also older than Paul and Kim.
Mary is the oldest.

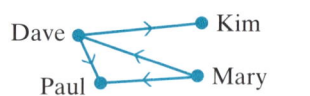

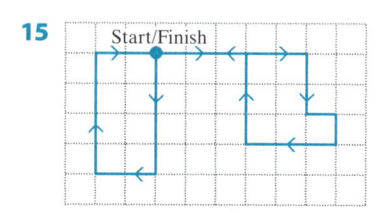

**15** Counting the units, there are 30 altogether.
So 30 units = 1.5 km
30 units = 1500 m
1 unit = (1500 ÷ 30) m
1 unit = 50 m

**16** 5 times $n$ = $5n$
The number 3 less than $5n$ is $5n - 3$
[Use numbers to help see what is happening. For example, the number 3 less than 5 times 2 is 7, $(5 \times 2 - 3)$]

### Advanced level questions

**Mini Test 21:** Number .................. Page 24

**1** B  **2** D  **3** 6%  **4** C  **5** B  **6** A  **7** D  **8** D
**9** −9 and 2  **10** A  **11** C  **12** B  **13** B  **14** $160
**15** D  **16** C  **17** A  **18** C

**1** The fractions all have a common denominator of 40.
$\frac{3}{5} = \frac{24}{40}$
$\frac{5}{8} = \frac{25}{40}$
$\frac{7}{10} = \frac{28}{40}$
$\frac{13}{20} = \frac{26}{40}$

So, in order, the fractions are $\frac{24}{40}, \frac{25}{40}, \frac{26}{40}, \frac{28}{40}$.
The order from lowest to highest is
$\frac{3}{5}, \frac{5}{8}, \frac{13}{20}, \frac{7}{10}$.

**2** $9^4 = 9 \times 9 \times 9 \times 9$
But $9 = 3 \times 3$
So $9^4 = 3 \times 3 \times 3 \times 3 \times 3 \times 3 \times 3 \times 3$
= $3^8$

**3** 30% received a medal.
Of these 20% received a gold medal.
Now 20% = $\frac{1}{5}$
So the percentage with a gold medal
= 30% ÷ 5
= 6%

**4** Consider the options:
$0.4 \times 0.8 = 0.32$
[There must be the same number of places after the decimal point in the answer as there were (in total) in the question.]
$0.12 + 0.2 = 0.32$
[0.12 + 0.20]
$6.4 \div 0.2 = 64 \div 2$
= 32
$1 - 0.68 = 0.32$
[1.00 − 0.68]
$6.4 \div 0.2$ is the calculation that is not equal to 0.32.

**5** [Write each number as a decimal.]
$\frac{1}{8} = 0.125$
$\left[ 8 \overline{) 1.0^2 0^4 0} \phantom{0} 0.1\,2\,5 \right]$
0.16
8% = 0.08
[8 ÷ 100]
$\frac{1}{9} = 0.1111...$
$\left[ 9 \overline{) 1.0^1 0^1 0} \phantom{0} 0.1\,1\,1 \right]$
The largest number is 0.16.

**6** $(0.3)^2 = 0.3 \times 0.3$
= 0.09
[There must be the same number of places after the decimal point in the answer as there were (in total) in the question.]

# YEAR 9 NUMERACY MINI TEST ANSWERS

**7** For every 5 boys there were 2 girls.
So 5 out of every 7 students were boys.
Now 28 ÷ 7 = 4
So there were 4 lots of 7 students.
Number of boys = 5 × 4
             = 20
Number of girls = 2 × 4
              = 8
Two girls joined the class.
New number of girls = 8 + 2
                   = 10
New ratio of boys to girls = 20 to 10
                          = 2 to 1

**8** Saving was 10%
Percentage to pay = 100% − 10%
                 = 90%
Sale price = 90% of $600
          = 0.9 × $600
          = $(0.9 × 600)
The calculation required is 600 × 0.9.

**9** The two numbers multiply to −18.
[One must be positive and one negative because they multiply to a negative number.]
They add to −7.
The two numbers are 2 and −9.

**10** $\sqrt{0.01} = 0.1$
[Try the options to see which one multiplied by itself will give 0.01: 0.1 × 0.1 = 0.01]

**11** Try each option:
3 × 4 × 5 = 60 but 4 is not a prime number so this is not the option.
2 × 3 × 5 = 30 so this is not the option.
2 × 2 × 3 × 5 = 60
This is the option.
2 × 3 × 3 × 5 = 90 so this is not the option.
60 written as a product of its prime factors is 2 × 2 × 3 × 5

**12** [All the fractions have a common denominator of 30.]
$\frac{1}{3} = \frac{10}{30}$
$\frac{2}{5} = \frac{12}{30}$
$\frac{3}{10} = \frac{9}{30}$
$\frac{11}{30}$

The largest fraction is $\frac{12}{30}$ or $\frac{2}{5}$.

**13** $\frac{1}{3}$ and $\frac{1}{5}$ have a common denominator of 15.
$\frac{1}{3} = \frac{5}{15}$
$\frac{1}{5} = \frac{3}{15}$
The number halfway between $\frac{3}{15}$ and $\frac{5}{15}$ is $\frac{4}{15}$.

**14** $\frac{3}{4}$ of the amount = $180
$\frac{1}{4}$ of the amount = $180 ÷ 3
                            = $60
The whole amount = 4 × $60
                = $240
$\frac{1}{3}$ of $240 = $240 ÷ 3
                     = $80
$\frac{2}{3}$ of $240 = 2 × $80
                     = $160

**15** Consider the options:
0.3 < 0.08 ?
0.30 > 0.08
This option is not correct.
−0.7 > −0.6 ?

−0.7 < −0.6
This option is not correct.
0.123 > 0.4 ?
0.123 < 0.400
This option is not correct.
−0.9 < −0.75 ?

This option is correct.
The correct statement is −0.9 < −0.75

**16** In 1991, Cathy was 16.
Jade was $\frac{1}{4}$ of 16 or 4.
Years later = 2011 − 1991
           = 20
Cathy's age in 2011 = 16 + 20
                   = 36

# YEAR 9 NUMERACY MINI TEST ANSWERS

Jade's age in 2011 = 4 + 20
= 24

Fraction of Cathy's age = $\frac{24}{36}$
= $\frac{2}{3}$

**17** Of the original 60 people, there were 7 adults for every 5 children.

So 7 out of 12 people were adults.

Now 60 ÷ 12 = 5 so there were 5 lots of 12 people.

Number of adults = 5 × 7
= 35

Number of children = 5 × 5
= 25

If 20 people left the party, 40 remained.

Of the remaining people there were 5 adults for every 3 children.

So 5 out of 8 people were adults.

Now 40 ÷ 8 = 5 so there were 5 lots of 8 people.

Number of adults = 5 × 5
= 25

Number of children = 5 × 3
= 15

Number of adults who left = 35 − 25
= 10

Number of children who left = 25 − 15
= 10

So 10 adults and 10 children left the party.

**18** $\frac{5}{12}$ of the balloons are red and $\frac{1}{3}$ are blue.

Fraction that is red and blue = $\frac{5}{12} + \frac{1}{3}$
= $\frac{5}{12} + \frac{4}{12}$
= $\frac{9}{12}$
= $\frac{3}{4}$

Fraction that is white = $1 - \frac{3}{4}$
= $\frac{1}{4}$

## Advanced level questions

**Mini Test 22:** Algebra .................... Page 25

**1** D  **2** A  **3** B  **4** $p = 2$  **5** C  **6** $x = 11$  **7** D
**8** C  **9** A  **10** B  **11** $x = 5$ and $y = 2$  **12** $-5x$
**13** D  **14** 9604  **15** C  **16** 95°F  **17** 3  **18** A

**1** $-5x + 3 = 3 − 5x$
[Simply rearranging the terms.]

**2** $3t^2 = 3 \times t^2$
When $t = -2$,
$3t^2 = 3 \times (-2)^2$
= $3 \times 4$
= 12

**3** [Consecutive numbers are numbers following one another like 17, 18 and 19.]
If $x$ is the first number, the second number is $x + 1$ and the third number is $x + 2$.
The largest number in the set is $x + 2$.

**4** $7p - 2 = 3p + 6$
[Add 2 to both sides.]
$7p = 3p + 8$
[Subtract 3p from both sides.]
$4p = 8$
[Divide by 4.]
$p = 2$

**5** $3(2a - 2) + 5a + 4 = 6a - 6 + 5a + 4$
= $6a + 5a - 6 + 4$
= $11a - 2$

**6** $y = 3x + 5$
If $y = 38$,
$38 = 3x + 5$
[Subtract 5 from both sides.]
$33 = 3x$
[Divide both sides by 3.]
$11 = x$
So $x = 11$

**7** $y > 3x - 7$
Try each option:
$x = 10$ and $y = 24$
$24 > 3 \times 10 - 7$
$24 > 23$
This option is correct.
$x = 5$ and $y = 10$
$10 > 3 \times 5 - 7$
$10 > 8$
This option is correct.

# YEAR 9 NUMERACY MINI TEST ANSWERS

$x = 2$ and $y = 0$
$0 > 3 \times 2 - 7$
$0 > -1$
This option is correct.
$x = 7$ and $y = 12$
$12 > 3 \times 7 - 7$
$12 > 14$
This option is not correct.
The pair of values that does not satisfy the inequality is $x = 7$ and $y = 12$.

**8** $3x^2 + 7x - 4$
Try each option:
$7x - 4 + 3x^2 = 3x^2 + 7x - 4$
This option is correct.
$-4 + 7x + 3x^2 = 3x^2 + 7x - 4$
This option is correct.
$4 - 7x - 3x^2 = -3x^2 - 7x - 4$
$= -(3x^2 + 7x + 4)$
This option is not correct.
$3x^2 - 4 + 7x = 3x^2 + 7x - 4$
This option is correct.
The expression that is not equivalent to $3x^2 + 7x - 4$ is $4 - 7x - 3x^2$

**9** $5m + 4 = 3m - 8$
[Subtract 4 from both sides.]
$5m = 3m - 12$
[Subtract $3m$ from both sides.]
$2m = -12$
[Divide both sides by 2.]
$m = -6$
[Or try each option to see which satisfies the equation.]

**10** $(3, 4)$ and $(14, 15)$
The $y$-value is one more than the $x$-value.
[So they will both lie on the line $y = x + 1$.]
Of the options, the only point with its $y$-value one more than its $x$-value is $(10, 11)$ so this point will lie on the line.

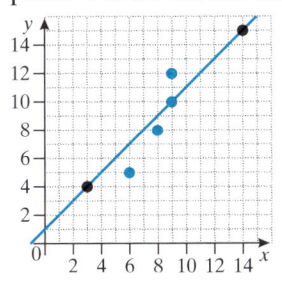

**11** $x + y = 7$
$x - y = 3$
[Add the two equations together and $y$ will be eliminated.]
$2x = 10$
[Divide by 2.]
$x = 5$
So $5 + y = 7$
[Subtract 5 from both sides.]
$y = 2$
So $x = 5$ and $y = 2$
[Check: $5 + 2 = 7$; $5 - 2 = 3$]

**12** $4(5x - 1) + 3 + \boxed{?} = 15x - 1$
$20x - 4 + 3 + \boxed{?} = 15x - 1$
$20x - 1 + \boxed{?} = 15x - 1$
[Add 1 to both sides.]
$20x + \boxed{?} = 15x$
But $20x - 5x = 15x$.
So the missing term is $-5x$.

**13** If $k = -3$,
$k^2 - 4k = (-3)^2 - 4 \times (-3)$
$= 9 + 12$
$= 21$

**14** $2^2 = 0 \times 4 + 4$
$3^2 = 1 \times 5 + 4$
$4^2 = 2 \times 6 + 4$
$5^2 = 3 \times 7 + 4$
$6^2 = 4 \times 8 + 4$
[The first number on the right-hand side is two less than the number that is squared on the left-hand side. The second number is two more than the number that is squared.]
Using the pattern:
$98^2 = 96 \times 100 + 4$
$= 9600 + 4$
$= 9604$

**15** $y = 3 - 2x$
P is the point $(-1, 5)$.
When $x = -1$,
$y = 3 - 2 \times -1$
$= 3 + 2$
$= 5$
So P lies on the line.
Q is the point $(-2, -1)$.

# YEAR 9 NUMERACY MINI TEST ANSWERS

When $x = -2$,
$y = 3 - 2 \times -2$
$\phantom{y} = 3 + 4$
$\phantom{y} = 7$ (not $-1$)
So Q does not lie on the line.
S is the point (1, 1).
When $x = 1$,
$y = 3 - 2 \times 1$
$\phantom{y} = 1$
So S lies on the line.
The line passes through P and S.

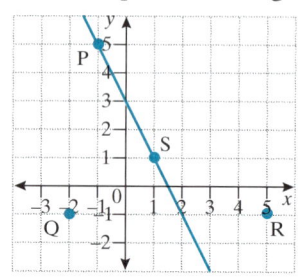

**16** $F = \dfrac{9}{5}C + 32$

When $C = 35$,
$F = \dfrac{9}{5} \times 35 + 32$
$[35 \div 5 = 7; 9 \times 7 = 63]$
$F = 63 + 32$
$\phantom{F} = 95$
The temperature would be 95°F.

**17** $\dfrac{3}{4} > \dfrac{2}{x}$

[Multiply both sides by $4x$.]
$3x > 8$
[Divide by 3.]
$x > 2\dfrac{2}{3}$
But $x$ is a whole number.
The smallest possible value of $x$ is 3.

**18** $\dfrac{x^2}{3} + \dfrac{2x^2}{3} = \dfrac{3x^2}{3}$
$\phantom{\dfrac{x^2}{3} + \dfrac{2x^2}{3}} = x^2$

## Advanced level questions

**Mini Test 23:** Space, Measurement and Data .................................... Page 26

**1** B  **2** D  **3** A  **4** A  **5** 60 km/h  **6** B  **7** C  **8** C
**9** A  **10** B  **11** 400  **12** D

**1**
The kite has two sides of length 30 metres.
Total length of those sides is 60 metres.
Perimeter = 160 m
Length of two remaining sides
$= (160 - 60)$ m
$= 100$ m
Length of each side $= 100$ m $\div 2$
$\phantom{Length of each side } = 50$ m

**2** The light is on for 20 seconds out of 25.

Probability that it is on $= \dfrac{20}{25}$
$\phantom{Probability that it is on } = \dfrac{4}{5}$
$\phantom{Probability that it is on } = \dfrac{4}{5} \times 100\%$
$\phantom{Probability that it is on } = 80\%$

**3** 76, 78, 83, 85, 87, 87, 88, 91, 94

The 10th score is 96.

The mean must increase because the score that is being included is higher than all the other scores.

The mode will not change.
[The score with the greatest frequency is still 87.]

The median will not change.
[The median of the nine scores is the fifth score: 87. The median of the ten scores is the average of the fifth and sixth scores, but they are both 87 so the median will still be 87.]

So, the mean increases but the mode and median do not change.

**4** The box is a rectangular prism, 5 cm long, 3 cm wide and 2 cm high.

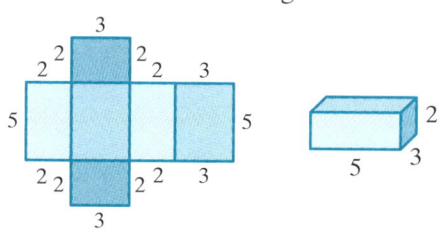

Volume = length × width × height
$\phantom{Volume} = (5 \times 3 \times 2)$ cm³
$\phantom{Volume} = 30$ cm³

# YEAR 9 NUMERACY MINI TEST ANSWERS

**5** Distance on map = 5 cm
Real distance = 5 × 6 km
= 30 km
Rosie travels 30 km in half an hour.
She would travel 60 km in one hour.
Her speed is 60 km/h.

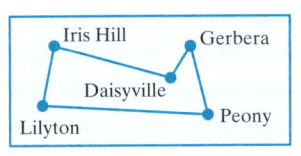

Scale: 1 cm represents 6 km

**6** Circumference = π × diameter
= π × 1.2 cm 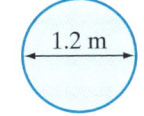
The value of π is a little bit more than 3.
Now 3 × 1.2 = 3.6
So π × 1.2 will be about 4.
The circumference of the tabletop is closest to 4 m.

**7** When a coin is tossed twice there are four possible outcomes: head head, head tail, tail head and tail tail.
A head each time is one of those four outcomes.
Probability of two heads = $\frac{1}{4}$

**8** The deck measurements are in metres but the board measurements are in millimetres.
The boards are 90 mm, or 0.09 metres wide and 4500 mm or 4.5 metres long.

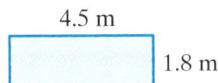

So the boards are the same length as the deck.
Number of boards will be the number of times that 0.09 goes into 1.8.
The correct calculation is 1.8 ÷ 0.09.

**9** If the original triangle is both right-angled and isosceles it will have one angle of 90° and two other angles of 45°.
The axis of symmetry passes through the right angle dividing it into two equal parts. So the two new triangles both have two angles of 45° (and one of 90°).
The new triangles are both right-angled and isosceles.

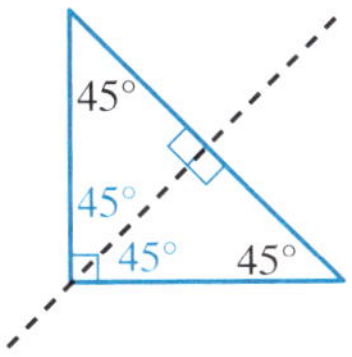

**10** The spinner is divided into six sections.
One of those sections shows 1 so the chance of getting 1 is $\frac{1}{6}$. 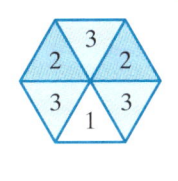
In 30 spins, you would expect 1 to occur $\frac{1}{6}$ × 30 times or 5 times.

Two of those sections show 2 so the chance of getting 2 is $\frac{2}{6}$ or $\frac{1}{3}$.
In 30 spins, you would expect 2 to occur $\frac{1}{3}$ × 30 times or 10 times.

Three of those sections show 3 so the chance of getting 3 is $\frac{3}{6}$ or $\frac{1}{2}$.
In 30 spins, you would expect 3 to occur $\frac{1}{2}$ × 30 times or 15 times.

The most likely result is

| Number spun | Number of spins |
|---|---|
| 1 | 5 |
| 2 | 10 |
| 3 | 15 |

**11** The bar chart is 6 cm long.
So a length of 6 cm represents 1200 people.
1 cm represents 1200 ÷ 6 people or 200 people.
Now the region for 'no' is 2 cm long.
Number of people who said 'no' is 2 × 200 or 400.

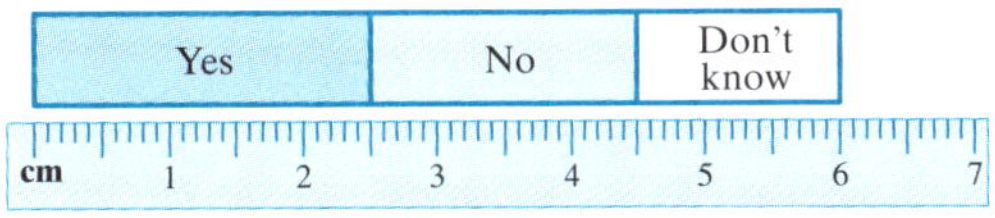

**12**

| Model | Capacity | Consumption |
|---|---|---|
| Sedan | 60 L | 8 L per 100 km |
| Coupe | 42 L | 6 L per 100 km |
| Van | 54 L | 9 L per 100 km |
| Wagon | 56 L | 7 L per 100 km |

Try each option:
The sedan uses 8 litres for every 100 km travelled. Its fuel tank holds 60 litres.
Distance = (60 ÷ 8) × 100 km
= 7.5 × 100 km
= 750 km

# YEAR 9 NUMERACY MINI TEST ANSWERS

The coupe uses 6 litres for every 100 km travelled. Its fuel tank holds 42 litres.
Distance = (42 ÷ 6) × 100 km
         = 7 × 100 km
         = 700 km

The van uses 9 litres for every 100 km travelled. Its fuel tank holds 54 litres.
Distance = (54 ÷ 9) × 100 km
         = 6 × 100 km
         = 600 km

The wagon uses 7 litres for every 100 km travelled. Its fuel tank holds 56 litres.
Distance = (56 ÷ 7) × 100 km
         = 8 × 100 km
         = 800 km

The wagon travels furthest on a full tank of fuel.

### Advanced level questions

**Mini Test 24:** Number .................... Page 27

**1** A   **2** 68%   **3** C   **4** C   **5** D   **6** D   **7** C   **8** 60
**9** $18 900   **10** D   **11** B   **12** 168   **13** B   **14** 9
**15** A   **16** 8 and 41   **17** 2 × 2 × 7 × 7   **19**   **18** B

1  $\frac{43.7 - 19.8}{\sqrt{183 + 79}} = \frac{23.9}{\sqrt{262}}$
     = 1.4765469…
     = 1.5 (to 1 decimal place)

2  Number of boys who start school
   = $\frac{3}{5}$ of 70
   = 42

   Number of girls who start school
   = $\frac{3}{4}$ of 80
   = 60

   Total starting school = 42 + 60
                         = 102
   Total pre-schoolers = 70 + 80
                       = 150
   Percentage starting school = $\frac{102}{150}$ × 100%
                              = 68%

3  Consider each option:
   $\frac{23}{5} = 4\frac{3}{5}$
   [5 divides into 23 four times with remainder 3]

$4.6 = 4\frac{6}{10}$
     $= 4\frac{3}{5}$

$4\frac{9}{25}$ cannot be simplified.

$460\% = \frac{460}{100}$
       $= 4\frac{60}{100}$
       $= 4\frac{3}{5}$

The number that is not equal to $4\frac{3}{5}$ is $4\frac{9}{25}$.

**4** At first there were 2 pink marshmallows for every 5 white ones.
So 2 out of every 7 marshmallows were pink.
Number of pink marshmallows = $\frac{2}{7}$ × 35
                            = 10
Number of white marshmallows = 35 − 10
                             = 25
After Emma ate 1 pink and 4 white marshmallows:
Number of pink marshmallows = 9
Number of white marshmallows = 21
New ratio = 9 to 21
          = 3 to 7

**5** Try each option:
1001 ÷ 7 = 143
1001 ÷ 11 = 91
1001 ÷ 13 = 77
1001 ÷ 17 = 58.88235…
So 17 is not a factor of 1001.

**6** $2^4 × 5^2$ = 2 × 2 × 2 × 2 × 5 × 5
         = 4 × 4 × 5 × 5
         = 4 × 5 × 4 × 5
         = 20 × 20
         = $20^2$

**7** Joe: $\frac{7}{12}$ × 100% = 58.3333…%

Harry: $\frac{8}{15}$ × 100% = 53.3333…%

Tom: $\frac{12}{19}$ × 100% = 63.1578…%

Rick: $\frac{15}{26}$ × 100% = 57.6923…%

The best success rate is 63.1578…%.
So Tom had the best success rate.

120

# YEAR 9 NUMERACY MINI TEST ANSWERS

8. Multiples of 12 are 12, 24, 36, 48, 60, 72, …
   Multiples of 15 are 15, 30, 45, 60, 75, …
   The smallest number that is a multiple of both 12 and 15 is 60.

9. Increase in income = 5% of $60 000
   $\qquad\qquad\qquad\qquad$ = $3000
   New income = $60 000 + $3000
   $\qquad\qquad\quad$ = $63 000
   Tax = 30% of $63 000
   $\quad\;\,$ = $18 900

10. If original value was 100% the new value is 140%.
    So 140% of the original value = $4200
    10% of the original value = $4200 ÷ 14
    $\qquad\qquad\qquad\qquad\qquad$ = $300
    100% of the original value = 10 × $300
    $\qquad\qquad\qquad\qquad\qquad\;$ = $3000

11. [To test whether a number is prime, you need to check the prime factors up to the square root of the number. Now $11^2$ = 121 so you only need to check the factors 2, 3, 5 and 7. (If 13 divided into one of the numbers, for example, it would need to do so less than 11 times.) None of the numbers are even, so none are divisible by 2. None end in 0 or 5 so none are divisible by 5.]
    Try divisibility by 3:
    111 ÷ 3 = 37
    So 117 will also be divisible by 3 and 113 and 119 will not.
    Try divisibility by 7:
    113 ÷ 7 = 16.142857…
    119 ÷ 7 = 17
    The number that is prime is 113.

12. After Kate added 1.5 her answer was 4.5.
    So before she added 1.5 it must have been 4.5 − 1.5 or 3.
    So after Kate divided by 63 her answer was 3. Before she divided by 63 it must have been 63 × 3 or 189.
    Now Kate should first have added 63.
    189 + 63 = 252
    Then she should have divided by 1.5.
    252 ÷ 1.5 = 168
    Kate's answer should have been 168.

13. The recipe uses 3 cups of flour and Elliott uses $7\frac{1}{2}$ cups.

    Number of times larger = $7\frac{1}{2} \div 3$
    $\qquad\qquad\qquad\qquad\;\;$ = $2\frac{1}{2}$
    So Elliott is making $2\frac{1}{2}$ times the recipe.
    Now the recipe uses $2\frac{1}{2}$ tablespoons of sugar.
    Required amount = $2\frac{1}{2} \times 2\frac{1}{2}$ tablespoons
    $\qquad\qquad\qquad$ = $6\frac{1}{4}$ tablespoons

14. The ratio of men to women was 7 to 3.
    So 7 out of 10 people were men.
    Number of men = $\frac{7}{10}$ of 120
    $\qquad\qquad\qquad$ = 84
    Number of women = 120 − 84
    $\qquad\qquad\qquad\quad\;$ = 36
    New number of people = 120 + 24
    $\qquad\qquad\qquad\qquad\;\;$ = 144
    New ratio of men to women is 11 to 5.
    So there are 11 men for every 5 women.
    So 5 out of 16 people are women.
    Number of women = $\frac{5}{16}$ of 144
    $\qquad\qquad\qquad\quad\;$ = 45
    Extra women = 45 − 36
    $\qquad\qquad\quad\;$ = 9

15. The answer 19668.6 is the charge in cents. In dollars this amount is $196.686 or $196.69 to the nearest cent.

16. 328 ÷ 2 = 164
    But 2 + 164 = 166 not 49
    328 ÷ 4 = 82
    But 4 + 82 = 86 not 49
    328 ÷ 8 = 41
    41 + 8 = 49
    So the numbers are 41 and 8.

17. [3724 is even so it is divisible by 2.]
    3724 ÷ 2 = 1862
    [1862 is even so it is also divisible by 2.]
    1862 ÷ 2 = 931
    [9 + 3 + 1 = 13; 13 is not divisible by 3 so 931 is not divisible by 3. 931 does not end in 0 or 5 so it is not divisible by 5.]
    931 ÷ 7 = 133
    133 ÷ 7 = 19

# YEAR 9 NUMERACY MINI TEST ANSWERS

So $3724 = 2 \times 2 \times 7 \times 7 \times 19$

[Or use a factor tree:
$$3724$$
$$2 \quad 1862$$
$$2 \quad 931$$
$$7 \quad 133$$
$$7 \quad 19$$
]

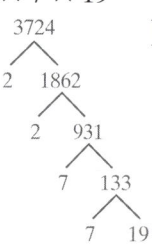

**18** $\frac{2}{5}$ of $\frac{3}{5}$ of the members are male pensioners.

Fraction $= \frac{2}{5} \times \frac{3}{5}$
$= \frac{6}{25}$

## Advanced level questions

**Mini Test 25:** Algebra—Patterns, Expressions and Number Plane............ Page 28

**1** C  **2** 1457  **3** B  **4** A  **5** 85  **6** 196  **7** D  **8** C  **9** C
**10** D  **11** B  **12** 79  **13** $4x$  **14** D  **15** A  **16** $\frac{11}{12}$

**1** $3(1 - p) - p = 3 - 3p - p$
$= 3 - 4p$

**2** The third number $= 17$
The fourth number $= 3 \times 17 + 2$
$= 51 + 2$
$= 53$
The fifth number $= 3 \times 53 + 2$
$= 159 + 2$
$= 161$
The sixth number $= 3 \times 161 + 2$
$= 483 + 2$
$= 485$
The seventh number $= 3 \times 485 + 2$
$= 1457$

**3** QR $= 8$ so Q is 8 units from R.
The co-ordinates of Q are $(-3, -2)$.
PQ $= 6$ so P is 6 units above Q.
The co-ordinates of P are $(-3, 4)$.

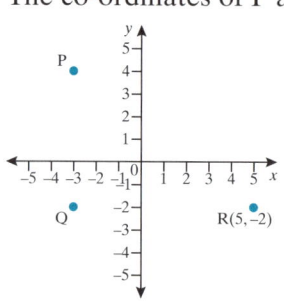

**4** $3(5x + 4) + 2(3x - 7) = 15x + 12 + 6x - 14$
$= 21x - 2$

**5**

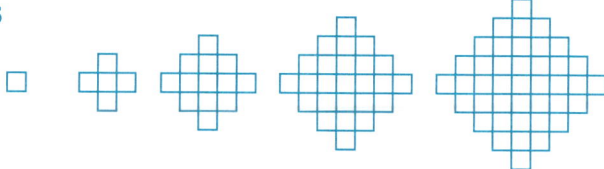

Shape 1  Shape 2  Shape 3  Shape 4  Shape 5

| Shape | 1 | 2 | 3 | 4 | 5 |
|---|---|---|---|---|---|
| Number of squares | 1 | 5 | 13 | 25 | 41 |
| Number of matches | 4 | 16 | 36 | 64 | 100 |

The number of squares increases by 4, then 8, then 12 and then 16.
The difference between the squares increases by 4 each time.
The next difference will be 20.
Shape 6 will have $41 + 20$ or 61 squares.
The next difference will be 24.
Shape 7 will have $61 + 24$ or 85 squares.

**6** The number of matches increases by 12, then 20, then 28 and then 36.
The difference between the number of matches increases by 8 each time.
The next difference will be 44.
Shape 6 will need $100 + 44$ or 144 matches.
The next difference will be 52.
Shape 7 will need $144 + 52$ or 196 matches.

**7** Try each option:
'$4 \times$ shape number'
There would be 4 matches for Shape 1.
There would be 8 matches for Shape 2.
This is not the rule.

'$3 \times$ number of squares $+ 1$'
When there is 1 square there would be 4 matches.
When there are 5 squares there would be 16 matches.
When there are 13 squares there would be 40 matches.
This is not the rule.

'$2 \times$ number of squares $+ 2$'
When there is 1 square there would be 4 matches.
When there are 5 squares there would be 12 matches.
This is not the rule.

# YEAR 9 NUMERACY MINI TEST ANSWERS

'(2 × shape number)²'

There would be (2 × 1)² or 4 matches for Shape 1.

There would be (2 × 2)² or 16 matches for Shape 2.

There would be (2 × 3)² or 36 matches for Shape 3.

There would be (2 × 4)² or 64 matches for Shape 4.

There would be (2 × 5)² or 100 matches for Shape 5.

This is the rule.

The rule is (2 × shape number)².

**8** [Use the rule found in the previous question and try each option.]

There would be (2 × 9)² or 324 matches needed for Shape 9.

There would be (2 × 10)² or 400 matches needed for Shape 10.

There would be (2 × 11)² or 484 matches needed for Shape 11.

There would be (2 × 12)² or 576 matches needed for Shape 12.

The largest number shape that can be made with 500 matches is Shape 11.

**9** [The shaded area is the area of a large rectangle minus the area of a small rectangle.]

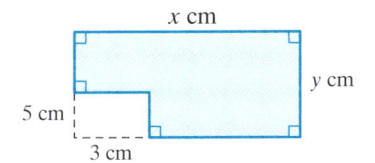

Area of large rectangle = length × width
= $x \times y$
= $xy$

Area of smaller rectangle = length × width
= 5 × 3
= 15

Shaded area = $(xy - 15)$ cm²

**10**

| $x$ | 1 | 2 | 3 | 4 | 5 |
|---|---|---|---|---|---|
| $y$ | 1 | 13 | 33 | 61 | 97 |

Try each option:

$y = x^2 + 1$

When $x = 1$,
$y = 1^2 + 1$
= 2

This is not the option.

$y = 2x^2 - 1$

When $x = 1$,
$y = 2 \times 1^2 - 1$
= 1

When $x = 2$,
$y = 2 \times 2^2 - 1$
= 7

This is not the option.

$y = 3x^2 - 2$

When $x = 1$,
$y = 3 \times 1^2 - 2$
= 1

When $x = 2$,
$y = 3 \times 2^2 - 2$
= 10

This is not the option.

$y = 4x^2 - 3$

When $x = 1$,
$y = 4 \times 1^2 - 3$
= 1

When $x = 2$,
$y = 4 \times 2^2 - 3$
= 13

When $x = 3$,
$y = 4 \times 3^2 - 3$
= 33

When $x = 4$,
$y = 4 \times 4^2 - 3$
= 61

When $x = 5$,
$y = 4 \times 5^2 - 3$
= 97

This is the option.

The rule is $y = 4x^2 - 3$.

**11** [If a line passes through a point the co-ordinates of that point must satisfy the equation of the line.]

The equation of the line is $y = 7 - 2x$.

Try each point:

At A, $x = 3$

When $x = 3$,
$y = 7 - 2 \times 3$
= 7 - 6
= 1 (not 4)

A does not lie on the line.

# YEAR 9 NUMERACY MINI TEST ANSWERS

At B, $x = 4$
When $x = 4$,
$y = 7 - 2 \times 4$
$= 7 - 8$
$= -1$
B does lie on the line.

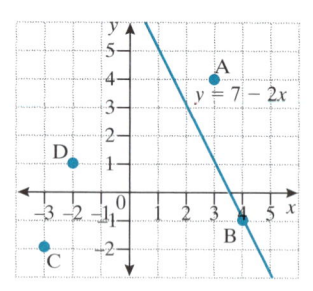

The point that lies on the line is B $(4, -1)$.

**12** 1, 4, 7, 10, 13, …

The numbers increase by 3 each time.
The first number is $3 \times 1 - 2$.
The second number is $3 \times 2 - 2$.
The third number is $3 \times 3 - 2$.
So, following this pattern,
the 27th number $= 3 \times 27 - 2$
$= 81 - 2$
$= 79$

**13** $3(2x - 1) + 5 + \boxed{?} = 10x + 2$

Now $3(2x - 1) + 5 = 6x - 3 + 5$
$= 6x + 2$

So the missing term is what must be added to $6x + 2$ to give $10x + 2$.

The missing term is $4x$.

**14** The line passes through $(1, 3)$ and $(7, 15)$.

The $y$-value in both points is 1 more than twice the $x$-value.

So that must be the equation of the line:
$y = 2x + 1$.

Considering the options, the only point with its $y$-value one more than twice its $x$-value is $(5, 11)$.

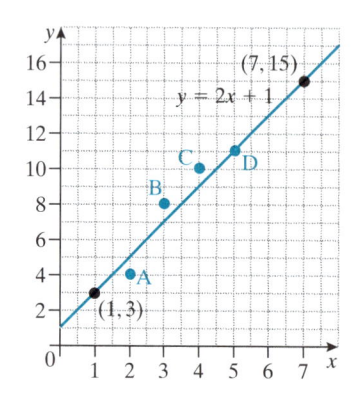

**15** $4 + x - x^2 = -x^2 + x + 4$
[4 and $x$ need to be added but $x^2$ needs to be subtracted.]

**16** $\frac{1}{2}, \frac{7}{12}, \frac{2}{3}, \frac{3}{4}, \frac{5}{6}, \ldots$

All the fractions have a common denominator of 12.
[Write the pattern using fractions whose denominator is 12.]
$\frac{6}{12}, \frac{7}{12}, \frac{8}{12}, \frac{9}{12}, \frac{10}{12}, \ldots$

The next number in the pattern will be $\frac{11}{12}$.

### Advanced level questions

**Mini Test 26:** Algebra—Substitution and Equations……………………………… Page 29

**1** D  **2** C  **3** D  **4** $m = 11$  **5** A  **6** 7 cm  **7** B
**8** 55  **9** C  **10** B  **11** A  **12** $x = -6$  **13** $n = 40$
**14** C  **15** 11.25  **16** D  **17** A  **18** 14

**1** When $x = -4$,
$3x - x^2 = 3 \times -4 - (-4)^2$
$= -12 - 16$
$= -28$

**2** If $a = 3$ and $b = -2$,
$2ab^2 = 2 \times 3 \times (-2)^2$
$= 2 \times 3 \times 4$
$= 24$

**3** $V = \frac{4}{3}\pi r^3$
When $r = 8$,
$V = \frac{4}{3} \times \pi \times 8^3$
$= 2144.6605\ldots$
$= 2145$ (nearest whole number)

The volume is closest to 2145 m³.

**4** $5(2m - 3) = 8m + 7$
[Remove the grouping symbols.]
$10m - 15 = 8m + 7$
[Add 15 to both sides.]
$10m = 8m + 22$
[Subtract $8m$ from both sides.]
$2m = 22$
[Divide both sides by 2.]
$m = 11$

# YEAR 9 NUMERACY MINI TEST ANSWERS

**5**  $y = 4 - 5x$
When $x = 1.2$,
$y = 4 - 5 \times 1.2$
$= 4 - 6$
$= -2$

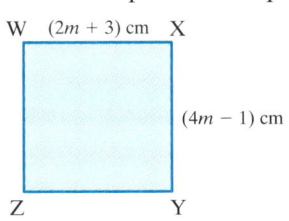

**6** The sides of a square are equal in length.

```
W  (2m + 3) cm  X



                (4m − 1) cm

Z               Y
```

So $4m - 1 = 2m + 3$
[Add 1 to both sides.]
$4m = 2m + 4$
[Subtract $2m$ from both sides.]
$2m = 4$
[Divide both sides by 2.]
$m = 2$
If $m = 2$,
$4m - 1 = 4 \times 2 - 1$
$= 8 - 1$
$= 7$
[And $2m + 3 = 2 \times 2 + 3 = 4 + 3 = 7$]
The length of each side is 7 cm.

**7** If $t = 6$,
$2t^2 - 3t = 2 \times 6^2 - 3 \times 6$
$= 2 \times 36 - 18$
$= 72 - 18$
$= 54$

**8** $P = 8n - 160$
When $P = 280$,
$280 = 8n - 160$
[Add 160 to both sides.]
$440 = 8n$
[Divide both sides by 8.]
$55 = n$
Kylie would need to sell 55 dolls to make a profit of $280.

**9** $\dfrac{m}{h^2} > 25$

Try each option:
When $m = 55$ and $h = 1.5$,
$\dfrac{m}{h^2} = \dfrac{55}{(1.5)^2}$
$= 24.44444..... (< 25)$

When $m = 60$ and $h = 1.6$,
$\dfrac{m}{h^2} = \dfrac{60}{(1.6)^2}$
$= 23.4375 (< 25)$
When $m = 75$ and $h = 1.7$,
$\dfrac{m}{h^2} = \dfrac{75}{(1.7)^2}$
$= 25.951557..... (> 25)$
When $m = 80$ and $h = 1.8$,
$\dfrac{m}{h^2} = \dfrac{80}{(1.8)^2}$
$= 24.691358..... (< 25)$
So, a person with weight 75 kg and height 1.7 m would be overweight.

**10** If $a = -1$,
$3 - 2a - a^2 = 3 - 2 \times -1 - (-1)^2$
$= 3 + 2 - 1$
$= 4$

**11** $c^2 = a^2 + b^2$
If $a = 8$ and $b = 15$,
$c^2 = 8^2 + 15^2$
$= 64 + 225$
$= 289$
$c = \sqrt{289}$ ($c > 0$)
$= 17$
[$c = -17$ would also be a valid answer, but it is not one of the options. (This formula is Pythagoras' theorem and is used to find the lengths of the sides of right-angled triangles which cannot be negative.)]

**12** $7x + 8 = 5x - 4$
[Subtract 8 from both sides.]
$7x = 5x - 12$
[Subtract $5x$ from both sides.]
$2x = -12$
[Divide both sides by 2.]
$x = -6$

**13** $C = \dfrac{360}{n}$

If $C = 9$,
$9 = \dfrac{360}{n}$
[Multiply both sides by $n$.]
$9n = 360$
[Divide both sides by 9.]
$n = 40$

# YEAR 9 NUMERACY MINI TEST ANSWERS

**14** $2x - 1 < 5$
[Add 1 to both sides.]
$\quad 2x < 6$
[Divide both sides by 2.]
$\quad x < 3$

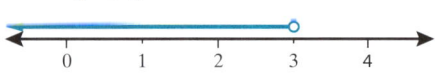

**15** $y = 5x^2$
When $x = 1.5$,
$y = 5 \times (1.5)^2$
$\quad = 5 \times 2.25$
$\quad = 11.25$

**16** $11 - 3x \geq 2$
Try each option:
If $x = -2$,
$11 - 3x = 11 - 3 \times -2$
$\quad\quad\quad = 11 + 6$
$\quad\quad\quad = 17 \;(> 2)$
This option does make the inequality true.
If $x = 0$,
$11 - 3x = 11 - 3 \times 0$
$\quad\quad\quad = 11 - 0$
$\quad\quad\quad = 11 \;(> 2)$
This option does make the inequality true.
If $x = 3$,
$11 - 3x = 11 - 3 \times 3$
$\quad\quad\quad = 11 - 9$
$\quad\quad\quad = 2 \;(= 2)$
This option does make the inequality true.
If $x = 6$,
$11 - 3x = 11 - 3 \times 6$
$\quad\quad\quad = 11 - 18$
$\quad\quad\quad = -7 \;(< 2)$
This option does not make the inequality true.
The value of $x$ that does not make the inequality true is $x = 6$.

**17** $C = \dfrac{nA}{n + 12}$
When $n = 4$ and $A = 20$,
$C = \dfrac{4 \times 20}{4 + 12}$
$\quad = \dfrac{80}{16}$
$\quad = 5$
The correct dose for a four-year-old child is 5 mL.

**18** $\dfrac{3}{8} > \dfrac{5}{x}$
[Multiply both sides by $8x$.]
$3x > 40$
[Divide both sides by 3,]
$x > 13.3333....$
So the smallest possible value of $x$ is 14.

### Advanced level questions

**Mini Test 27:** Angles ............................................... Page 30

**1** 45  **2** B  **3** D  **4** 120°  **5** B  **6** 75  **7** A  **8** 115
**9** 105°  **10** 60  **11** 150°  **12** C  **13** D  **14** A
**15** 60  **16** D

**1** Angle sum of an octagon $= (8 - 2) \times 180°$
$\quad\quad\quad\quad\quad\quad\quad\quad\quad\quad = 6 \times 180°$
$\quad\quad\quad\quad\quad\quad\quad\quad\quad\quad = 1080°$
Each angle of a regular octagon $= 1080° \div 8$
$\quad\quad\quad\quad\quad\quad\quad\quad\quad\quad\quad\quad\quad = 135°$
The quadrilateral formed inside the octagon is a rectangle.
Each angle of a rectangle $= 90°$
So $x = 135 - 90$
$\quad\quad = 45$

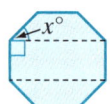

**2** Try each option:
Angle sum of a pentagon $= (5 - 2) \times 180°$
$\quad\quad\quad\quad\quad\quad\quad\quad\quad\quad = 3 \times 180°$
$\quad\quad\quad\quad\quad\quad\quad\quad\quad\quad = 540°$
If there were two angles of 90° and three of 135°, angle sum $= 2 \times 90° + 3 \times 135°$
$\quad\quad\quad\quad\quad\quad\quad\quad\quad\quad = 180° + 405°$
$\quad\quad\quad\quad\quad\quad\quad\quad\quad\quad = 585°$
So the polygon is not a pentagon.
Angle sum of a hexagon $= (6 - 2) \times 180°$
$\quad\quad\quad\quad\quad\quad\quad\quad\quad\quad = 4 \times 180°$
$\quad\quad\quad\quad\quad\quad\quad\quad\quad\quad = 720°$
If there were two angles of 90° and four of 135°, angle sum $= 2 \times 90° + 4 \times 135°$
$\quad\quad\quad\quad\quad\quad\quad\quad\quad\quad = 180° + 540°$
$\quad\quad\quad\quad\quad\quad\quad\quad\quad\quad = 720°$
So the polygon is a hexagon.

# YEAR 9 NUMERACY MINI TEST ANSWERS

**3** Draw a line through the right angle, parallel to both *l* and *m*.

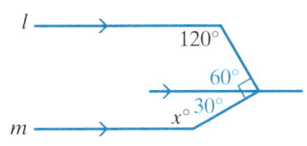

The angle above the line, co-interior to the angle of 120° must be 60°.
[Co-interior angles, formed by parallel lines, add to 180°.]
So the angle below the line is 90° − 60° or 30°.
Now $x + 30 = 180$ (co-interior angles, parallel lines)
$x = 180 − 30$
$= 150$

**4** The polygon has five angles so it is a pentagon.
Angle sum of a pentagon $= (5 − 2) × 180°$
$= 3 × 180°$
$= 540°$

Now there are three angles of 100°.
Sum of 3 angles $= 3 × 100°$
$= 300°$
Sum of remaining angles $= 540° − 300°$
$= 240°$
But those two angles are equal.
Each angle $= 240° ÷ 2$
$= 120°$

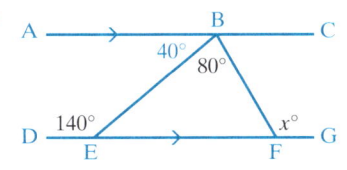

**5** ∠ABE + ∠BED = 180° (co-interior angles, parallel lines)
So ∠ABE = 40°
∠ABF = 40° + 80°
= 120°
∠ABF = ∠BFG (alternate angles, parallel lines)
So $x = 120$

[If you didn't know that the lines were parallel you could still find the answer. The angle beside the one of 140° on the straight line must be 40° and then, because it is the exterior angle of the triangle, $x = 40 + 80$.]

**6** Angle sum of an octagon $= (8 − 2) × 180°$
$= 6 × 180°$
$= 1080°$
Each angle of a regular octagon $= 1080° ÷ 8$
$= 135°$
Each angle of an equilateral triangle is 60°.
Each angle of a square is 90°.

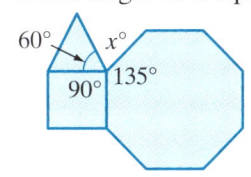

Angles at a point add to 360°.
So $x + 135 + 90 + 60 = 360$
$x + 285 = 360$
$x = 360 − 285$
$x = 75$

**7** Draw a line through the unknown angle, parallel to both *m* and *n*.

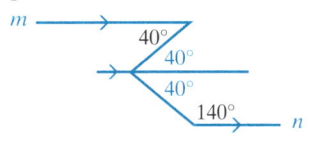

Because alternate angles formed by parallel lines are equal, the top part of the unknown angle is 40°.
Because co-interior angles formed by parallel lines add to 180°, the bottom part of the unknown angle is 40°.
So $x = 40 + 40$
$= 80$

**8** The shape is a pentagon.
Angle sum of a pentagon $= (5 − 2) × 180°$
$= 3 × 180°$
$= 540°$

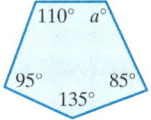

So $a + 85 + 135 + 95 + 110 = 540$
$a + 425 = 540$
$a = 540 − 425$
$= 115$

**9** ∠BAC + ∠ABC + ∠BCA = 180° (angle sum of a triangle)
Now ∠ABC = 30°,
so ∠BAC + ∠BCA = 150°
But ∠BAC = ∠BCA (angles opposite equal sides in an isosceles triangle)

# YEAR 9 NUMERACY MINI TEST ANSWERS

So ∠BCA = 150° ÷ 2
= 75°

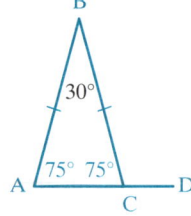

∠BCD + ∠BCA = 180° (angles in a straight line)

So ∠BCD = 180° − 75°
= 105°

**10** Because co-interior angles formed by parallel lines add to 180°, the angle on the left at the top is 55°, and the angle on the right is 65°.

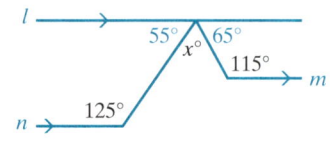

Now angles in a straight line add to 180°.
So $x + 55 + 65 = 180$
$x + 120 = 180$
$x = 180 − 120$
$= 60$

**11** A clock face is divided into 12 parts.
So each part is 360° ÷ 12 = 30°

There are five parts in the obtuse angle between the hands at seven o'clock.

Angle = 5 × 30°
= 150°

**12** Consider the options:

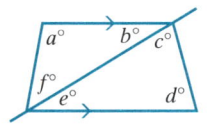

$a + b + f = 180$ (angle sum of a triangle)
$a + f + e = 180$ (co-interior angles, parallel lines)
$a + b + c$ is not necessarily equal to 180.
$b + c + d = 180$ (co-interior angles, parallel lines)

The expression that is not necessarily equal to 180 is $a + b + c$.

[If the other pair of sides of the trapezium were parallel (i.e. the trapezium was in fact a parallelogram) then $a + b + c$ would equal 180. If those sides are not parallel, then $a + b + c$ would not equal 180.]

**13** Consider the options.
If the polygon had 6 sides then:
angle sum = (6 − 2) × 180°
= 4 × 180°
= 720°

Each angle = 720° ÷ 6
= 120°

So the polygon does not have 6 sides.
If the polygon had 7 sides then:
angle sum = (7 − 2) × 180°
= 5 × 180°
= 900°

Each angle = 900° ÷ 7
= 128.57…°

So the polygon does not have 7 sides.
If the polygon had 8 sides then:
angle sum = (8 − 2) × 180°
= 6 × 180°
= 1080°

Each angle = 1080° ÷ 8
= 135°

So the polygon does not have 8 sides.
If the polygon had 9 sides then:
angle sum = (9 − 2) × 180°
= 7 × 180°
= 1260°

Each angle = 1260° ÷ 9
= 140°

So the polygon does have 9 sides.

**14** ∠ABD = ∠BAD (opposite equal sides, isosceles triangle)

So ∠ABD = 50°
∠ABC + ∠BAD = 180° (co-interior angles, parallel lines)

So ∠ABC = 130°
∠CBD = 130° − 50°
= 80°

∠CDB = ∠CBD (angles opposite equal sides, isosceles triangle)

So ∠CDB = 80°

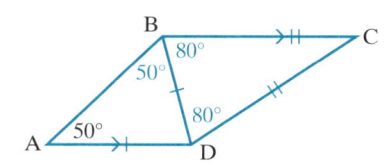

# YEAR 9 NUMERACY MINI TEST ANSWERS

∠CBD + ∠CDB + ∠BCD = 180° (angle sum of a triangle)
80° + 80° + ∠BCD = 180°
∠BCD = 180° − 160°
= 20°

**15** Draw a line through the unknown angle, parallel to both *l* and *m*.

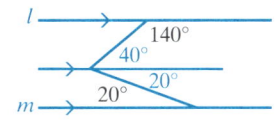

Because co-interior angles formed by parallel lines add to 180°, the top part of the unknown angle is 40°.

Because alternate angles formed by parallel lines are equal, the bottom part of the unknown angle is 20°.

So x = 40 + 20
= 60

**16** Angle sum of a hexagon = (6 − 2) × 180°
= 4 × 180°
= 720°

Each angle = 720° ÷ 6
= 120°

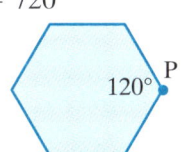

Now angles at a point add to 360°.
Remaining angle = 360° − 120°
= 240°

Now try the options.
Two regular hexagons:
2 × 120° = 240°
So two regular hexagons could fill the space.
Four equilateral triangles:
Each angle of an equilateral triangle is 60°.
4 × 60° = 240°
So four equilateral triangles could fill the space.
Two squares and an equilateral triangle:
Each angle of a square is 90°.
2 × 90° + 60° = 180° + 60°
= 240°
So two squares and an equilateral triangle could fill the space.
One regular octagon and one square:
Angle sum of an octagon = (8 − 2) × 180°
= 6 × 180°
= 1080°

Each angle of a regular octagon = 1080° ÷ 8
= 135°
135° + 90° = 225°
So a regular octagon and a square will not fill the space.

### Advanced level questions

**Mini Test 28:** Measurement .......... Page 31

**1** 500 km  **2** B  **3** C  **4** A  **5** 36 m²  **6** 1650 mL
**7** C  **8** D  **9** B  **10** 20  **11** 288 m²  **12** 42 m
**13** A  **14** 318 km  **15** D

**1** Amount of petrol = (54 ÷ 1.35) L
= 40 L
Distance travelled = (40 ÷ 8) × 100 km
= 500 km

**2** Circumference of circle = π × D
= π × 5 m
= 15.70796… m

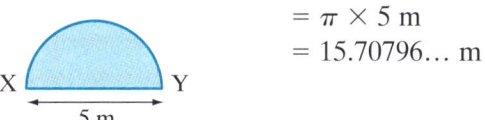

Curved distance from X to Y is half the circumference of a circle.
Distance = (15.7096… ÷ 2) m
= 7.85398… m
Of the options, the closest distance is 7.9 metres.

**3** Volume of cube = (length of side)³
Length of side = $\sqrt[3]{1728}$ cm
= 12 cm
Area of each face = (12 × 12) cm²
= 144 cm²
There are six faces.
Total area of all faces = 6 × 144 cm²
= 864 cm²

**4** Time taken = (336 ÷ 64) h
= 5.25 h
= $5\frac{1}{4}$ h
= 5 h 15 min
5 hours after 8:10 am is 1:10 pm.
15 minutes after 1:10 pm is 1:25 pm.
The journey finished at 1:25 pm.

129

# YEAR 9 NUMERACY MINI TEST ANSWERS

**5** Area of 2 triangular faces
$= 2 \times (\frac{1}{2} \times \text{base} \times \text{height})$
$= (2 \times \frac{1}{2} \times 3 \times 4)$ m²
$= 12$ m²

Area of 3 rectangular faces
$= (3 \times 2 + 4 \times 2 + 5 \times 2)$ m²
$= 24$ m²

Total area $= (12 + 24)$ m²
$= 36$ m²

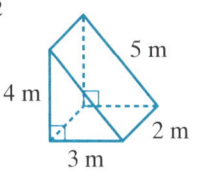

**6** The amount of juice in the jug is 2.4 litres or 2400 mL.

Juice in six glasses $= 6 \times 125$ mL
$= 750$ mL

Amount remaining $= (2400 - 750)$ mL
$= 1650$ mL

**7** When it is 8:15 am Friday in Melbourne, it is 10:15 pm Thursday in London.

London is 10 hours behind Melbourne time.

When it is 2:30 pm Thursday in Melbourne, it is 11:30 pm Wednesday in New York.

New York is 15 hours behind Melbourne time.
So New York is 5 hours behind London time.
London is 5 hours ahead of New York time.
When it is 9 am Monday in New York it will be 2 pm Monday in London.

**8** First prism has volume 12 m³.

The length of the second prism is twice that of the first.

The width of the second prism is twice that of the first.

The height of the second prism is twice that of the first.

So the number of times that the volume is greater $= 2 \times 2 \times 2$
$= 8$

The volume of the second prism $= 8 \times 12$ m³
$= 96$ m³

**9** 1 ML = 1 000 000 L
1 kL = 1000 L
So 1 ML = 1000 kL
18 ML = 18 000 kL

**10** 25 t = 25 000 kg
Number of containers $= 25\,000 \div 1200$
$= 20.8333....$

So the truck can carry at most 20 of the containers.

[The answer is closer to 21, but 21 containers would exceed the maximum load limit.]

**11** Perimeter = 72 m
Length + width $= (72 \div 2)$ m
$= 36$ m
Length $= (36 - 12)$ m
$= 24$ m

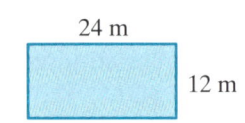

Area = length × width
$= (24 \times 12)$ m²
$= 288$ m²

**12** William's height is $\frac{1.8}{1.5}$ or 1.2 times the length of the shadow.

The height of the tree will also be 1.2 times the length of its shadow.

Height of tree $= 1.2 \times 35$ m
$= 42$ m

**13** The area of the shaded rectangle is half the area of the trapezium.

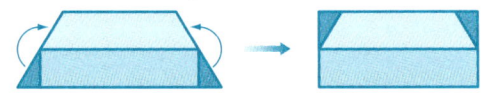

Area of rectangle $= (168 \div 2)$ m²
$= 84$ m²

**14** Distance from Brisbane to Rockhampton
$= (1114 - 398)$ km
$= 716$ km

So the distance from Bundaberg to Mackay is also 716 km.

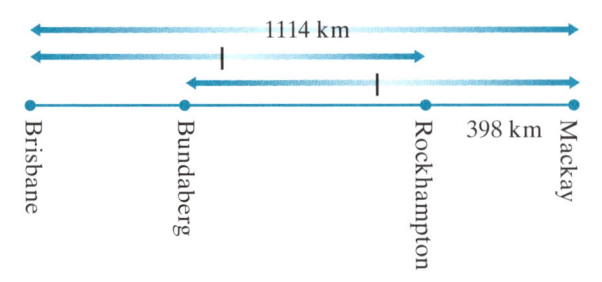

The distance from Bundaberg to Rockhampton $= (716 - 398)$ km
$= 318$ km

# YEAR 9 NUMERACY MINI TEST ANSWERS

**15** Total distance is 250 km in $3\frac{1}{2}$ hours.

Darren's driving time = (130 ÷ 65) h
= 2 h

Remaining distance = (250 − 130) km
= 120 km

Remaining time = $(3\frac{1}{2} - 2)$ h
= $1\frac{1}{2}$ h

Dane's average speed = $(120 \div 1\frac{1}{2})$ km/h
= 80 km/h

## Advanced level questions

**Mini Test 29:** Plane Figures and Solids..................... Page 32

**1** 1.44 m² **2** D **3** D **4** 6 cm **5** A **6** 116 cm
**7** C **8** B **9** 27 cm³ **10** 14 cm² **11** B **12** C

**1** From the diagram you can see that the rectangle has the same width as the small square, so it is 10 cm wide. It is twice as long as it is wide so the rectangle is 20 cm long. The large square is the same length as the rectangle, so it is 20 cm by 20 cm.

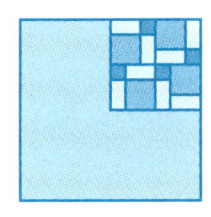

The tiling pattern shown is 60 cm long and 60 cm wide.

So the tabletop is 120 cm or 1.2 metres long and 1.2 metres wide.

Area = (1.2 × 1.2) m²
= 1.44 m²

**2** Consider the options:

If both pairs of opposite sides of a quadrilateral are equal, the quadrilateral must be a parallelogram.

If a pair of opposite sides of a quadrilateral is equal and parallel, the quadrilateral must be a parallelogram.

If all sides of a quadrilateral are equal, it must be a parallelogram.
[It must be a rhombus, but a rhombus is a special parallelogram.]

A quadrilateral can have diagonals that are equal and not be a parallelogram.
[The diagonals of a parallelogram are not usually equal.]

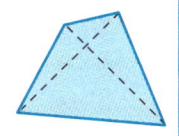

The property that does not mean that a quadrilateral must be a parallelogram is both diagonals being equal.

**3** The square has 4 axes of symmetry.

The regular hexagon has 6 axes of symmetry.

The dodecagon has 4 axes of symmetry.

The regular heptagon has 7 axes of symmetry.

The shape that has the most axes of symmetry is the regular heptagon.

**4** Volume = length × width × height
So 12 × 8 × h = 576
96 × h = 576
h = 576 ÷ 96
= 6

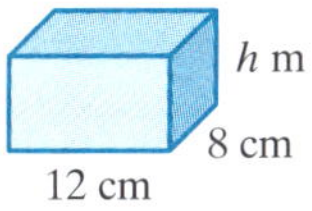

The height of the prism is 6 cm.

**5** Jai can see 16 faces at the front, so there will also be 16 faces at the back.

There are 10 faces on the right side, so there will be 10 on the left side.

There are 8 faces at the top.

Total visible faces = 2 × 16 + 2 × 10 + 8
= 60

Total faces on 32 cubes = 32 × 6
= 192

Faces that cannot be seen = 192 − 60
= 132

# YEAR 9 NUMERACY MINI TEST ANSWERS

**6** Horizontal ribbon:
length = (2 × 20 + 2 × 15) cm
= 70 cm
Second ribbon:
length = (2 × 15 + 2 × 8) cm
= 46 cm
Total length = (70 + 46) cm
= 116 cm

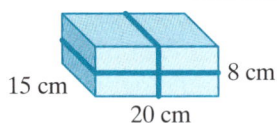

**7** PQTS is a trapezium.
[A trapezium is a quadrilateral with one pair of sides parallel. Sides PS and QT are parallel because they were (part of) the sides of a square.]

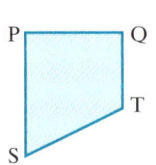

**8** 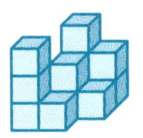 The view from the top is

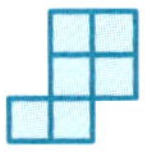

The view from the back is

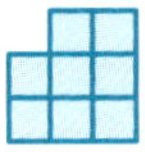

The view from the right side, or from the left side, is

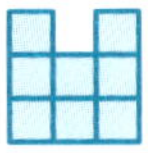

The view that cannot be seen is

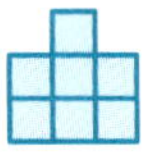

**9** The cube has 12 edges.
All the edges of a cube are equal. 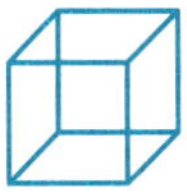
Each edge = (36 ÷ 12) cm
= 3 cm
Volume = side$^3$
= 3$^3$ cm$^3$
= 27 cm$^3$

**10** The area of triangle PRT is half the area of the rectangle. So the area of triangle PQR plus the area of triangle TRS will equal 32 cm$^2$. 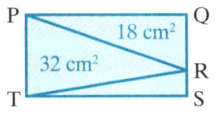
Area of triangle TRS = (32 − 18) cm$^2$
= 14 cm$^2$

**11** Together the object and its image have six sides.
So the shape is a hexagon.

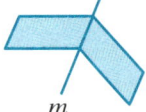

**12** 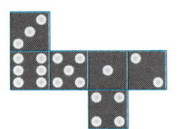 The cube that cannot be made from this net is

[If one is on the top face and five on the right side, three will be on the front face. But, the dots on the three are on the wrong diagonal compared with the net.]

### Advanced level questions

**Mini Test 30:** Chance and Data .................. Page 33

**1** D **2** C **3** D **4** B **5** 108° **6** D **7** C **8** A
**9** B **10** B **11** A **12** 1.73 m

**1** Mean of 8 numbers is 56.
Sum of 8 numbers = 8 × 56
= 448
The mean of 7 numbers is 54.
Sum of 7 numbers = 7 × 54
= 378
Difference = 448 − 378
= 70
The number left out was 70.

**2** There are 8 different possibilities:
HHH, HHT, HTH, HTT, THH, THT, TTH, TTT.
Three of the possibilities involve two heads and a tail.
Probability of 2 heads and 1 tail = $\frac{3}{8}$

**3**

| Week | 1 | 2 | 3 | 4 | 5 | 6 | 7 |
|---|---|---|---|---|---|---|---|
| Mark | 18 | 17 | 19 | 16 | 17 | 15 | 17 |

In order, from lowest to highest, the scores are: 15, 16, 17, 17, 17, 18, 19.
There are more scores of 17 than any other so the mode is 17.
The middle score is the fourth one of the seven. So the median is 17.
The sum of the scores
= 15 + 16 + 3 × 17 + 18 + 19
= 119
Mean = 119 ÷ 7
= 17
So the mean, mode and median are all equal.

# YEAR 9 NUMERACY MINI TEST ANSWERS

**4** Sum of the ages of the juniors = 25 × 15
= 375
Sum of the ages of the seniors = 15 × 31
= 465
Total of all the ages = 375 + 465
= 840
Total number of members = 25 + 15
= 40
Average age of the members = 840 ÷ 40
= 21

**5**

| Colour | Number of rosebushes |
|---|---|
| Red | 18 |
| Orange | 9 |
| Yellow | 7 |
| White | 12 |
| Pink | 14 |

Total rosebushes = 18 + 9 + 7 + 12 + 14
= 60

Fraction of red rosebushes = $\frac{18}{60}$
= $\frac{3}{10}$

Total degrees in a sector graph = 360°
Degrees needed for red rosebushes
= $\frac{3}{10}$ × 360°
= 108°

**6**

|  | Lulu said true | Lulu said false |
|---|---|---|
| Was True | 36 | 16 |
| Was False | 21 | 27 |

Of the questions that were true, Lulu said 36 were true. So she got 36 of the true questions correct.

Of the questions that were false, Lulu said 27 were false. So she got 27 of the false questions correct.

Total correct questions = 36 + 27
= 63

**7** There are 36 possible outcomes.
There are 3 different ways of scoring 4:
1 + 3, 2 + 2 and 3 + 1.
So the probability of scoring 4 = $\frac{3}{36}$
= $\frac{1}{12}$

**8** The average of 9 tests is 78.
Total marks from 9 tests = 9 × 78
= 702

In order to have an average of 80 after 10 tests:
Total marks from 10 tests = 10 × 80
= 800
Extra marks needed = 800 − 702
= 98
Joe would need to score 98% in his tenth test.

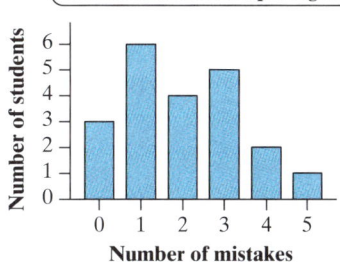

**9** Mistakes made in a spelling test

More students made 1 mistake than any other number of mistakes so the mode is 1.

Total number of students
= 3 + 6 + 4 + 5 + 2 + 1
= 21

So, there will be 21 scores altogether.

The middle score will be the 11th score.
It will be 2.

So the median is 2.
[If written out in order they would be 0, 0, 0, 1, 1, 1, 1, 1, 1, 2, 2, 2, 2, 3, …]

Total mistakes made
= 6 × 1 + 4 × 2 + 5 × 3 + 2 × 4 + 1 × 5
= 42

Mean = 42 ÷ 21
= 2

So the median and mean are both 2 but the mode is 1.
So mode ≠ median = mean.

**10** 22, 22, 22, 23, 23, 24, 25
There are 7 scores.
The sum of the scores
= 3 × 22 + 2 × 23 + 24 + 25
= 161
Mean = 161 ÷ 7
= 23
So, because the mean is 23 a score of 23 can be left out and the mean will not change.

**11** 1, 1, 2, 3, 3, 3, 3, 4, 4, 4, 5
There are 11 scores.
The median is the sixth score.
Median = 3

# YEAR 9 NUMERACY MINI TEST ANSWERS

There are more 3s than any other number.
Mode = 3
The sum of the scores
$= 2 \times 1 + 2 + 4 \times 3 + 3 \times 4 + 5$
$= 33$
Mean $= 33 \div 11$
$= 3$
Now if one score of 3 changes to 4:
1, 1, 2, 3, 3, 3, 4, 4, 4, 4, 5
The median is still the sixth score. It is still 3.
The mode changes to 4.
The sum of the scores
$= 2 \times 1 + 2 + 3 \times 3 + 4 \times 4 + 5$
$= 34$
Mean $= 34 \div 11$
$= 3.090909\ldots$
So the mean and mode increase but the median stays the same.
[It wasn't necessary to calculate the mean; if one score is increased the mean must also increase.]

**12** The average height of 6 players is 1.75 m.
The sum of the 6 heights $= 6 \times 1.75$ m
$= 10.5$ m
The sum of the 7 heights $= (10.5 + 1.61)$ m
$= 12.11$ m
Average height of 7 players $= (12.11 \div 7)$ m
$= 1.73$ m

### Advanced level questions

**Mini Test 31:** Mixed Questions.................... Page 34

**1** D  **2** A  **3** C  **4** B  **5** C  **6** A  **7** A  **8** D  **9** D
**10** C  **11** 12 L  **12** 6%  **13** D  **14** 0.3  **15** B  **16** B

**1** Divide the rectangle into 12 parts.
[The top has been divided in half and the bottom in thirds, so first divide into sixths, because 6 is the lowest common multiple of 2 and 3.]
7 of the parts are shaded.
The fraction of the rectangle that is shaded is $\frac{7}{12}$.

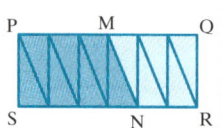

**2** If $a = -1$,
$5a - 2a^2 = 5 \times -1 - 2 \times (-1)^2$
$= -5 - 2 \times 1$
$= -5 - 2$
$= -7$

**3** $3^2 \times 9^3 = 3 \times 3 \times 9 \times 9 \times 9$
But $3 \times 3 = 9$
So $3^2 \times 9^3 = 9 \times 9 \times 9 \times 9$
[It is also $3 \times 3 \times 3 \times 3 \times 3 \times 3 \times 3 \times 3$ but that is not one of the options.]

**4** Write each list with a common denominator.
$\frac{1}{3}, \frac{2}{5}, \frac{7}{15}$
The common denominator is 15.
$\frac{1}{3} = \frac{5}{15}$
$\frac{2}{5} = \frac{6}{15}$
So $\frac{1}{3}, \frac{2}{5}, \frac{7}{15}$ is in ascending order.

$\frac{2}{3}, \frac{3}{4}, \frac{7}{12}$
The common denominator is 12.
$\frac{2}{3} = \frac{8}{12}$
$\frac{3}{4} = \frac{9}{12}$
So $\frac{2}{3}, \frac{3}{4}, \frac{7}{12}$ is not in ascending order.

The fractions that are not in order from lowest to highest are $\frac{2}{3}, \frac{3}{4}, \frac{7}{12}$.

**5** Co-interior angles formed by parallel lines add to 180°.
So the angle co-interior to that of 140° is 40° and the angle co-interior to that of 100° is 80°.

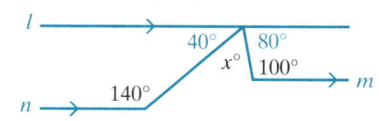

Now, angles in a straight line add to 180°.
So $x + 40 + 80 = 180$
$x + 120 = 180$
$x = 180 - 120$
$= 60$

**6** $y = 2x + 7$
When $x = -1$,
$y = 2 \times -1 + 7$
$= -2 + 7$
$= 5$
So P lies on the line.

# YEAR 9 NUMERACY MINI TEST ANSWERS

When $x = -4$,
$y = 2 \times -4 + 7$
$\quad = -8 + 7$
$\quad = -1$
So Q lies on the line.
P and Q both lie on the line.

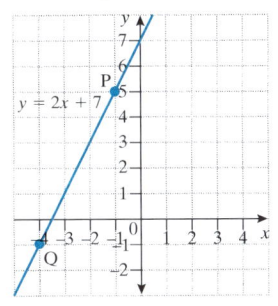

**7** 2, 2, 2, 2, 3, 4, 4, 5
Mode = 2
It will remain 2 if 3 is left out.
Range = 5 − 2
$\quad\quad\;\; = 3$
It will still be 3 if 3 is left out.
Sum of scores = $4 \times 2 + 3 + 2 \times 4 + 5$
$\quad\quad\quad\quad\quad\;\; = 24$
Mean = $24 \div 8$
$\quad\quad\;\, = 3$
It will still be 3 if 3 is left out.
Median = $\dfrac{2 + 3}{2}$
$\quad\quad\;\;\, = 2\dfrac{1}{2}$
It will change to 2 if 3 is left out.
The median will change if 3 is left out of the scores.

**8** For every 2 new books there were 3 old ones.
So 2 out of every 5 books were new.
Now $600 \div 5 = 120$
$2 \times 120 = 240$
So 240 books were new.
$3 \times 120 = 360$
So 360 books were old.
30 new books were sold.
Number of new books = 240 − 30
$\quad\quad\quad\quad\quad\quad\quad\;\; = 210$
10 old books were sold.
Number of old books = 360 − 10
$\quad\quad\quad\quad\quad\quad\quad\; = 350$
Ratio of new to old books = 210 to 350
$\quad\quad\quad\quad\quad\quad\quad\quad\quad\;\; = 21$ to $35$
$\quad\quad\quad\quad\quad\quad\quad\quad\quad\;\; = 3$ to $5$

**9** $4t^2 - 3t + 5t + t^2 = (4t^2 + t^2) - 3t + 5t$
$\quad\quad\quad\quad\quad\quad\quad\quad\;\; = 5t^2 + 2t$

**10** There are 8 different arrangements of three children in a family.
There are 3 different arrangements of 1 girl and 2 boys: girl, boy, boy; boy, girl, boy and boy, boy, girl.
Probability of 1 girl and 2 boys = $\dfrac{3}{8}$

**11** Distance travelled
$= (2\dfrac{1}{2} \times 60)$ km
$= (2 \times 60 + \dfrac{1}{2}$ of 60) km
$= (120 + 30)$ km
$= 150$ km
Petrol used = 8 L for 100 km
$\quad\quad\quad\quad\;\; = 4$ L for 50 km
Fuel used = 12 L for 150 km
So 12 litres of fuel were used.

**12** Percentage that is first-year students
$= 40\%$
Percentage that is first-year law students
$= 30\%$ of $40\%$
$= \dfrac{30}{100} \times 40\%$
$= 12\%$
Percentage that is male first-year law students
$= \dfrac{1}{2}$ of $12\%$
$= 6\%$

**13** Five different faces can be seen.

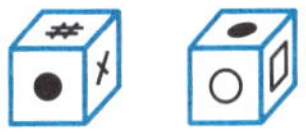

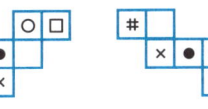

The face with the dot can be seen in both views. The face that cannot be seen in either view is opposite the dot.
So the blank face must be opposite the dot.
So these cannot be the net because the blank face is not opposite the dot.
This cannot be the net because if the cross is to the right of the dot the hashed face must be on the top but here it would be on the bottom. 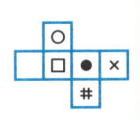
The correct net is

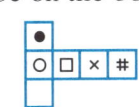

# YEAR 9 NUMERACY MINI TEST ANSWERS

**14** $0.3 \times 0.3 = 0.09$
So $\sqrt{0.09} = 0.3$

**15** $\dfrac{2}{5} > \dfrac{a}{b}$

[Multiply both sides by 5b.]
$2b > 5a$
Now try each option:
$a = 1$ and $b = 2$
$2 \times 2 > 5 \times 1$ ?
$\quad 4 > 5$ ✗
This option is not correct.
$a = 3$ and $b = 8$
$2 \times 8 > 5 \times 3$ ?
$\quad 16 > 15$ ✓
This option is correct.
The values of $a$ and $b$ that make the inequality true are $a = 3$ and $b = 8$.

**16** [The length and width are in metres but the depth is in centimetres. Change the depth to metres.]
25 cm = 0.25 m
Volume = $(2.5 \times 2 \times 0.25)$ m³
$\quad\quad\quad = (5 \times 0.25)$ m³
$\quad\quad\quad = 1.25$ m³
Capacity = $1.25 \times 1000$ L
$\quad\quad\quad = 1250$ L

## Advanced level questions

**Mini Test 32:** Mixed Questions ............. Page 35

**1** 4.5 min  **2** 20  **3** C  **4** 276 m²  **5** C  **6** D  **7** B
**8** 44%  **9** A  **10** 4  **11** 1.75 m  **12** 7  **13** C
**14** A  **15** D  **16** B

**1** Distance = 42 km
Time = 3 h 9 min
$\quad\quad = (3 \times 60 + 9)$ min
$\quad\quad = 189$ min
Time per kilometre = $(189 \div 42)$ min
$\quad\quad\quad\quad\quad\quad\quad = 4\dfrac{1}{2}$ min

**2** The sector graph is broken up into 16 parts.
Now $64 \div 16 = 4$
So each part represents 4 people.
The sector for 2 cars is 5 parts.

Number of people = $5 \times 4$
$\quad\quad\quad\quad\quad\quad = 20$

**3** The mean of 4 numbers is 9.
Sum of the numbers = $4 \times 9$
$\quad\quad\quad\quad\quad\quad\quad\quad = 36$
Now $3 + 15 + 7 = 25$
So $x = 36 - 25$
$\quad\quad = 11$

**4** $a = 16, b = 30$ and $h = 12$
$A = \dfrac{h}{2}(a + b)$
$\quad = \dfrac{12}{2}(16 + 30)$
$\quad = 6 \times 46$
$\quad = 276$
The area of the trapezium is 276 m².

**5** Alternate angles formed by parallel lines are equal.

Angles at a point add to 360°.
So $x + 117 + 128 = 360$
$\quad\quad x + 245 = 360$
$\quad\quad\quad\quad x = 360 - 245$
$\quad\quad\quad\quad\quad = 115$

**6** The area of the outer rectangle = $x$ m $\times y$ m
$\quad\quad\quad\quad\quad\quad\quad\quad\quad\quad\quad\quad = xy$ m²
The area of the inner rectangle = 12 m $\times$ 5 m
$\quad\quad\quad\quad\quad\quad\quad\quad\quad\quad\quad\quad = 60$ m²
So the paved area = $(xy - 60)$ m²

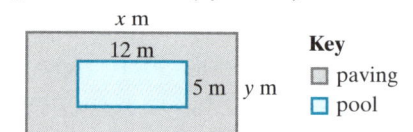

**Key**
▨ paving
☐ pool

**7** When $n = -3$,
$2n^2 - 5n + 3 = 2 \times (-3)^2 - 5 \times (-3) + 3$
$\quad\quad\quad\quad\quad\quad = 2 \times 9 + 15 + 3$
$\quad\quad\quad\quad\quad\quad = 18 + 15 + 3$
$\quad\quad\quad\quad\quad\quad = 36$

**8** Of the 28 students in 7C, there are 3 boys for every 4 girls.
So 3 out of 7 students are boys.
Number of boys in 7C = $\dfrac{3}{7}$ of 28
$\quad\quad\quad\quad\quad\quad\quad\quad\quad = 12$

# YEAR 9 NUMERACY MINI TEST ANSWERS

Of the 22 students in 7H, there are 5 boys for every 6 girls.
So 5 out of 11 students are boys.
Number of boys in 7H $= \dfrac{5}{11}$ of 22
$\qquad\qquad\qquad\qquad\ = 10$

Total boys in Year 7 $= 12 + 10$
$\qquad\qquad\qquad\quad\ = 22$

Total students in Year 7 $= 28 + 22$
$\qquad\qquad\qquad\qquad\quad = 50$

Percentage of boys $= \dfrac{22}{50} \times 100\%$
$\qquad\qquad\qquad\quad = 44\%$

**9** The radius is 9 metres. 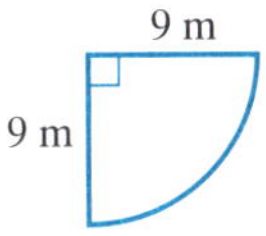
The diameter is 18 metres.
Length of arc $= \dfrac{1}{4} \times \pi \times 18$ m
$\qquad\qquad\ \ = 14.137...$ m

Length of concrete strip
$= (14.137... + 9 + 9)$ m
$= 32.137...$ m

Of the options, the closest to the length of the strip is 32 metres.

**10** $5(3x + 1) - 7x + \boxed{\phantom{0}} = 8x + 9$
Now $5(3x + 1) - 7x = 15x + 5 - 7x$
$\qquad\qquad\qquad\qquad\ = 8x + 5$
$8x + 5 + 4 = 8x + 9$
So the missing term is 4.

**11** [The two triangles are similar so the sides are in proportion.]
$\dfrac{h}{7} = \dfrac{1}{4}$
$h = \dfrac{1}{4} \times 7$
$\ \ = 1\dfrac{3}{4}$
$\ \ = 1.75$

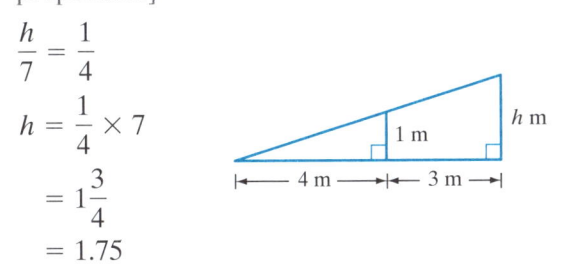

The ramp is 1.75 metres high at its highest point.

**12** $1750 = 10 \times 175$
Now $10 = 2 \times 5$ and $175 = 5 \times 35$
So $1750 = 2 \times 5 \times 5 \times 35$
$\qquad\quad = 2 \times 5 \times 5 \times 5 \times 7$

The highest prime factor of 1750 is 7.

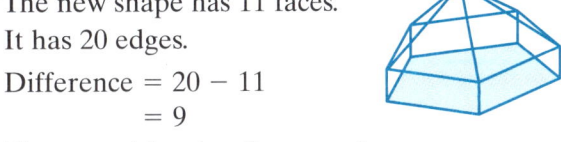

**13** The new shape has 11 faces.
It has 20 edges.
Difference $= 20 - 11$
$\qquad\qquad = 9$
The new object has 9 more edges than faces.

**14** There are 9 possible outcomes, each of which is equally likely to occur.
$[1 + 1, 1 + 2, 1 + 3, 2 + 1, 2 + 2, 2 + 3,$
$3 + 1, 3 + 2, 3 + 3]$
The ways to get a result of 4 are
$1 + 3, 2 + 2$ and $3 + 1$. 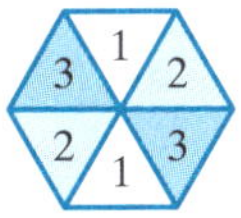
There are 3 ways to get a result of 4.
Probability of 4 $= \dfrac{3}{9}$
$\qquad\qquad\qquad = \dfrac{1}{3}$

**15** $\dfrac{1}{15}, \dfrac{3}{5}, 1\dfrac{2}{15}, 1\dfrac{2}{3}$

$\dfrac{3}{5} - \dfrac{1}{15} = \dfrac{8}{15}$

$1\dfrac{2}{15} - \dfrac{3}{5} = \dfrac{8}{15}$

$1\dfrac{2}{3} - 1\dfrac{2}{15} = \dfrac{8}{15}$

So the numbers are increasing by $\dfrac{8}{15}$ each time.

The next number $= 1\dfrac{2}{3} + \dfrac{8}{15}$
$\qquad\qquad\qquad = 2\dfrac{1}{5}$

**16** Total goals scored in first 5 games $= 5 \times 52$
$\qquad\qquad\qquad\qquad\qquad\qquad\qquad = 260$

Total goals scored in last 10 games $= 10 \times 67$
$\qquad\qquad\qquad\qquad\qquad\qquad\qquad = 670$

Total goals scored in the season $= 260 + 670$
$\qquad\qquad\qquad\qquad\qquad\qquad\ = 930$

Total games $= 5 + 10$
$\qquad\qquad\ \ = 15$

Goals per game $= 930 \div 15$
$\qquad\qquad\qquad\ = 62$

# Year 9 Numeracy — Sample Test Answers

**Non-calculator**

**YEAR 9 Numeracy Sample Test 1**  Pages 36–43

1 **C** (Basic level)
2 **B** (Basic level)
3 **A** (Basic level)
4 **10.8** (Basic level)
5 **D** (Basic level)
6 **D** (Basic level)
7 **C** (Basic level)
8 **A** (Intermediate level)
9 **C** (Intermediate level)
10 **D** (Basic level)
11 **21 m²** (Intermediate level)
12 **C** (Basic level)
13 **A** (Intermediate level)
14 **A** (Intermediate level)
15 **C** (Intermediate level)
16 **B** (Intermediate level)
17 **D** (Intermediate level)
18 **A** (Basic level)
19 **D** (Intermediate level)
20 $x = 6$ (Intermediate level)
21 **1750 mL** (Intermediate level)
22 **18** (Advanced level)
23 **1°C** (Intermediate level)
24 **C** (Advanced level)
25 **100** (Intermediate level)
26 **B** (Advanced level)
27 **D** (Advanced level)
28 **3 h** (Advanced level)
29 **B** (Advanced level)
30 **NZ$75** (Advanced level)
31 **B** (Advanced level)
32 **B** (Advanced level)

1  29 is closer to 30 than 20.
57 is closer to 60 than 50.
32 is closer to 30 than 40.
78 is closer to 80 than 70.
The best estimate for $29 + 57 \times 32 + 78$ is $30 + 60 \times 30 + 80$.

2  The face numbered 4 will be on the face opposite the face numbered 1.
[If 1 was on the bottom, 2, 3, 5 and 6 would wrap around the middle and 4 would be on top.]

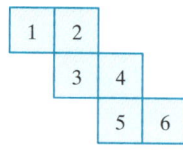

3  15 out of the 40 tickets are blue.
So, probability of blue $= \dfrac{15}{40}$
$= \dfrac{3}{8}$

4  1.2, 2.4, 3.6, 4.8, 6
The numbers increase by 1.2 each time.
The ninth number will be $9 \times 1.2$ or 10.8.

5  1 m = 1000 mm
So 1 m + 35 mm = (1000 + 35) mm
= 1035 mm

6  $0.6 \div 0.02 = 60 \div 2$
$= 30$
[Move the decimal point so that you divide by a whole number. The decimal point must be moved the same number of places in both parts of the question.]

7  An obtuse angle measures more than 90° but less than 180°.
The obtuse angle is C.
[A and B are reflex angles. D is a right angle.]

8  When $p = -4$,
$2 - 3p = 2 - 3 \times -4$
$= 2 + 12$
$= 14$

9  $3\dfrac{4}{5} = \dfrac{3 \times 5 + 4}{5}$
$= \dfrac{19}{5}$

10  4, 4, 6, 6, 6, 7, 9
Mean $= \dfrac{4 + 4 + 6 + 6 + 6 + 7 + 9}{7}$
$= \dfrac{42}{7}$
$= 6$
The median is the fourth score.
The median is 6.
There are more 6s than any other number.
The mode is 6.
Range $= 9 - 4$
$= 5$
The range is not equal to 6.

11  Perimeter = 20 m
So length + width = 10 m
But the width is 3 metres, so the length must be 7 metres.
Area = length × width
= (3 × 7) m²
= 21 m²

12  [Fill in more positions on the number line.]

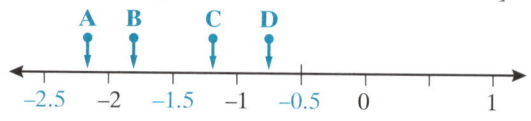

138

# YEAR 9 NUMERACY SAMPLE TEST ANSWERS

−1.2 is between −1.5 and −1.
C is pointing to −1.2.

**13** $5 - (2x + 3) = 5 - 2x - 3$
$\phantom{5 - (2x + 3)} = -2x + 2$

**14** For every 3 boys at the party there are 5 girls.
So 3 out of every 8 children at the party are boys.
Now $40 \div 8 = 5$
So there are 5 lots of 8 children.
Number of boys $= 5 \times 3$
$\phantom{Number of boys} = 15$

**15** A quarter to two in the afternoon is 1:45 pm.
$\frac{3}{4}$ hour is 45 minutes.
So $\frac{3}{4}$ hour before 1:45 pm is 1:00 pm.
Another 6 hours before that is 7:00 am.

**16** [Write each number with the same number of places after the decimal point.]
0.080
0.400
0.317
0.250
So the largest number is 0.4.

**17** A rhombus is a parallelogram so its opposite sides are parallel.

All the sides of a rhombus are equal so the opposite sides are equal and the adjacent sides are equal.

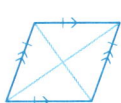

The property that is not always true for a rhombus is that the diagonals are equal.
[If the diagonals of a rhombus are equal then the rhombus is a square.]

**18** $19 \times 36 + 24 \times 19 = 36 \times 19 + 24 \times 19$
$\phantom{19 \times 36 + 24 \times 19} = (36 + 24) \times 19$
$\phantom{19 \times 36 + 24 \times 19} = 60 \times 19$

**19**

| △ | 1 | 2 | 3 | 4 | 5 |
|---|---|---|---|---|---|
| ○ | 3 | 12 | 27 | 48 | 75 |

Consider each option:
○ = 3 × △
When △ = 1,
○ = 3 × 1
  = 3 ✓
When △ = 2,
○ = 3 × 2
  = 6 ✗
The rule is not ○ = 3 × △

○ = 9 × △ − 6
When △ = 1,
○ = 9 × 1 − 6
  = 3 ✓
When △ = 2,
○ = 9 × 2 − 6
  = 12 ✓
When △ = 3,
○ = 9 × 3 − 6
  = 21 ✗
The rule is not ○ = 9 × △ − 6

○ = △ × △ + 2
When △ = 1,
○ = 1 × 1 + 2
  = 3 ✓
When △ = 2,
○ = 2 × 2 + 2
  = 6 ✗
The rule is not ○ = △ × △ + 2

○ = 3 × △ × △
When △ = 1,
○ = 3 × 1 × 1
  = 3 ✓
When △ = 2,
○ = 3 × 2 × 2
  = 12 ✓
When △ = 3,
○ = 3 × 3 × 3
  = 27 ✓
When △ = 4,
○ = 3 × 4 × 4
  = 48 ✓
When △ = 5,
○ = 3 × 5 × 5
  = 75 ✓
The rule is ○ = 3 × △ × △

**20** $7x - 3 = 5x + 9$
[Subtract $5x$ from both sides.]
$2x - 3 = 9$
[Add 3 to both sides.]
$\phantom{xx}2x = 12$
[Divide both sides by 2.]
$\phantom{xxxx}x = 6$

139

# YEAR 9 NUMERACY SAMPLE TEST ANSWERS

**21** The drum currently holds 2.5 litres.
2.5 L = 2500 mL
Amount remaining
= (2500 − 750) mL
= 1750 mL

**22** Number of red cars = 15% of 160
Now 10% of 160 = 16
So 5% of 160 = 8
15% of 160 = 16 + 8
= 24
So there are 24 red cars in the car park.
Number of red sedans = $\frac{3}{4}$ of 24
Now 24 ÷ 4 = 6
and 3 × 6 = 18
So 18 cars are red sedans.

**23** The temperature at 11 pm was −2°C.
At 5 am it was 6°C colder.
Temperature at 5 am = (−2 − 6)°C
= −8°C
At 9 am it was 9° warmer.
Temperature at 9 am = (−8 + 9)°C
= 1°C

**24** $4^2 \times 2^3$ = 4 × 4 × 2 × 2 × 2
[But this is not one of the options.]
Now 2 × 2 = 4
So $4^2 \times 2^3$ = 4 × 4 × 4 × 2

**25** The exterior angle of a triangle is equal to the sum of the interior opposite angles.
Now 80 + 50 = 130
So the angle in the triangle, adjacent to the angle marked x°, must be 80°.

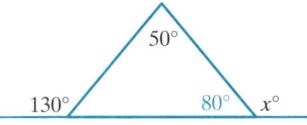

Now, angles in a straight line add to 180°.
So  x + 80 = 180
x = 100

**26** $\frac{1}{4} = \frac{6}{24}$
and $\frac{1}{6} = \frac{4}{24}$
The number halfway between $\frac{1}{4}$ and $\frac{1}{6}$ is the number halfway between $\frac{6}{24}$ and $\frac{4}{24}$.
It is $\frac{5}{24}$.

**27** The average of 5 numbers is 8.
Sum of those 5 numbers = 5 × 8
= 40
The average of 4 numbers is 7.
The sum of those 4 numbers = 4 × 7
= 28
Difference = 40 − 28
= 12
So the number that was left out must have been 12.

**28** The distance on the map is 5 cm.

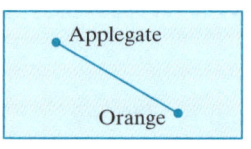

Scale: 1 cm represents 15 km

So, the actual distance = 5 × 15 km
= 75 km
The average speed = 25 km/h
Time = (75 ÷ 25) h
= 3 h

**29** y = 2 − 3x
When x = 0,
y = 2 − 3 × 0
= 2
When x = 1,
y = 2 − 3 × 1
= −1
[So you can draw the line on the grid.]

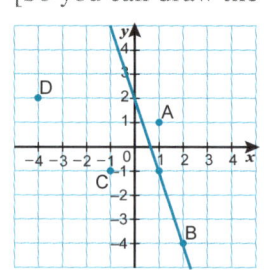

The line passes through point B.
[Or substitute the coordinates of each point into the equation. B is the point (2, −4). When x = 2,
y = 2 − 3 × 2
= −4
So B lies on the line.]

# YEAR 9 NUMERACY SAMPLE TEST ANSWERS

**30** $45US = $60 Australian

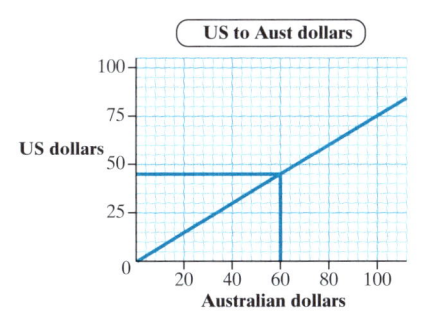

*US to Aust dollars* (graph)

$60 Australian = NZ$75

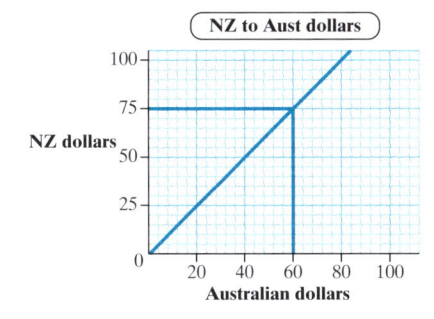

*NZ to Aust dollars* (graph)

**31** Sid travelled for $5\frac{1}{2}$ hours at an average speed of 72 km/h.

Distance travelled in km = 72 × 5.5

Number of lots of 100 km = (72 × 5.5) ÷ 100

The car used 8 litres for every 100 km travelled.

Petrol used = (72 × 5.5 ÷ 100) × 8
= 72 × 5.5 × 8 ÷ 100

The calculation is 72 × 5.5 × 8 ÷ 100

**32** $l < 3h − 5$ ($6 \leq h \leq 25$)

Try each option:
$l = 18, h = 8$
$18 < 3 × 8 − 5$ ?
$18 < 19$ ✓

The inequality is true if $l = 18$ and $h = 8$.

$l = 24, h = 9$
$24 < 3 × 9 − 5$ ?
$24 < 22$ ✗

The inequality is not true if $l = 24$ and $h = 9$. A letter could not be posted at the cheaper rate if the length was 24 cm and height 9 cm.

---

## Calculator Allowed

### YEAR 9 Numeracy Sample Test 1 — Pages 44–51

| | | | |
|---|---|---|---|
| **1** | **$0.85** (Basic level) | **18** | **D** (Intermediate level) |
| **2** | **A** (Basic level) | **19** | **D** (Basic level) |
| **3** | **A** (Intermediate level) | **20** | **96 cm** (Intermediate level) |
| **4** | **9 km** (Basic level) | **21** | **C** (Intermediate level) |
| **5** | **40** (Intermediate level) | **22** | **B** (Intermediate level) |
| **6** | **C** (Basic level) | **23** | **−2 and −3** (Intermediate level) |
| **7** | **B** (Basic level) | **24** | **a = 10** (Intermediate level) |
| **8** | **A** (Intermediate level) | **25** | **D** (Advanced level) |
| **9** | **B** (Intermediate level) | **26** | **A** (Advanced level) |
| **10** | **C** (Intermediate level) | **27** | **52%** (Advanced level) |
| **11** | **B** (Intermediate level) | **28** | **A** (Advanced level) |
| **12** | **D** (Intermediate level) | **29** | **10 runs/over** (Advanced level) |
| **13** | **47 km** (Intermediate level) | **30** | **B** (Advanced level) |
| **14** | **C** (Advanced level) | **31** | **C** (Intermediate level) |
| **15** | **B** (Basic level) | **32** | **$1450** (Advanced level) |
| **16** | **D** (Basic level) | | |
| **17** | **120°** (Advanced level) | | |

**1** Price per apple = $6.80 ÷ 8
= $0.85

**2** The opening in the shed faces south-east.

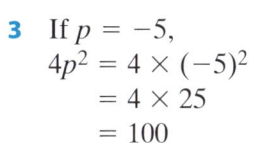

**3** If $p = −5$,
$4p^2 = 4 × (−5)^2$
$= 4 × 25$
$= 100$

**4** Time taken = 45 min
$= \frac{3}{4}$ h

Speed = 12 km every hour

Distance = $\frac{3}{4}$ of 12 km
= 9 km

**5** The exterior angle of a triangle is equal to the sum of the interior opposite angles.

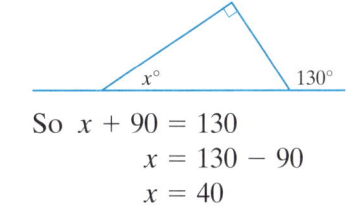

So $x + 90 = 130$
$x = 130 − 90$
$x = 40$

# YEAR 9 NUMERACY SAMPLE TEST ANSWERS

**6** 1 kg = 1000 g
So 1 kg + 80 g = (1000 + 80) g
= 1080 g

**7**

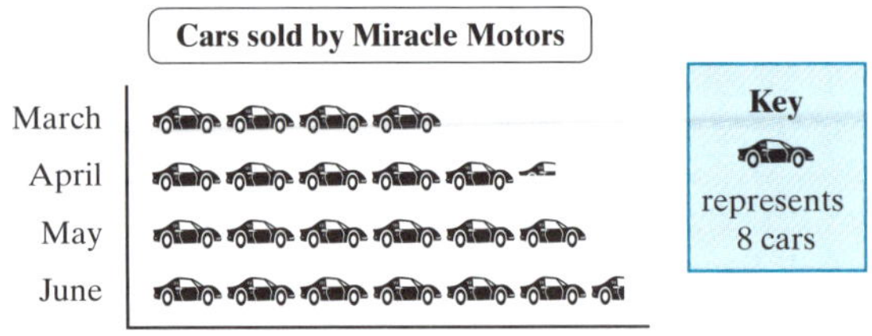

Cars sold by Miracle Motors

March
April
May
June

Key — represents 8 cars

Each symbol represents 8 cars.
So 42 cars would be represented by (42 ÷ 8) symbols or $5\frac{1}{4}$ symbols.
The month that has $5\frac{1}{4}$ symbols is April, so April is the month in which 42 cars were sold.

**8** [Change each number to a decimal.]
29% = 0.29
$\frac{2}{9}$ = 0.22222... [2 ÷ 9]
0.209
0.2009

Writing each number with four digits after the decimal point the numbers are 0.2900, 0.2222, 0.2090 and 0.2009.
The largest is 0.2900.
So the largest of the numbers is 29%.

**9** From 7:25 until 8:00 is 35 minutes.
So from 7:25 until 8:05 is 40 minutes.
From 8:05 am until 5:05 pm is 9 hours.
So the total time is 9 h 40 min.

**10** $3(4a - 1) = 3 \times 4a - 3 \times 1$
$= 12a - 3$

**11**

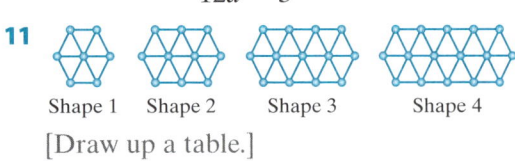

Shape 1    Shape 2    Shape 3    Shape 4

[Draw up a table.]

| Shape | 1 | 2 | 3 | 4 |
|---|---|---|---|---|
| Number of pins | 7 | 10 | 13 | 16 |

The number of pins is increasing by 3 each time.
The rule is:
the number of pins = 3 × shape number + 4
Now 40 − 4 = 36
So   3 × shape number = 36
       shape number = 36 ÷ 3
                    = 12
So 40 pins will be needed for Shape 12.

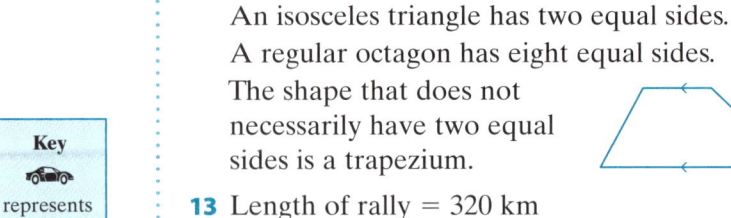

**12** A rhombus has four equal sides.
An isosceles triangle has two equal sides.
A regular octagon has eight equal sides.
The shape that does not necessarily have two equal sides is a trapezium.

**13** Length of rally = 320 km

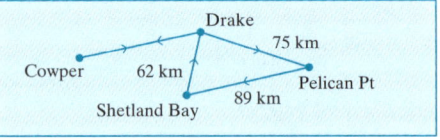

Drake 75 km
Cowper 62 km
Pelican Pt
Shetland Bay 89 km

Lengths in diagram = (75 + 89 + 62) km
= 226 km
Remaining length = (320 − 226) km
= 94 km
Distance from Cowper to Drake
= (94 ÷ 2) km
= 47 km

**14** Sum of male ages = 20 × 13
= 260
Sum of female ages = 40 × 19
= 760
Total of all ages = 260 + 760
= 1020
Total number in choir = 20 + 40
= 60
Average age = 1020 ÷ 60
= 17

**15** The temperature is −2.4°C.

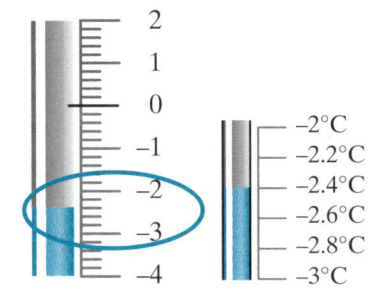

**16** [Find the volume of each prism.]
$V = (5 \times 4 \times 3)$ m$^3$
$= 60$ m$^3$

$V = (7 \times 3 \times 3)$ m$^3$
$= 63$ m$^3$

$V = (11 \times 2 \times 3)$ m$^3$
$= 66$ m$^3$

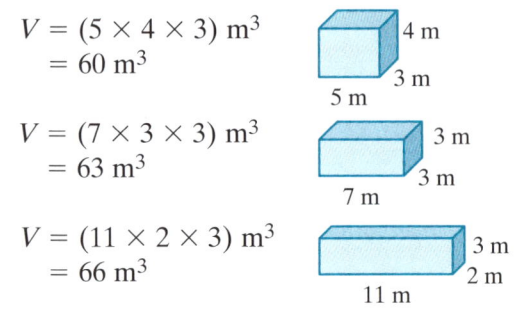

142

# YEAR 9 NUMERACY SAMPLE TEST ANSWERS

$V = (7 \times 5 \times 2)$ m$^3$
$= 70$ m$^3$

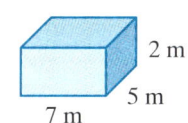

The largest volume is 70 m$^3$.
The rectangular prism with the greatest volume is D.

**17** The polygon has 8 angles so it is an octagon.
Angle sum of an octagon $= (8 - 2) \times 180°$
$= 6 \times 180°$
$= 1080°$
Now 4 angles measure 150°.
Total of those angles $= 4 \times 150°$
$= 600°$
Total of remaining angles $= 1080° - 600°$
$= 480°$
Size of each remaining angle $= 480° \div 4$
$= 120°$

**18** There are 36 possible results.
Possible results giving 8 are:
$2 + 6, 3 + 5, 4 + 4, 5 + 3$ and $6 + 2$.
So there are 5 outcomes that give 8.
Probability of 8 $= \dfrac{5}{36}$

**19** All four views could be Mel's object.

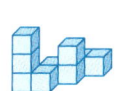

The first view could be Mel's object viewed from the front. The side view is the right side.

The second view could be Mel's object viewed from the front. The side view is the left side.

The third view could be Mel's object viewed from the back. The side view is the left side.

The fourth view could be Mel's object viewed from the front. The side view is the right side.

**20** The photo was 7.5 cm wide and is now 60 cm wide.
Number of times larger $= 60 \div 7.5$
$= 8$
The photo was 12 cm long.
New length $= 8 \times 12$ cm
$= 96$ cm

**21**

| $x$ | 1 | 1.5 | 2 | 3 | 6 |
|---|---|---|---|---|---|
| $y$ | 6 | 4 | 3 | 2 | 1 |

[Consider each option.]
$y = 6x$

When $x = 1$,
$y = 6 \times 1$
$= 6$
When $x = 1.5$,
$y = 6 \times 1.5$
$= 9$ (not 6)
This option is not correct.

$y = \dfrac{x}{6}$

When $x = 1$,
$y = \dfrac{1}{6}$ (not 6)
This option is not correct.

$y = \dfrac{6}{x}$

When $x = 1$,
$y = \dfrac{6}{1}$
$= 6$
When $x = 1.5$,
$y = \dfrac{6}{1.5}$
$= 4$
When $x = 2$,
$y = \dfrac{6}{2}$
$= 3$
When $x = 3$,
$y = \dfrac{6}{3}$
$= 2$
When $x = 6$,
$y = \dfrac{6}{6}$
$= 1$
This option is correct.
The correct rule is $y = \dfrac{6}{x}$.

**22** [Try each option.]
$6789 \div 31 = 219$
So 31 is a factor of 6789.
$6789 \div 53 = 128.094339...$
So 53 is not a factor of 6789.
$6789 \div 73 = 93$
So 73 and 93 are factors of 6789.
53 is not a factor of 6789

**23** [The two numbers multiply to give a positive number so they have the same sign.

143

# YEAR 9 NUMERACY SAMPLE TEST ANSWERS

The two numbers also add to give a negative number, so both must be negative.]
$-2 + (-3) = -5$
$-2 \times -3 = 6$
The numbers are $-2$ and $-3$.
[Or 3 and $-2$]

**24** $7a - 15 = 3a + 25$
[Add 15 to both sides.]
$7a = 3a + 40$
[Subtract $3a$ from both sides.]
$4a = 40$
[Divide both sides by 4.]
$a = 10$

**25** The circle is divided into eight sectors. 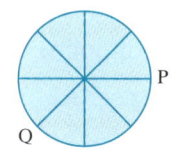
So Q is $\frac{3}{8}$ of the way around the circle.
The radius is 5 cm so the diameter is 10 cm.
The distance from P to Q $= \frac{3}{8} \times \pi \times 10$ cm
$= 11.78…$ cm
Of the options, the best estimate for the distance is 12 cm.

**26** Angles in a triangle add to 180°.
So $\angle EAB + \angle AEB + \angle ABE = 180°$
$50° + 60° + \angle ABE = 180°$
$110° + \angle ABE = 180°$
$\angle ABE = 180° - 110°$
$= 70°$

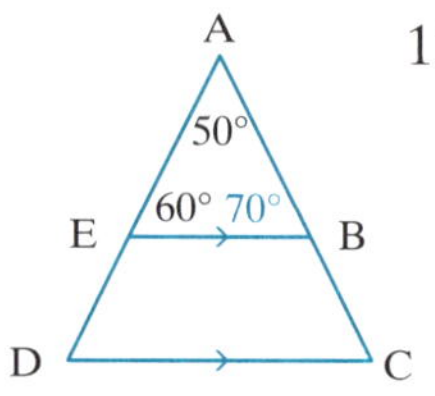

Now $\angle ACD = \angle ABE$ (alternate angles, EB is parallel to DC)
So $\angle ACD = 70°$

**27** Number of boys who had seen the movie
$= 40\%$ of 60
$= \frac{40}{100} \times 60$
$= 24$

Number of girls who had seen the movie
$= 60\%$ of 90
$= \frac{60}{100} \times 90$
$= 54$

Number who had seen the movie
$= 24 + 54$
$= 78$

Total number of boys and girls
$= 60 + 90$
$= 150$

Percentage who had seen the movie
$= \frac{78}{150} \times 100\%$
$= 52\%$

**28** 0, 1, 4, 5, 6, 6, 10
Mean $= (0 + 1 + 4 + 5 + 6 + 6 + 10) \div 7$
$= 32 \div 7$
$= 4.57…$

There are two scores of 6 and only one of all the others.
So the mode is 6.
There are 7 scores, so the middle score is the fourth score.
So the median is 5.
So mean $<$ median $<$ mode

**29** Number of runs still needed $= 185 - 65$
$= 120$
Number of overs remaining $= 20 - 8$
$= 12$
So 120 more runs are needed off 12 overs.
Required run rate $= (120 \div 12)$ runs/over
$= 10$ runs per over

**30** (1, 9) and (5, 1)
The rule that both points obey is
$2x + y = 11$
[$2 \times 1 + 9 = 11$; $2 \times 5 + 1 = 11$]
Of the options, the only point that obeys this rule is (3, 5).
[$2 \times 3 + 5 = 11$]

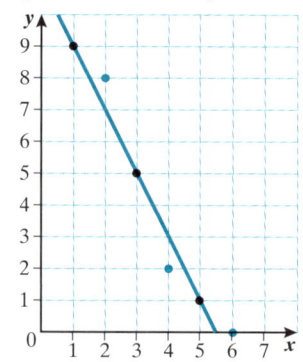

The point that also lies on the line is (3, 5).

**31** 2.7 million seconds
$= 2\,700\,000$ s
$= (2\,700\,000 \div 60)$ min

144

# YEAR 9 NUMERACY SAMPLE TEST ANSWERS

= 45 000 min
= (45 000 ÷ 60) h
= 750 h
= (750 ÷ 24) days
= 31.25 days

So 2.7 million seconds is about 1 month.

**32** $C = 350 + 25n$

When $n = 180$,

$C = 350 + 25 \times 180$
$= 350 + 4500$
$= 4850$

So the cost to make 180 gnomes is $4850.

The money received from the sale of
180 gnomes = 180 × $35
= $6300

Profit = $6300 − $4850
= $1450

## Non-calculator

### YEAR 9 Numeracy Sample Test 2
Pages 52–59

- **1** C (Basic level)
- **2** 60 (Basic level)
- **3** D (Basic level)
- **4** 51 (Intermediate level)
- **5** C (Basic level)
- **6** C (Basic level)
- **7** A (Intermediate level)
- **8** A (Basic level)
- **9** D (Intermediate level)
- **10** 10 (Intermediate level)
- **11** A (Basic level)
- **12** B (Intermediate level)
- **13** 57° (Intermediate level)
- **14** D (Intermediate level)
- **15** C (Advanced level)
- **16** 36 (Intermediate level)
- **17** C (Basic level)
- **18** $x = 3$ (Intermediate level)
- **19** A (Intermediate level)
- **20** 140 (Intermediate level)
- **21** D (Advanced level)
- **22** B (Intermediate level)
- **23** B (Intermediate level)
- **24** D (Advanced level)
- **25** 90 km/h (Advanced level)
- **26** B (Advanced level)
- **27** D (Advanced level)
- **28** A (Advanced level)
- **29** B (Advanced level)
- **30** 456 cm² and 480 cm³ (Advanced level)
- **31** B (Advanced level)
- **32** C (Advanced level)

**1** Donna is travelling south-east.

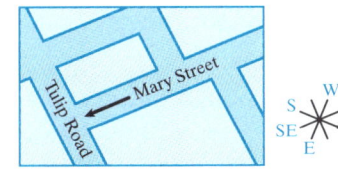

**2** 25% are casual workers.
Now 25% is one-quarter.
Number of casual workers = 80 ÷ 4
= 20
Number of permanent staff = 80 − 20
= 60

**3** There are 6 possible outcomes when a die is tossed. 5 is one of those outcomes.

Probability of 5 = $\frac{1}{6}$

**4** First number = 2
Second number = 2 × 2 + 5
= 4 + 5
= 9
Third number = 2 × 9 + 5
= 18 + 5
= 23
Fourth number = 2 × 23 + 5
= 46 + 5
= 51

**5** [Remove one block from each side.]

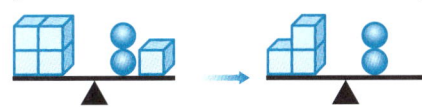

3 blocks balance 2 balls.
So 3 × 3 blocks will balance 3 × 2 balls.
9 blocks will balance 6 balls.

**6** Kate is taller than both Ann and Judith.
Ann is taller than both Judith and Skye.
Both Judith and Skye are taller than Claire.

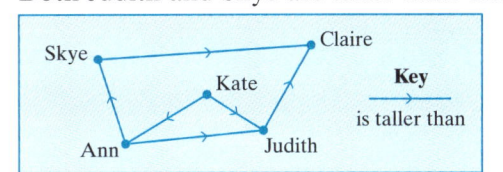

Claire is the shortest.

**7** From 8:50 am until 9:00 am is 10 minutes.
From 9 am until 4 pm is 7 hours.
From 4 pm until 4:15 pm is 15 minutes.
Total time = 10 min + 7 h + 15 min
= 7h 25 min

**8** There are 12 cubes altogether. 
When viewed from the front there are two rows on the far left, one row in the second position from the left, three rows in the third position from the left and just one row on the right.

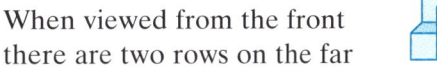

# YEAR 9 NUMERACY SAMPLE TEST ANSWERS

The view from the top is

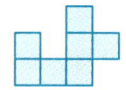

**9** $12 \div \frac{1}{2} = 12 \times 2$
$= 24$

[There are two halves in every one whole. So, there are 24 halves in 12.]

**10** Total of the angles = 360°
Given angles = 120° + 80° + 100°
$= 300°$
Remaining angle = 360° − 300°
$= 60°$
Fraction who chose sci-fi movies = $\frac{60}{360}$
$= \frac{1}{6}$

Now, the whole graph represents 60 people.
Number who chose sci-fi movies = 60 ÷ 6
$= 10$

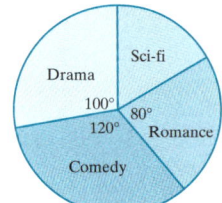

**11** 1 m = 100 cm
So 1 m + 85 cm = 185 cm
[But this is not one of the options.]
Now 1 cm = 10 mm
So 185 cm = 1850 mm
1 m + 85 cm = 1850 mm

**12** When $a = 2$ and $b = 5$,
$3ab^2 = 3 \times 2 \times 5^2$
$= 3 \times 2 \times 25$
$= 150$

**13** ∠PQR = 57°
[R is to the right of the vertex Q and so the inside scale on the protractor is used.]

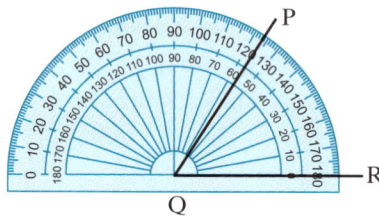

**14** A parallelogram is a quadrilateral with both pairs of opposite sides parallel.

Rectangles, rhombuses and squares are all quadrilaterals with both pairs of opposite sides parallel so they are all parallelograms.

A trapezium has one pair of opposite sides parallel. It is not a parallelogram. [But all parallelograms are trapeziums.]

**15** $-x^2 + 5x = 5x - x^2$
[$-x^2$ and $5x$ are unlike terms so they cannot be added together. $x(x - 5) = x^2 - 5x$
$= -(-x^2 + 5x)$]

**16** There are 60 red apples.
The ratio of red to green apples is 5 to 3.
So for every 5 red apples there are 3 green ones.
Now 60 ÷ 5 = 12
So there are 12 lots of 5 red apples.
[So there will be 12 lots of 3 green apples.]
Number of green apples = 3 × 12
$= 36$

**17** Area = $\frac{1}{2}$ × base × perpendicular height
$= \frac{1}{2} \times 45 \times 40$

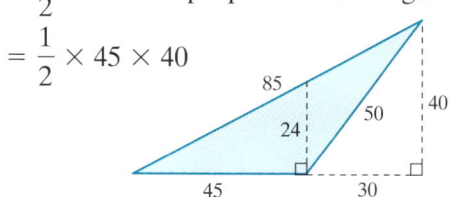

[The height must be the perpendicular height so it is not 85 or 50 because those measurements are not at right angles to the base. The measurement 24 is at right angles to the base but does not give the height of the triangle.]

**18** $3(2x + 1) = 9x - 6$
[Remove brackets]
$6x + 3 = 9x - 6$
[Add 6 to both sides.]
$6x + 9 = 9x$
[Subtract $6x$ from both sides.]
$9 = 3x$
[Divide both sides by 3.]
$3 = x$
So $x = 3$

**19** The larger rectangular prism is 3 times longer, 3 times wider and 3 times higher than the smaller prism.
The number of times that the volume is greater = 3 × 3 × 3
$= 27$
[If the smaller prism has length $l$, breadth $b$ and height $h$ its volume is $lbh$. The larger prism has volume $3l \times 3b \times 3h = 27lbh$.]

**20** Selma received 220 votes.
The sector for Alice is a quadrant.
So Alice received one quarter of the votes.

# YEAR 9 NUMERACY SAMPLE TEST ANSWERS

Number of votes for Alice = 480 ÷ 4
= 120

Mary received the remaining votes.

Number of votes for Mary = 480 − 220 − 120
= 140

21 [Change each fraction so they all have the same denominator, 24.]

$\frac{2}{3} = \frac{16}{24}$

$\frac{3}{4} = \frac{18}{24}$

$\frac{5}{8} = \frac{15}{24}$

$\frac{7}{12} = \frac{14}{24}$

So from lowest to highest the fractions are $\frac{14}{24}, \frac{15}{24}, \frac{16}{24}, \frac{18}{24}$.

The set of fractions in order from lowest to highest is $\frac{7}{12}, \frac{5}{8}, \frac{2}{3}, \frac{3}{4}$.

22 Consider each option:

0.3 < 0.04 ?

0.30 > 0.04

This option is not correct.

−0.6 > −0.7 ?

This option is correct.

−0.2 < −0.235 ?

−0.200 > −0.235

This option is not correct.

−2.5 > −1.8 ?

−2.5 < −1.8

This option is not correct.

The correct statement is −0.6 > −0.7.

23 The pattern has four shapes that repeat.

Every fourth shape will be 🦆.

So the 88th shape will be 🦆.

The 89th shape will be 🔺 and the 90th shape will be 🦆.

24 The triangles will be right-angled but not isosceles.

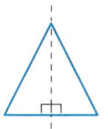

25 Distance = 315 km

From 9:40 am until 12:40 pm is 3 hours.

From 12:40 pm until 1:10 pm is 30 minutes or half an hour.

Time taken = 3.5 h

Average speed = (315 ÷ 3.5) km/h
= (630 ÷ 7) km/h
= 90 km/h

26 The fourth vertex will be at (−3, −2).

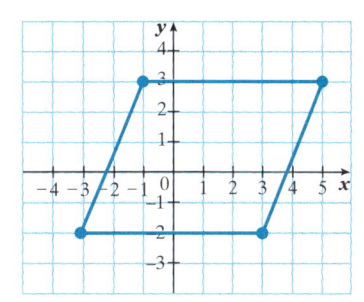

27 The price has increased by 5%.

Now 5% = 5 ÷ 100
= 0.05

So the increase in price is 0.05 × 560.

The new price is 560 + 0.05 × 560
= 560 × 1 + 560 × 0.05
= 560 × (1 + 0.05)
= 560 × 1.05

28 $4^3 = 4 \times 4 \times 4$

But $4 = 2 \times 2$

So $4^3 = 2 \times 2 \times 2 \times 2 \times 2 \times 2$
$= 2^6$

$[4^3 = (2^2)^3 = 2^{2 \times 3} = 2^6]$

29 When lines are parallel, the co-interior angles add to 180°.

So an angle of 60° is at the top right.

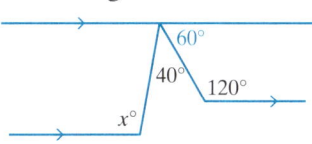

When lines are parallel, the alternate angles are equal.

So $x = 40 + 60$
$= 100$

# YEAR 9 NUMERACY SAMPLE TEST ANSWERS

**30** The front and back triangular faces both have area 48 cm². 

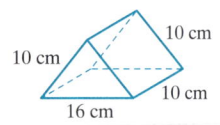

There are three rectangular faces.
Total area of the rectangular faces
= (16 × 10 + 10 × 10 + 10 × 10) cm²
= (160 + 100 + 100) cm²
= 360 cm²
Total surface area = (2 × 48 + 360) cm²
= (96 + 360) cm²
= 456 cm²

$V = Ah$
$= 48 × 10$
$= 480$
The volume is 480 cm³.

**31** Rose Bay is due south of Lavender so, as Begonia is west of Azalea, it will be at the bottom of the map.

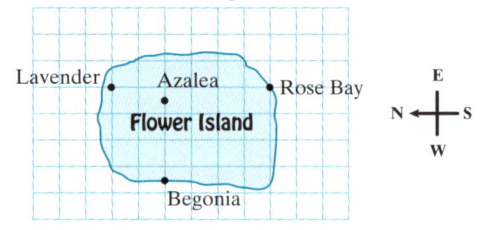

From Lavender to Rose Bay on the map is 6 units.
So 6 units represents 180 km.
1 unit will represent (180 ÷ 6) km or 30 km.
The distance from Azalea to Begonia is about 3 units on the map.
So the real distance is about 3 × 30 km or 90 km.

**32** Probability of blue = $\frac{1}{4}$

Probability of yellow = $\frac{1}{3}$

Probability of blue or yellow = $\frac{1}{4} + \frac{1}{3}$

$= \frac{3}{12} + \frac{4}{12}$

$= \frac{7}{12}$

Probability of green = $1 - \frac{7}{12}$

$= \frac{5}{12}$

---

### Calculator Allowed

### YEAR 9 Numeracy Sample Test 2  *Pages 60–67*

| | |
|---|---|
| **1 B** (Basic level) | **17 31** (Intermediate level) |
| **2 C** (Basic level) | **18 B** (Advanced level) |
| **3 D** (Basic level) | **19 D** (Intermediate level) |
| **4 18** (Basic level) | **20 C** (Intermediate level) |
| **5 B** (Basic level) | **21 C** (Advanced level) |
| **6 36** (Intermediate level) | **22 A** (Intermediate level) |
| **7 A** (Intermediate level) | **23 47** (Intermediate level) |
| **8 11 m** (Basic level) | **24 C** (Intermediate level) |
| **9 700 mL** (Intermediate level) | **25 B** (Intermediate level) |
| | **26 A** (Advanced level) |
| **10 225°** (Intermediate level) | **27 4.6** (Advanced level) |
| **11 D** (Advanced level) | **28 221** (Advanced level) |
| **12 9** (Basic level) | **29 A** (Advanced level) |
| **13 8:09** (Basic level) | **30 5 × 7 × 17** (Advanced level) |
| **14 C** (Intermediate level) | |
| **15 B** (Advanced level) | **31 D** (Advanced level) |
| **16 D** (Intermediate level) | **32 7x** (Advanced level) |

**1** 23 287 564 = 23 290 000 to the nearest ten thousand
[23 287 564 is closer to 23 290 000 than 23 280 000. 23 300 000 is the population to the nearest hundred thousand and 23 288 000 is the population to the nearest thousand.]

**2** The letter M is the only one that maps onto itself when folded along the dotted line.

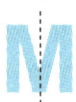

The dotted line is an axis of symmetry in option C.

**3** Eric turns into Hill Street.

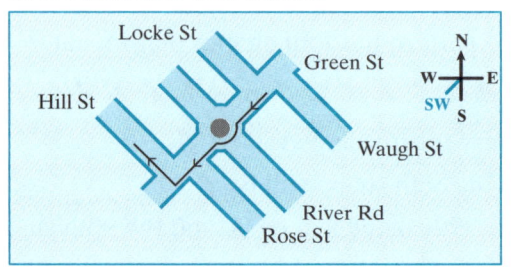

**4** After multiplying by 7 the answer was 203. Before multiplying by 7 the number must have been 203 ÷ 7 or 29.

148

# YEAR 9 NUMERACY SAMPLE TEST ANSWERS

So when 11 is added to a number the result is 29.

The number is 29 − 11 or 18.

5  When $n = 4$, $\dfrac{3n}{n-1} = \dfrac{3 \times 4}{4-1}$
$= \dfrac{12}{3}$
$= 4$

6  There are 3 boys for every 5 girls at the dance.
There are 60 girls at the dance.
Number of boys = 3 × (60 ÷ 5)
= 3 × 12
= 36

7  **Scores of Class 9P**

| Stem | Leaf |
|------|------|
| 6 | 4 5 6 8 9 |
| 7 | 1 3 5 7 ⑧ |
| 8 | 1 2 2 4 6 9 |
| 9 | 0 3 5 |

**Key**
9 | 0 is a score of 90

There are 19 scores in total, so the middle score is the 10th score.
The median is 78.

8  Perimeter = 36 m
Length + width = (36 ÷ 2) m
= 18 m
But the width is 7 metres.
Length = (18 − 7) m
= 11 m

9  1 litre = 1000 mL 
Each litre on the jug is divided into 5.
Each mark represents (1000 ÷ 5) mL or 200 mL.
So the jug holds 1200 mL.
Amount removed = 2 × 250 mL
= 500 mL
Amount remaining = (1200 − 500) mL
= 700 mL

10  In two rotations, the arrow turns through 360° + 90° or 450°.
Angle of rotation = (450 ÷ 2)°
= 225°

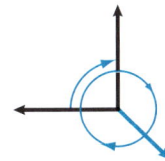

11  $x − x^2 = −x^2 + x$

12  The probability that a ball is white is $\dfrac{1}{3}$ so $\dfrac{1}{3}$ of the balls must be white.
But there are 18 white balls.
So the total number of balls = 3 × 18
= 54
Now 15 + 12 + 18 = 45
The remaining balls are red.
Number of red balls = 54 − 45
= 9

13

| Fingal | 7:17 | 7:59 | 8:30 | 9:09 |
|--------|------|------|------|------|
| Paget | 7:31 | 8:18 | 8:47 | 9:23 |
| Malak | 7:52 | 8:40 | 9:08 | 9:42 |
| City | 8:05 | 8:53 | 9:21 | 9:54 |

A quarter past nine is 9:15.
So the latest train that Sam can catch is the one that arrives in the city at 8:53.
This train leaves Paget station at 8:18.
The latest time that Sam can leave home is 9 minutes before 8:18 or 8:09.

14  Number of students = 360
Number of part-time students = 360 ÷ 4
= 90
Number of full-time students = 360 − 90
= 270
Number of mature-aged full-time students
= 30% of 270
= 81

15  Total mass = (4.69 ÷ 4.97) kg
= 0.94366... kg
= 943.66... g
Average mass = (943.66... ÷ 6) g
= 157.2769... g
≈ 160 g

16  Triangle C is isosceles because it has two equal sides.
[Find the remaining angle in each of the other triangles.]

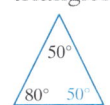

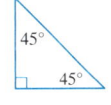

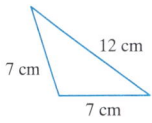

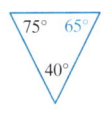

Triangles A and B are both isosceles because they both have two equal angles.

149

# YEAR 9 NUMERACY SAMPLE TEST ANSWERS

Triangle D has three different angles. It is not an isosceles triangle. (It is scalene.)

**17** Number of pens Caitlin has = $12 \times 7 + 5$
$= 84 + 5$
$= 89$

Total number needed = $12 \times 10$
$= 120$

Number of extra pens needed = $120 - 89$
$= 31$

**18** The area of a triangle is half that of a parallelogram with the same base and height. So if both the area and height are the same, the base of the triangle would need to be twice as long as that of the parallelogram.
[Or

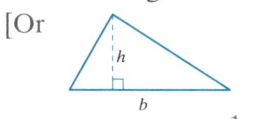

Area of triangle = $\frac{1}{2}bh$

Area of parallelogram = $Bh$

So $\frac{1}{2}bh = Bh$

$\frac{1}{2}b = B$ (after dividing by $h$)

$b = 2B$ (after multiplying by 2)

So the base of the triangle is twice that of the parallelogram.]

**19** $5x - 2 > 3x$
[Add 2 to both sides.]
$5x > 3x + 2$
[Subtract $3x$ from both sides.]
$2x > 2$
[Divide both sides by 2.]
$x > 1$

So, of the options, the only value of $x$ greater than 1 is $x = 2$.

The value of $x$ that will make the inequality true is $x = 2$.

[Or substitute each option into the inequality to see which is correct.]

**20** Tom's scores (in order from lowest to highest) are 77, 79, 82, 82, 85.

Mode = 82

Mean = $(77 + 79 + 82 + 82 + 85) \div 5$
$= 405 \div 5$
$= 81$

Median = 82

A score of 81 is included.

The mode will still be 82.

The mean will still be 81.
[Because the number included is equal to the original mean.]

The median will be $\frac{81 + 82}{2}$ or 81.5.

So the mode and mean will not change but the median will change.

**21** $y = 5x - 7$
$y = 3x + 5$

[If both equations are satisfied at the same time then $5x - 7$ and $3x + 5$ will have the same value (the value of $y$).]

$5x - 7 = 3x + 5$
[Add 7 to both sides.]
$5x = 3x + 12$
[Subtract $3x$ from both sides.]
$2x = 12$
[Divide both sides by 2.]
$x = 6$

**22** Q is 3 units above R so Q has coordinates (9, 7).

P is 4 units to the left of Q so it has coordinates (5, 7).

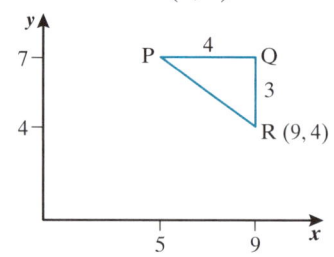

**23** Zoe has placed 17 blocks in her cube.

The cube is 4 units high at the back, so it must also be 4 units long and 4 units wide.

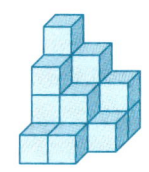

Total number of blocks = $4 \times 4 \times 4$
$= 64$

Extra blocks needed = $64 - 17$
$= 47$

**24** The value has increased by 60%.

So the value is now 160% of what it was four years ago.

Now 160% = $1200

1% = $1200 ÷ 160
= $7.50

100% = $7.50 × 100
= $750

# YEAR 9 NUMERACY SAMPLE TEST ANSWERS

The value four years ago was $750.

**25**

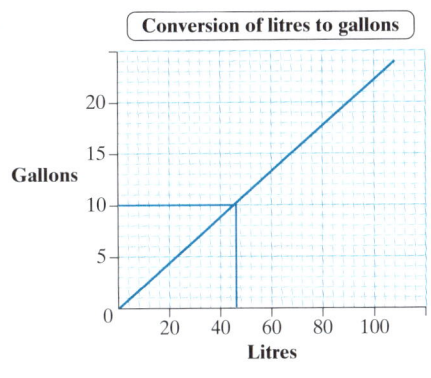

*Conversion of litres to gallons*

From the graph, 10 gallons is about 45 litres.
Number of 3-litre bottles = 45 ÷ 3
= 15

**26** Time for first part of the journey
= (175 ÷ 70) h
= 2.5 h
Now 2 hours after 7:50 am is 9:50 am.
Half an hour, or 30 minutes, after that is 10:20 am.
40 minutes after 10:20 am is 11:00 am.
So Liam set off again at 11:00 am.
He arrived at 12:30 pm so the time for the second part of the journey was 1.5 hours.
Distance travelled = (1.5 × 84) km
= 126 km
Total distance = (175 + 126) km
= 301 km

**27** The triangle is right-angled.
Area of triangle:
$A = \frac{1}{2}bh$
$= \frac{1}{2} \times 12 \times 5$
$= 30$
The area of the triangle is 30 m².
But the area of the triangle can also be found using the base of 13 m.
$A = \frac{1}{2}bh$
$30 = \frac{1}{2} \times 13 \times h$
$= 6.5 \times h$
$h = 30 ÷ 6.5$
$= 4.6153846…$
$= 4.6$ [1 d.p.]

**28** The first number is 4.
Now 5 × 4 = 20
The second number is 11.
20 − 9 = 11
So the number that is subtracted is 9.
The third number = 5 × 11 − 9
= 55 − 9
= 46
The fourth number = 5 × 46 − 9
= 230 − 9
= 221

**29** Co-interior angles formed by parallel lines add to 180°.
Now 180° − 110° = 70°
So the angle that is co-interior to 110° is 70°.
Now alternate angles, formed by parallel lines, are equal.
So $x + 70 = 80$
$x = 10$

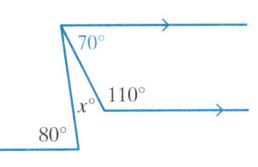

**30** Because it ends in 5, 595 is divisible by 5.
Now 595 ÷ 5 = 119
[So now we need to find the prime factors of 119.]
119 is not divisible by 3, because the digits (1 + 1 + 9) add to 11 which is not divisible by 3.
119 is not divisible by 5.
Try 7:
119 ÷ 7 = 17
17 is prime.
So 595 = 5 × 7 × 17

**31** The average of 8 numbers is 47.
Sum of those 8 numbers = 8 × 47
= 376
The average of 7 numbers is 43.
Sum of those 7 numbers = 7 × 43
= 301
Difference = 376 − 301
= 75
So the number Cody left out was 75.

**32** $5(2x − 1) + 3(x + 2) − \square = 6x + 1$
$10x − 5 + 3x + 6 − \square = 6x + 1$
$13x + 1 − \square = 6x + 1$
[Subtract 1 from both sides.]
$13x − \square = 6x$
So $\square = 7x$

151

# YEAR 9 NUMERACY SAMPLE TEST ANSWERS

**Non-calculator**

**YEAR 9 Numeracy Sample Test 3**  Pages 68–75

1. **D** (Basic level)
2. ☐ = **3** (Basic level)
3. **C** (Basic level)
4. **A** (Intermediate level)
5. **D** (Intermediate level)
6. **A** (Basic level)
7. **B** (Basic level)
8. **0.4** (Basic level)
9. **B** (Intermediate level)
10. **B** (Basic level)
11. **20 km** (Basic level)
12. **−1.6** (Basic level)
13. **C** (Intermediate level)
14. **A** (Intermediate level)
15. **D** (Intermediate level)
16. **D** (Intermediate level)
17. **150** (Advanced level)
18. **B** (Intermediate level)
19. **9409** (Intermediate level)
20. **40 cm** (Intermediate level)
21. **C** (Intermediate level)
22. **C** (Advanced level)
23. **C** (Advanced level)
24. **C** (Intermediate level)
25. **800 km** (Advanced level)
26. **D** (Intermediate level)
27. **A** (Advanced level)
28. **D** (Advanced level)
29. **12%** (Intermediate level)
30. **B** (Advanced level)
31. **17** (Advanced level)
32. **A** (Advanced level)

1  The object could be a rectangular pyramid.

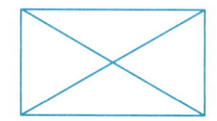

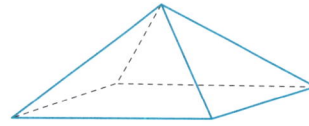

[When viewed from the top the top vertex appears as a point in the centre of the rectangular base. The edges joining the top vertex to the base appear as lines.]

2  $48 \div 12 = 12 \div \square$
Now $48 \div 12 = 4$
So $12 \div \square = 4$
So ☐ = 3 because $12 \div 3 = 4$

3  [Fill in the missing measurements.]

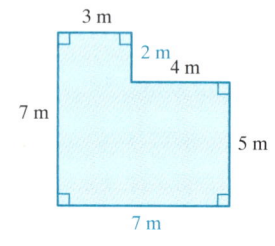

Perimeter $= 2 \times (7 + 7)$ m
$= 2 \times 14$ m
$= 28$ m

4  There are 12 sectors on the spinner.
So in 60 spins each sector should occur $60 \div 12$ or 5 times. 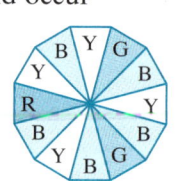
So the colour that appears on only one section would be the colour that you would expect to occur 5 times.
You would expect red (R) to appear 5 times.

5  $2x − 3 + x + 5 = (2x + x) − 3 + 5$
$= 3x + 2$

6  Decrease $= 300 − 240$
$= 60$
Percentage decrease $= \dfrac{60}{300} \times 100\%$
$= \dfrac{20}{100} \times 100\%$
$= 20\%$

7  Total pegs $= 12 + 15 + 8 + 25$
$= 60$
Number of blue pegs $= 12$
Probability of blue peg $= \dfrac{12}{60}$
$= \dfrac{1}{5}$

8  8.4, 7.6, 6.8, 6, …
The numbers are decreasing by 0.8 each time.
The 11th number will have 0.8 subtracted from the first number 10 times.
Now $10 \times 0.8 = 8$
So the 11th number $= 8.4 − 8$
$= 0.4$
[Or continue the pattern:
8.4, 7.6, 6.8, 6, 5.2, 4.4, 3.6, 2.8, 2, 1.2, 0.4]
The 11th number is 0.4.

9  The exterior angle of a triangle is equal to the sum of the interior opposite angles.
Now $40 + 80 = 120$
So the exterior angle is 120°.

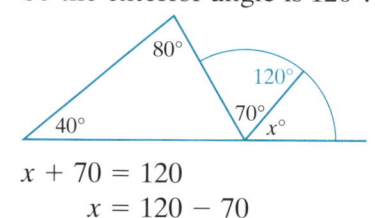

$x + 70 = 120$
$x = 120 − 70$
$x = 50$

# YEAR 9 NUMERACY SAMPLE TEST ANSWERS

**10** [Find the area of each paddock.]

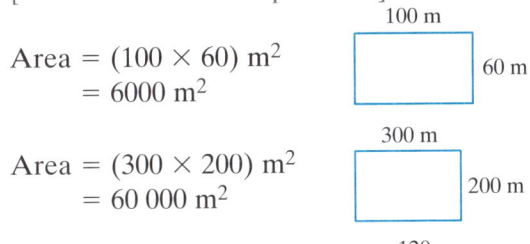

Area = $(100 \times 60)$ m$^2$
= 6000 m$^2$

Area = $(300 \times 200)$ m$^2$
= 60 000 m$^2$

Area = $(120 \times 50)$ m$^2$
= 6000 m$^2$

Area = $(1500 \times 400)$ m$^2$
= 600 000 m$^2$

Now 1 ha = 10 000 m$^2$
So 6 ha = 60 000 m$^2$

The paddock that is 300 metres long and 200 metres wide has an area of 6 ha.

**11** Average speed = 30 km/h.
So Dan travels 30 km in 60 minutes.
So he would travel 10 km in 20 minutes and 20 km in 40 minutes.

**12** The arrow is pointing to $-1.6$ (or $-1\frac{3}{5}$).

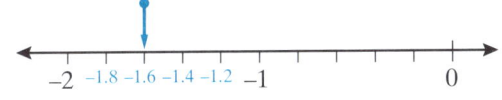

**13** When $t = -3$,
$2t^2 = 2 \times (-3)^2$
$= 2 \times 9$
$= 18$

**14** $20^2 = 20 \times 20$
$= 400$
So $\sqrt{250}$ must be less than 20.
$\sqrt{250}$ is about 16.
[$16^2 = 256$]

**15** $2\frac{5}{7} = \frac{2 \times 7 + 5}{7}$
$= \frac{19}{7}$

**16** $3(2n + 1) = 3 \times 2n + 3 \times 1$
$= 6n + 3$

**17** $\angle$QRS = 90° (angle of a square)
$\angle$TRS = 60° (angle of an equilateral triangle)
So $\angle$QRT = 90° − 60°
= 30°
$\angle$TQR + $\angle$RTQ + $\angle$QRT = 180° (angle sum of a triangle)

But $\angle$TQR = $\angle$RTQ (angles of an isosceles triangle, QR = TR)
$2\angle$RTQ + 30° = 180°
$2\angle$RTQ = 180° − 30°
$2\angle$RTQ = 150°
$\angle$RTQ = 150° ÷ 2
$\angle$RTQ = 75°

Similarly, $\angle$PTS = 75°
$\angle$STR = 60° (angle of an equilateral triangle)
Angles at a point add to 360°.

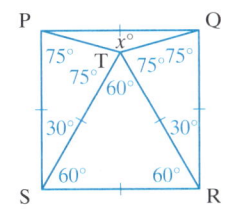

So $x + 75 + 60 + 75 = 360$
$x + 210 = 360$
$x = 360 − 210$
$x = 150$

**18** $0.03 \div 0.5 = 0.3 \div 5$
$= 0.06$

$\phantom{5)}0.0\,6$
$5)\overline{0.3\,^30}$

**19** $4^2 = 1 \times 7 + 9$
$5^2 = 2 \times 8 + 9$
$6^2 = 3 \times 9 + 9$
$7^2 = 4 \times 10 + 9$
$8^2 = 5 \times 11 + 9$

[The first number on the right-hand side is 3 less than the number that is squared on the left-hand side. The second number on the right-hand side is 3 more than the number that is squared. The last number is always 9.]

So, using the pattern:
$97^2 = 94 \times 100 + 9$
$= 9400 + 9$
$= 9409$

**20** Area = 100 cm$^2$
Each side = $\sqrt{100}$ cm
= 10 cm
Perimeter = 4 × 10 cm
= 40 cm

**21** $56 \times 73 = 4088$
[There are two digits after the decimal points in the question so there must be two digits after the decimal point in the answer.]
So $5.6 \times 7.3 = 40.88$
[Or use estimation: $5.6 \times 7.3$ is about $6 \times 7$ or 42.]

153

# YEAR 9 NUMERACY SAMPLE TEST ANSWERS

**22** [Divide the rectangle into equal pieces.]
There are 18 triangles.
4 of the triangles are shaded. 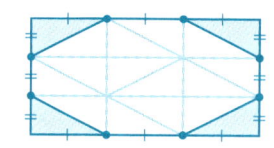
Fraction shaded $= \dfrac{4}{18}$
$= \dfrac{2}{9}$

**23** The rectangle has two axes of symmetry.
The parallelogram has no axes of symmetry.
The rhombus has two axes of symmetry.

rectangle   parallelogram   rhombus

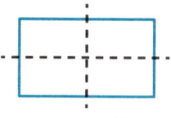

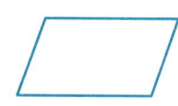

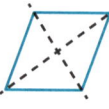

So the two shapes that have the same number of axes of symmetry are the rectangle and the rhombus.

**24** The time on the clock is 2:30.
Now the clock face is divided into 12 sections.
A complete revolution is 360°.
Angle for each section $= 360° \div 12$
$= 30°$
Now $240 \div 30 = 8$
So the hand will turn through 8 sections.
Each section represents 5 minutes. 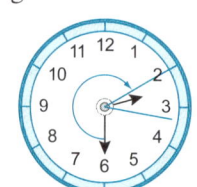
So the time will increase by 40 minutes.
The time will be 3:10.

**25** Fuel used $= 7$ L/100 km
Now 56 litres $= 8 \times 7$ L
So the distance travelled $= 8 \times 100$ km
$= 800$ km

**26** $\dfrac{17}{100} + \dfrac{3}{10} = 0.17 + 0.3$
$= 0.47$

$\phantom{+\ }0.17$
$+\ 0.30$
$\overline{\phantom{+\ }0.47}$

**27** $n$ is the smallest number.
The next number is one more than that.
Second number $= n + 1$
The third number is one more than the second number.
Third number $= n + 1 + 1$
$= n + 2$

The fourth number is one more than the third number.
Fourth number $= n + 2 + 1$
$= n + 3$
The largest number is $n + 3$.

**28** After 3 more boys enrolled there were 18 boys.
Before they enrolled there were 15 boys.
Now the ratio of boys to girls was 3 to 4.
So, for every 3 boys, there were 4 girls.
Now $15 \div 3 = 5$
So there were 5 lots of 3 boys.
Number of girls $= 5 \times 4$
$= 20$
New ratio $= 18$ to $20$
$= 9$ to $10$

**29** There were 25 balloons altogether.
Total in table $= 7 + 4 + 6 + 5$
$= 22$
Number of orange balloons $= 25 - 22$
$= 3$

| Colour | Number |
|---|---|
| Red | 7 |
| White | 4 |
| Blue | 6 |
| Green | 5 |
| Orange |  |

Fraction of orange balloons $= \dfrac{3}{25}$
$= \dfrac{12}{100}$
Percentage of orange balloons $= 12\%$

**30** The route from Seascape to Hilltop covers 7 units on the map.

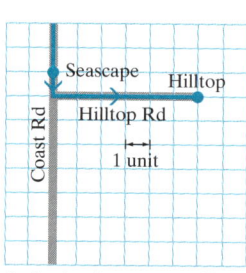

Actual distance
$= 7 \times 20$ km
$= 140$ km

Scale : 1 unit represents 20 km

Average speed $= 70$ km/h
Time taken $= (140 \div 70)$ h
$= 2$ h
So Julie would need to leave at about 8 am to be in Hilltop at around 10 am.

**31** $\dfrac{3}{10} > \dfrac{5}{x}$
[Multiply both sides by $10x$.]
$3x > 50$
[Divide both sides by 3.]
$x > 16.666\ldots$

# YEAR 9 NUMERACY SAMPLE TEST ANSWERS

But $x$ is a whole number.
So the smallest possible value of $x$ is 17.

**32** The line passes through $(1, 3)$ and $(-1, -1)$.
So when $x = 1$, $y = 3$ and
when $x = -1$, $y = -1$
Try each option:
$y = 2x + 1$
When $x = 1$, $y = 2 \times 1 + 1$
$\phantom{When x = 1, y} = 2 + 1$
$\phantom{When x = 1, y} = 3 \checkmark$
When $x = -1$, $y = 2 \times -1 + 1$
$\phantom{When x = -1, y} = -2 + 1$
$\phantom{When x = -1, y} = -1 \checkmark$
So the equation of the line is $y = 2x + 1$.

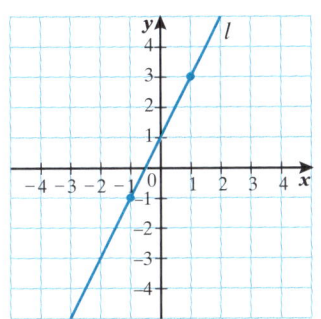

### Calculator Allowed

## YEAR 9 Numeracy Sample Test 3   Pages 76–83

- **1** A (Basic level)
- **2** 46 (Basic level)
- **3** A (Basic level)
- **4** B (Basic level)
- **5** 50 min (Basic level)
- **6** C (Intermediate level)
- **7** D (Basic level)
- **8** A (Advanced level)
- **9** D (Intermediate level)
- **10** D (Basic level)
- **11** B (Intermediate level)
- **12** B (Intermediate level)
- **13** A (Basic level)
- **14** B (Advanced level)
- **15** 90 cm (Intermediate level)
- **16** 70 (Intermediate level)
- **17** C (Intermediate level)
- **18** D (Basic level)
- **19** A (Advanced level)
- **20** C (Intermediate level)
- **21** C (Intermediate level)
- **22** D (Intermediate level)
- **23** B (Intermediate level)
- **24** A (Intermediate level)
- **25** B (Intermediate level)
- **26** A (Advanced level)
- **27** D (Advanced level)
- **28** B (Advanced level)
- **29** C (Advanced level)
- **30** C (Advanced level)
- **31** 98% (Advanced level)
- **32** 3:4 (Advanced level)

**1** ◆ is on the face opposite ●
[All of the other shapes will be on faces that are next to ●]

**2** 1, 2, 4, 7, 11, 16
The differences between the numbers in the pattern are 1, then 2, then 3, 4 and 5.
So the difference is increasing by 1 each time.
The seventh number $= 16 + 6$
$\phantom{The seventh number } = 22$
The eighth number $= 22 + 7$
$\phantom{The eighth number } = 29$
The ninth number $= 29 + 8$
$\phantom{The ninth number } = 37$
The tenth number $= 37 + 9$
$\phantom{The tenth number } = 46$

**3** $8^2 + 15^2 = 64 + 225$
$\phantom{8^2 + 15^2 } = 289$
$\phantom{8^2 + 15^2 } = 17^2$

**4** 750 km $= 7.5 \times 100$ km
Petrol used $= 7.5 \times 6.5$ L
$\phantom{Petrol used } = 48.75$ L
The best approximation for the amount of fuel used is 50 litres.

**5**

| Day | Time |
| --- | --- |
| Monday | 20 min |
| Tuesday | 1 h 10 min |
| Wednesday | 45 min |
| Thursday | 1 h 15 min |
| Friday | 40 min |

1h 10 min = 70 min
1 h 15 min = 75 min
Total minutes $= 20 + 70 + 45 + 75 + 40$
$\phantom{Total minutes } = 250$
Average $= (250 \div 5)$ min
$\phantom{Average } = 50$ min

**6** $\frac{2}{3}$ of the number $= 72$
$\frac{1}{3}$ of the number $= 72 \div 2$
$\phantom{\frac{1}{3} of the number } = 36$
The number $= 36 \times 3$
$\phantom{The number } = 108$
$\frac{3}{4}$ of $108 = 81$

**7** 1 tonne = 1000 kg

155

# YEAR 9 NUMERACY SAMPLE TEST ANSWERS

$$1 \text{ tonne} + 80 \text{ kg} = (1000 + 80) \text{ kg}$$
$$= 1080 \text{ kg}$$
$$= 1.08 \text{ t}$$

**8** If $x = 6$,
$2x - x^2 = 2 \times 6 - 6^2$
$\phantom{2x - x^2} = 12 - 36$
$\phantom{2x - x^2} = -24$

**9** Angles in a straight line add to 180°.

So the angle that forms a straight line with the angle of 120° will be 60° and the angle that forms a straight line with the angle of 100° will be 80°.

Now the exterior angle of a triangle is equal to the sum of the interior opposite angles.

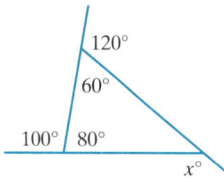

So $x = 60 + 80$
$\phantom{So }x = 140$

**10** Total marbles $= 10 + 15 + 25$
$\phantom{Total marbles }= 50$

Chance of blue marble $= \dfrac{15}{50}$
$\phantom{Chance of blue marble }= \dfrac{30}{100}$
$\phantom{Chance of blue marble }= 30\%$

**11**

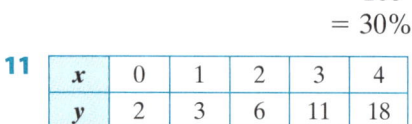

| x | 0 | 1 | 2 | 3 | 4 |
|---|---|---|---|---|---|
| y | 2 | 3 | 6 | 11 | 18 |

Try each option:
$y = x + 2$
When $x = 0$, $y = 0 + 2$
$\phantom{When x = 0, y} = 2$ ✓
When $x = 1$, $y = 1 + 2$
$\phantom{When x = 1, y} = 3$ ✓
When $x = 2$, $y = 2 + 2$
$\phantom{When x = 2, y} = 4$ ✗

The rule is not $y = x + 2$
$y = x^2 + 2$
When $x = 0$, $y = 0^2 + 2$
$\phantom{When x = 0, y} = 0 + 2$
$\phantom{When x = 0, y} = 2$ ✓
When $x = 1$, $y = 1^2 + 2$
$\phantom{When x = 1, y} = 1 + 2$
$\phantom{When x = 1, y} = 3$ ✓
When $x = 2$, $y = 2^2 + 2$
$\phantom{When x = 2, y} = 4 + 2$
$\phantom{When x = 2, y} = 6$ ✓

When $x = 3$, $y = 3^2 + 2$
$\phantom{When x = 3, y} = 9 + 2$
$\phantom{When x = 3, y} = 11$ ✓
When $x = 4$, $y = 4^2 + 2$
$\phantom{When x = 4, y} = 16 + 2$
$\phantom{When x = 4, y} = 18$ ✓
The rule is $y = x^2 + 2$

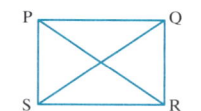

**12** The diagonals of a rectangle are always equal.

PR = QS

[The diagonals of a rhombus, kite or trapezium are not always equal.

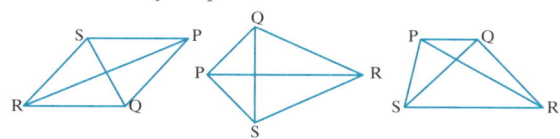

For example, in each case PR is longer than QS. (If the diagonals of a rhombus or kite are equal then the quadrilateral is also a square. If the diagonals of a trapezium are equal, the trapezium is also a rectangle.)]

**13** The cut will produce a triangle.

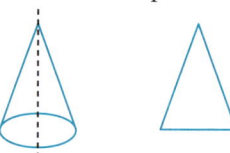

**14** $-5p + p^2 = p^2 - 5p$
[$p^2$ is positive, $5p$ is negative.]

**15** The plan is 8 cm long and the actual table is 1.6 metres long.

Now 1.6 metres is 160 cm.
So 8 cm represents 160 cm.
1 cm represents (160 ÷ 8) cm or 20 cm.
4.5 cm represents 4.5 × 20 cm or 90 cm.
So the table is 90 cm wide.

**16** Angles of a triangle add to 180°.
So the remaining angles add to 180° − 40° or 140°.

Now the triangle is isosceles.
So the two remaining angles are equal.
[They are the two angles opposite the equal sides.]
So $x = 140 ÷ 2$
$\phantom{So }x = 70$

156

# YEAR 9 NUMERACY SAMPLE TEST ANSWERS

**17** The number halfway between 0.12 and 0.4 is the average.
Sum = 0.12 + 0.40
      = 0.52
Average = 0.52 ÷ 2
            = 0.26
The number halfway between 0.12 and 0.4 is 0.26.

**18** Holiday Q is shorter than holiday R but costs more.

**Hilltop Holiday Tours**

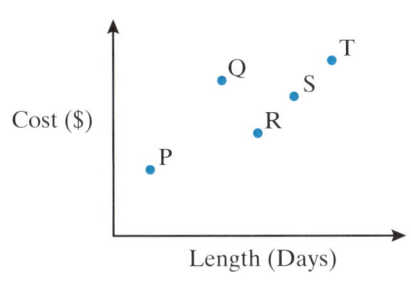

Of the options, the two tours that show that 'the higher the cost the longer the tour' is not always correct are R and Q.

**19** The fence is made up of three sides of a square and half the circumference of a circle.

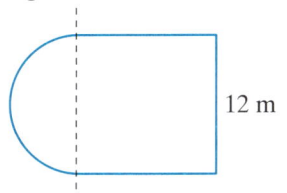

Total length of the fence
= $(3 \times 12 + \frac{1}{2} \times \pi \times 12)$ m
= (36 + 18.84955…) m
= 54.84955… m
Of the options, the best approximation for the length of the fence is 55 metres.

**20** Saving = $17\frac{1}{2}$% of $640
         = 0.175 × $640
         = $112
Price paid = $640 − $112
             = $528

**21** 1 km = 1000 m
1 km² = 1000 m × 1000 m
        = 1 000 000 m²
2 km² = 2 000 000 m²

**22** $h = \frac{3V}{\pi r^2}$
When $V = 1.5$ and $r = 0.8$,
$h = \frac{3 \times 1.5}{\pi \times (0.8)^2}$
   = 2.23811…
Of the options, the height is closest to 2.2 metres.

**23**

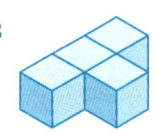

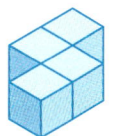

The object that Shelly cannot make is option B.

**24** When it is 5 pm in Melbourne it is 7 am in London.
From 7 am until 5 pm on the same day is 10 hours.
So Melbourne is 10 hours ahead of London.
10 hours ahead of 5 pm Monday is 3 am Tuesday.

**25** Time taken = (90 ÷ 72) h
               = 1.25 h
               = 1 h 15 min

**26** Total area of all faces = 24 m²
A cube has six faces.
Area of each face = (24 ÷ 6) m²
                        = 4 m²
Now each face is a square. If the area of a square is 4 m² each side will be 2 metres long.
Volume = (2 × 2 × 2) m³
          = 8 m³

**27** $3^3 \times 9^2 = 3 \times 3 \times 3 \times 9 \times 9$
[But this is not one of the options.]
Now 9 = 3 × 3
So $3^3 \times 9^2 = 3 \times 3 \times 3 \times 3 \times 3 \times 9$

**28** Because the two triangles have a common angle and both have right angles they are similar. This means that their sides are in proportion.

(not to scale)

# YEAR 9 NUMERACY SAMPLE TEST ANSWERS

$$\frac{x}{3+4} = \frac{2}{4}$$

$$\frac{x}{7} = \frac{1}{2}$$

$$x = \frac{1}{2} \times 7$$

$$= 3\frac{1}{2}$$

So $x = 3.5$

**29** $\frac{a}{5} > \frac{b}{3}$

[Multiply both sides by 15.]

$3a > 5b$

Now try each option:

$a = 3$ and $b = 2$

$3 \times 3 > 5 \times 2$ ?

$9 < 10$

So this option is not correct.

$a = 4$ and $b = 3$

$3 \times 4 > 5 \times 3$ ?

$12 < 15$

So this option is not correct.

$a = 7$ and $b = 4$

$3 \times 7 > 5 \times 4$ ?

$21 > 20$

This option is correct.

**30** The polygon has three angles of 150° and others of 126°.

Try each option:

Angle sum of a pentagon = $(5 - 2) \times 180°$
$= 3 \times 180°$
$= 540°$

A pentagon has five angles, so there would need to be two angles of 126°.

Now $3 \times 150° + 2 \times 126° = 450° + 252°$
$= 702°$ (not 540°)

The polygon is not a pentagon.

Angle sum of a hexagon = $(6 - 2) \times 180°$
$= 4 \times 180°$
$= 720°$

A hexagon has six angles, so there would need to be three angles of 126°.

Now $3 \times 150° + 3 \times 126° = 450° + 378°$
$= 828°$ (not 720°)

The polygon is not a hexagon.

Angle sum of an octagon = $(8 - 2) \times 180°$
$= 6 \times 180°$
$= 1080°$

An octagon has eight angles, so there would need to be five angles of 126°.

Now $3 \times 150° + 5 \times 126° = 450° + 630°$
$= 1080°$

The polygon is an octagon.

**31** Average of 24 scores = 73

Sum of 24 scores = $24 \times 73$
$= 1752$

Average of 25 scores = 74

Sum of 25 scores = $25 \times 74$
$= 1850$

Difference = $1850 - 1752$
$= 98$

Callum's mark must have been 98%.

**32** There were originally 36 people.

For every 4 adults there were 5 children.

So 4 out of every 9 people were adults.

Number of adults = $\frac{4}{9} \times 36$
$= 16$

Number of children = $36 - 16$
$= 20$

Now 2 more adults and 4 more children arrive.

New number of adults = $16 + 2$
$= 18$

New number of children = $20 + 4$
$= 24$

New ratio of adults to children = $18:24$
$= 3:4$